Cruel

CRUEL HARVEST

US Intervention in the
Afghan Drug Trade

Julien Mercille

PlutoPress
www.plutobooks.com

First published 2013 by Pluto Press
345 Archway Road, London N6 5AA

www.plutobooks.com

Distributed in the United States of America exclusively by
Palgrave Macmillan, a division of St. Martin's Press LLC,
175 Fifth Avenue, New York, NY 10010

British Library Cataloguing in Publication Data
A catalogue record for this book is available from the British Library

ISBN   978 0 7453 3233 8   Hardback
ISBN   978 0 7453 3232 1   Paperback
ISBN   978 1 8496 4776 2   PDF eBook
ISBN   978 1 8496 4778 6   Kindle eBook
ISBN   978 1 8496 4777 9   EPUB eBook

1006993 02X

Library of Congress Cataloging in Publication Data applied for

This book is printed on paper suitable for recycling and made from fully managed
and sustained forest sources. Logging, pulping and manufacturing processes are
expected to conform to the environmental standards of the country of origin.

10   9   8   7   6   5   4   3   2   1

Designed and produced for Pluto Press by Chase Publishing Services Ltd
Typeset from disk by Stanford DTP Services, Northampton, England
Simultaneously printed digitally by CPI Antony Rowe, Chippenham, UK and
Edwards Bros in the United States of America

Contents

Abbreviations

AREU	Afghanistan Research and Evaluation Unit
BCCI	Bank of Credit and Commerce International
CAT	Civil Air Transport
CIA	Central Intelligence Agency
CSTO	Collective Security Treaty Organization
DEA	Drug Enforcement Administration
EU	European Union
FARC	Fuerzas Armadas Revolucionarias de Colombia (Revolutionary Armed Forces of Colombia)
GAO	Government Accountability Office (United States)
GATT	General Agreement on Tariffs and Trade
GDP	Gross Domestic Product
ICOS	International Council on Security and Development (formerly Senlis Council)
INCB	International Narcotics Control Board
INL	Department of State's Bureau of International Narcotics and Law Enforcement Affairs (United States)
ISAF	International Security Assistance Force
ISI	Inter-Services Intelligence (Pakistan)
KMT	Kuomintang
NATO	North Atlantic Treaty Organization
NSP	Needle and syringe exchange programs
NWFP	North-West Frontier Province (Pakistan)
RAWA	Revolutionary Association of the Women of Afghanistan
RDF	Rapid Deployment Force
SCO	Shanghai Cooperation Organization
TAP	Turkmenistan-Afghanistan-Pakistan pipeline (Trans-Afghanistan Pipeline)
UN	United Nations
UNAMA	United Nations Assistance Mission in Afghanistan
UNDCP	United Nations International Drug Control Program
UNODC	United Nations Office on Drugs and Crime
UNSCR	United Nations Security Council Resolution
WHO	World Health Organization

Acknowledgements

Thank you to all who agreed to be interviewed for this book or provided material and information at UNODC, the National Security Archive, the US military and government, DEA, NATO, and organizations in Afghanistan, the United States and elsewhere. Thank you also to Sonali Kolhatkar, James Ingalls, Enda Murphy and others for comments on earlier drafts, as well as to the staff at Pluto Press for editing and publishing support.

1
Introduction

Afghanistan is the world's uncontested leader in heroin production, accounting for as much as 90 percent of global supply, leading some commentators to label it a "narco-state."[1] Counternarcotics operations in the country have been intensified over the last few years, led by the United States with the participation of NATO allies. The stakes are high, we are told, because drugs fund the insurgency, corrupt the political process, and increase addiction around the world. The Taliban are invariably depicted as the main culprits and beneficiaries of the drug trade, along with a host of corrupt government officials. It is thus claimed that eliminating the narcotics industry would weaken the insurgency and allow the United States to preside over the establishment of a stable and democratic Afghan polity.

This book's position differs and documents the United States' complicity in drug trafficking and repeated failure to reduce drug problems. For example, Washington has long supported or tolerated traffickers around the world, has looked the other way while the global financial system launders large sums of narcotics money every year, and has consistently adopted the counterdrug strategies known not to work. Counternarcotics missions abroad mostly target individuals and groups that are considered enemies or who have outlived their usefulness, while allies are rarely prosecuted. This, in fact, seems to have become President Obama's official policy in Afghanistan, as when his administration specified in 2009 that it is drug traffickers *with links to the insurgency* that will be targeted (see chapter 6). The book suggests that so-called "drug wars" have, in effect, served to facilitate intervention overseas.

A few days before the US-UK attack on Afghanistan in October 2001, the British prime minister, Tony Blair, declared that the Taliban is a regime "funded on the drugs trade. The biggest drugs hoard in the world is in Afghanistan, controlled by the Taliban. Ninety per cent of the heroin on British streets originates in Afghanistan. The arms the Taliban are buying today are paid for with the lives of young British people buying their drugs on British streets. That is another part of their regime that we should seek to destroy." The war was seemingly going to be more acceptable to the public if the Taliban adversary was explicitly linked to narcotics. While referring to al-Qaeda's responsibility for 9/11, Blair further claimed that Osama bin Laden and the Taliban "jointly exploited the drugs trade" and warned that we should be prepared for a "new invasion" of al-Qaeda's opium. In short, as the Transnational Institute correctly observed about the prime minister's statements: "Everything nasty is combined to paint a black image of the 'evil' enemy, never mind reality," a recurring principle that will be described throughout this book.[2]

President George W. Bush conveyed similar ideas worth quoting at length:

> You know, I'm asked all the time, "How can I help fight against terror? What can I do, what can I as a citizen do to defend America?" Well, one thing you can do is not purchase illegal drugs. Make no mistake about it, if you're buying illegal drugs in America, it is likely that money is going to end up in the hands of terrorist organizations. Just think about the Taliban in Afghanistan: 70 percent of the world's opium trade came from Afghanistan, resulting in significant income to the Taliban, significant amount of money to the people that were harboring and feeding and hiding those who attacked and killed thousands of innocent Americans on September the 11th. When we fight drugs, we fight the war on terror.[3]

Or again, when he answered a student's question:

> I don't know if you know this or not, but the Taliban Government and Al Qaida—the evil ones—use heroin trafficking in order to fund their murder. And one of our objectives is to make sure that Afghanistan is never used for that purpose again.[4]

The book examines American policy toward Afghanistan since the late 1970s, as related to narcotics. In the 1980s, during the Soviet invasion and occupation of the country, the United States, through the CIA, supported mujahideen fighters against the Russians, and some of those rebels were involved in drug production. As such, the protection and support the CIA offered them resulted in the expansion of the drug industry, which until then had remained relatively small and regional in scope. It grew eightfold over the decade, opium production increasing from about 200 tons in 1981 to 1,600 tons in 1990. The mujahideen's trafficking in narcotics was tolerated because it provided them with extra resources to "bleed the Russians," the American objective.

In the first half of the 1990s, a civil war raged among the mujahideen factions, causing much destruction and hardship. But Washington disengaged from Afghanistan and looked the other way as narcotics production rose from 1,600 tons in 1990 to 3,100 tons in 1994—hardly an example of concern for drug control. When the Taliban took power from 1996 to 2001, the US government initially sought to engage them, hoping that they would bring stability to the war-torn country and permit American company Unocal to lay down pipelines across their land. However, when Washington linked the 1998 American embassy bombings in Africa to Osama bin Laden, who was then living in Afghanistan, the Taliban were labeled a "rogue" regime due to their refusal to expel him. Nevertheless, the Taliban managed to implement a successful ban on opium production in 2000–01. It would have been expected that the most successful drug control operation to have taken place anywhere since China's anti-narcotics campaign in the aftermath of the 1949 revolution, would warm up relations with the United States, if drug control had indeed been an important objective. On the contrary, Washington reacted by slapping sanctions on Afghanistan, while the United Nations Office on Drugs and Crime (UNODC)[5] broke its promise of financial assistance, underfunded by world powers more inclined toward isolating the Taliban than implementing narcotics control programs.

Since 2001, heroin production has literally skyrocketed, coinciding with the invasion and occupation of the country. In a similar strategy to that in the 1980s, the United States has supported individuals involved in trafficking. This time, allied warlords and strongmen and their militias have contributed to chasing the Taliban from power in 2001, and have been empowered by foreign troops to maintain "stability" in the country, although the insurgency has been threatening the Afghan government for some years now. Not surprisingly, the result has been an increase in opium production, since many of the industry's key players have been tolerated or directly supported by the international coalition. Although mainstream commentary has associated heroin with the Taliban, it will be seen that in fact, the United States and NATO share a large part of responsibility for the expansion of the drug traffic, while the Taliban, according to the available data, play a relatively minor role. For instance, they capture only about 5 percent of total drug revenues in Afghanistan, while the remainder of the funds goes to government officials, traffickers, police and local commanders, many of which are either supported or tolerated by Washington. Western powers also contribute to sustaining the narcotics industry indirectly by regulating only lightly a global financial system that launders its proceeds, while the West is a significant source of chemical precursors used to transform opium into heroin (see chapter 6).

Finally, the book will examine the many solutions that have been proposed to address the problem of Afghanistan's drugs and reduce the addiction they cause globally. The weakness of conventional debate on the subject is that the proposed alternatives are almost entirely confined to solutions within Afghanistan, even if research indicates that those are the least effective ones. The best strategies are those that reduce demand in consumer countries—in this case, primarily Europe and Russia—through provision of treatment services for addicts and prevention campaigns. The fact that the West and Russia have for decades promoted the solutions that are proven to be futile while neglecting those that work is further evidence that the war on drugs is less about reducing narcotics problems than about maintaining power prerogatives, as will be seen in chapter 7.

Overall, the book focuses on US drug policy and responsibility for the expansion of trafficking in Afghanistan since the late 1970s. However, this is not to say that other countries or institutions do not share a part of responsibility as well, such as Afghan drug lords themselves and the many individuals who allow their business to flourish. Nevertheless, because the United States has had a significant impact in the country, in particular since 2001, and that conventional analyses do not highlight its role in the trade, it is hoped that the book will be valuable in telling a different story. Also, to argue that the United States shares a part of responsibility in the narcotics traffic is not to say that to protect it is a goal in itself, as suggested by some authors who have taken a somewhat conspiratorial view. On the contrary, this book suggests that Washington is not too concerned about drugs themselves one way or another. Drugs are not strategic commodities like oil or raw materials, and they mostly serve an instrumental purpose within the broader scheme of American foreign policy, such as providing additional funds to local allies. One of the book's claims is that policy is shaped by political economic factors which have very little to do with drugs.

Before discussing the above points in detail in subsequent chapters, the following section sketches the nature of the Afghan narcotics industry and its evolution over time, and puts it in the context of the global drug trade.

THE AFGHAN DRUG INDUSTRY[6]

Afghanistan specializes in the production of opiates (opium, morphine, and heroin). In simple terms, the production process is as follows.[7] Poppy plants are grown by farmers (a field of one hectare can bear from 60,000 to 120,000 poppies) and four months after planting, the opium is harvested from the poppy capsules at the tip of the plant's stalk. This task is very labor-intensive and time-consuming and consists in creating incisions (lancing) on each capsule with a small blade. The opium sap is then left to ooze and dry before farmers scrape it off. An experienced worker can lance 150–200 capsules per hour. After a few days, the process may be repeated (up to six or seven times) to extract more opium. Once the opium gum is fully harvested, it is then mixed with various chemicals in small-scale "laboratories" to transform it into morphine, and further into heroin.

The global illegal drug industry has an estimated annual value of US$13 billion at the production level, $94 billion at the wholesale level and $322 billion at the retail level (street prices). At the retail level, cannabis products (marijuana and hashish) account for $142 billion, followed by cocaine ($71 billion), opiates ($65 billion) and amphetamine-type stimulants (ATS—methamphetamine, amphetamine and ecstasy) ($44 billion).[8]

The global supply of illegal opiates is produced in three main areas: Afghanistan, Southeast Asia (mainly Myanmar) and Latin America (Mexico and Colombia). In recent years, Afghanistan has produced up to 8,200 metric tons of raw opium annually, accounting for 90 percent of global production and valued at about $3 billion in Afghanistan (production level) and $60 billion on the streets worldwide. Much less publicized but still remarkable is the fact that the country is also thought to have become the world's leading producer of hashish, of which it exports an estimated 1,500 to 3,500 tons annually. Its export value is unknown, but is likely to be substantially less than for opiates (about 15 percent of opiates'

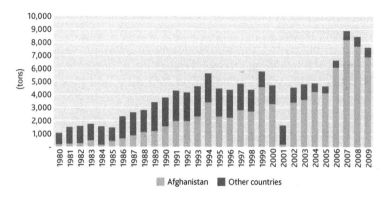

Figure 1.1   Global Potential Opium Production, 1980–2009

Source: UNODC, *Addiction, Crime and Insurgency: The Transnational Threat of Afghan Opium* (Vienna: UNODC), p. 10.

value, according to some estimates). This book is restricted to opiates since our knowledge of the hashish industry is very limited.[9]

Afghan production has increased steadily over the last three decades, both in absolute terms and relative to other opium producers (Figure 1.1). In 1981, the country produced only 225 tons of opium, compared to 5,800 tons in 2011. The largest harvest ever recorded was 8,200 tons, in 2007. Production in 2010 was only 3,600 tons, a 48 percent decrease from 2009, due in part to plant diseases that affected poppy fields, but it recovered in 2011. The most notable exception to the steady increase in yields over the last three decades is in 2001, when only 185 tons were harvested, mostly in the northern provinces not controlled by the Taliban regime then ruling over most of the country. The Taliban had implemented a ban on cultivation that reduced the harvest drastically.[10]

The drug industry is very important to the Afghan economy. For example, in 2008, total revenues from opiates amounted to $3.4 billion, which represents about 25 percent of Afghanistan's total GDP (including the drug industry). In the years immediately after 2001, this percentage was even higher given the smaller economy. The drug trade is also vital to farmers who harvest and sell the opium: for example, their revenues amounted to $730 million in 2008, or about $2,000 for each of the 366,500 households that grew poppies that year. Thus, narcotics generate much needed income and employment in the countryside. In 2008, about 2.4 million Afghans, or 10 percent of the population, were involved in poppy cultivation.[11] Yet, Afghans capture only a fraction of the $60 billion generated by the sale of their products worldwide, as prices increase as the drugs are transported to their final destination in the rich consumer markets. Smugglers, traffickers, corrupt officials and customs agents all take a cut along the way as compensation for their contribution to bringing the substances from Asia to Russia, Europe and beyond.

Today, poppy growing takes place mostly in the country's south, although in previous years it was more scattered geographically. The processing of opium into heroin occurs mostly within Afghanistan as well, although earlier, in the 1980s and 1990s, Turkey processed a large portion of Afghan morphine into heroin, along with the Federally Administered Tribal Areas (FATA) in northwestern Pakistan. For example, in 1994, 100 laboratories were estimated to be in operation in the latter area, producing some 70 tons of heroin annually. During the 1990s, labs spread in the southeastern and northeastern provinces of Afghanistan, and in the following years heroin production became increasingly concentrated within the country. The largest refining facilities are now thought to be located in the south, although they are present in other areas as well. Estimates of the total number of laboratories in Afghanistan range from 100 to 500.[12]

Raw opium and heroin are shipped to consumer markets via three main routes (Figure 1.2): through Iran to Turkey and Western Europe; through Pakistan to Africa, Asia, the Middle East, and Iran; and through Central Asia to Russia. A relatively small amount of Afghan heroin reaches the United States, whose main suppliers are Mexico and Colombia.

UNODC estimates that worldwide, there are 12–14 million heroin users who consume 375 tons of the substance annually, in addition to 4 million users consuming 1,100 tons of opium. Although estimates vary, the largest heroin consumers are Europe (in particular, the United Kingdom, Italy, France, and Germany) and Russia, which account respectively for 26 percent and 21 percent of global consumption (in quantity terms). The United States and Canada together account for 6 percent. Opium is mostly used in Asia, especially in Iran, which accounts for 42 percent of global consumption, compared to 9 percent for Europe and 5 percent for Russia. It takes about 7 tons of opium to make 1 ton of heroin. Therefore, if total opiate consumption is calculated in terms of "opium equivalents," the leading consumers are Europe (710 tons), Russia and Iran (550 tons each), and China (460 tons).[13] In monetary terms, the global heroin market in 2008 was worth $55

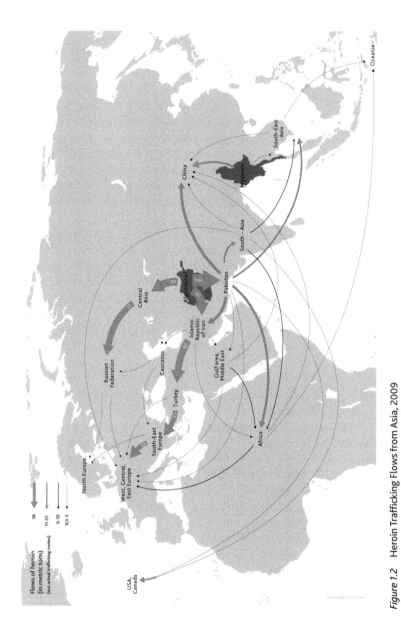

Figure 1.2 Heroin Trafficking Flows from Asia, 2009

Source: UNODC, *The Global Afghan Opium Trade: A Threat Assessment*, July 2011 (Vienna: UNODC), p. 8.

billion (retail value) while the opium market amounted to $7–10 billion, for an annual total as large as $65 billion. The leading countries in market value are Europe (retail market of $20 billion), Russia ($13 billion), China and the United States/Canada ($8–9 billion each).[14]

The next chapter discusses in detail the conventional view of drugs, drug wars and US involvement in Afghanistan. It then presents an alternative interpretation, which subsequent chapters will illustrate.

2
Perspectives

This chapter first reviews the conventional interpretation of the Afghan drug trade and the US position relative to it. This view assumes that the Taliban are the main culprits behind the dramatic increase in the size of the narcotics industry, along with corrupt Afghan government officials, and that drugs should be eliminated from the country because they finance the insurgency, make Afghanistan more difficult to govern, and raise addiction levels in the West and elsewhere. The second section presents a more critical interpretation, which highlights American complicity in trafficking.[1]

THE CONVENTIONAL INTERPRETATION

The conventional view of counternarcotics operations in Afghanistan has been presented by a number of American officials and in various congressional reports. International drug control institutions such as UNODC have more or less adopted the same position, as have many scholars and journalists. Since 9/11, the rhetoric of the global war on drugs has meshed with that of the "war on terror." For example, President Bush said to Drug Enforcement Administration (DEA) agents in 2003 that by "keeping drug money from financing terror, you're playing an important part of this war" on terror. Senator Dianne Feinstein recently claimed that "we can all agree that the Taliban has morphed into a hybrid. It is one part terrorist organization, one part global drug trafficking organization." A UNODC report even warned that some insurgent groups in Afghanistan are turning into "narco-cartels."[3]

Although differences are evident among analysts, the conventional view essentially makes the following points:

- The United States and NATO are conducting a war on drugs in Afghanistan.
- The Taliban are the driving force behind the drug industry, while drugs fuel the insurgency by financing it. This "narco-terrorist nexus" must be defeated.

- Heroin is the world's deadliest drug and is flooding Europe, adding to the urgency of reducing supply.
- The fact that poppy cultivation is concentrated in the south of Afghanistan, where the Taliban are most active, shows that insurgents are responsible for the skyrocketing narcotics production.
- The Taliban have recently become involved in the chemical precursors business, giving them an additional source of profits. (Precursors are chemicals that are shipped illegally into Afghanistan and are used to transform opium into morphine and heroin.)
- The Taliban and traffickers launder their drug money using the opaque *hawala* financial system, therefore, tracking drug money is difficult.
- Corrupt Afghan government officials and police are also involved in trafficking and benefit financially from it. Narcotics fuel corruption and thus destabilize the Afghan government and prevent the coalition from establishing a stable polity.
- The solution to the problem combines eradication of poppy fields, arrests of drug traffickers and support for rural development projects to shift farmers toward legal crops or occupations.

Thus, it is claimed that the US government and military are concerned about drugs because they are dangerous and harmful substances linked to crime and insurgency that destabilize the nation-building project in Afghanistan. Because the Taliban are important players in the drug trade—perhaps even the most important ones, according to some analysts—insurgency and drugs reinforce one another in a vicious cycle: the Taliban encourage poppy cultivation, and in turn, trafficking finances their operations. Therefore, reducing drug supply will weaken the insurgency, while eliminating militants will lead to a drop in poppy cultivation. It is recognized that Afghan government officials and the police derive profits from the drug business, but corruption is blamed, giving the impression that what is needed is to clean up the "bad apples" instead of any radical policy reorientation. Finally, drug warriors are keen to emphasize operations in supplier countries but almost never mention actions in consumer countries.

Before giving a number of examples of this view, a brief comment is in order in relation to the much-discussed "narco-terrorist nexus." Although it is true that some terrorists are involved in trafficking, the concept should nevertheless be put in perspective. According to the US government definition, a "narco-terrorist organization is an organized group that is complicit in the activities of drug trafficking to further or fund premeditated, politically motivated violence to influence a government or group of people."[5] Groups like the Taliban or the FARC in Colombia are often mentioned in this respect. However, by this definition, the US government and NATO also appear to be narco-terrorist organizations, since they clearly are and have been for a long time "complicit in the activities of drug trafficking" in order to "further or fund" violence, as will be seen in later chapters. Nevertheless, one would be hard put to find this mentioned in the media or scholarship, the label being reserved for enemies.[6]

Some of the official rationales for counternarcotics operations have to do with an alleged desire to reduce drug use and associated health problems and crime. For example, a US Senate report stated that Afghanistan's annual production "is enough to supply every opium and heroin addict in the world for two years," an urgent matter because it "has caused drug use epidemics in Iran and Russia, and contributed to drug crime in the United Kingdom and other European countries." If cultivation is allowed to increase, warns the *US Counternarcotics Strategy for Afghanistan*, this will mean "lower prices, increasing purity, increasing numbers of users, and more drug-related deaths." The United States has itself been relatively insulated from Afghan opiates as only about 5 percent of its heroin comes from Afghanistan, but it is ready to help affected countries, like Russia, which is losing "30,000 lives a year to the Afghan drug trade." Nevertheless, the situation is seen as precarious because trafficking and consumption patterns "can and have shifted quickly in the past; there is no assurance that relatively low level American dependence on Afghan-origin opiates will continue." Indeed, "Afghan heroin reaches the western hemisphere via Canada, where it accounts for about 50% of all heroin consumed," and therefore it could easily be diverted to the United States.[7]

But there is worse, as "the heroin itself is a weapon of the insurgency and terrorists." In fact, the CIA estimated that Afghanistan could have produced up to 650 tons of heroin in 2009, "a massive amount that could kill hundreds of thousands" worldwide. Moreover, convicted Afghan narco-terrorist Khan Mohammed once declared, "may God turn all the infidels into dead corpses ... Whether it is by opium or by shooting, this is our common goal."[8]

The links between narcotics and insurgents are always emphasized. As ISAF Commanding General Dan McNeill stated: "When I see a poppy field, I see it turning into money and then into IEDs [improvised explosive devices], AKs [assault rifles], and RPGs [rocket propelled grenades]." General David Petraeus told the Senate that "drug money has been the oxygen in the air" that allows the Taliban to operate.[9] The Department of State has also painted an image of close cooperation between the Taliban and drug traffickers, declaring that:

A symbiotic relationship exists between the insurgency and narcotics trafficking in Afghanistan. Traffickers provide weapons, funding, and other material support to the insurgency in exchange for the protection of drug trade routes, fields, laboratories, and their organizations, while others provide the same support because they are ideologically aligned with the Taliban. Some insurgent commanders engage directly in drug trafficking to finance their operations.[10]

Moreover, the "insurgents profit from every aspect of the opium trade. They tax farmers and traffickers, offer protection for travel on drug transit routes, and develop high-level contacts for joining the Jihad with narco-trafficking." Allegedly, "drug traffickers are co-equals with the Taliban ... They work by consensus." Their collaboration is close, so that traffickers "act as intelligence collection officers for the Taliban," a problem because they are "able to collect information such as the troop movements of U.S., NATO, and Afghan forces and provide it to the Taliban." The geography of poppy cultivation is further taken to demonstrate the significance of the narco-terrorist nexus, as "nearly all significant poppy cultivation now occurs in areas with active insurgent elements. Cultivation [is] largely confined to six provinces in the south and west of the country."[11] Some believe that the situation has deteriorated because "anti-government elements" have now involved themselves more deeply in trafficking. For example, journalist Gretchen Peters maintains that "the Taliban has transformed itself into something closer to the Mafia than a traditional insurgency, particularly in its stronghold of southern Afghanistan." In short, "The Sopranos are the real model for the Taliban."[12]

The hawala system and traditional trading networks crossing porous borders also make it difficult to regulate the industry: "Following the money is a time-tested means of assembling criminal cases against drug traffickers and corrupt government officials, but that task is probably harder in Afghanistan than anywhere in the world because of the ancient and secretive system called hawala." Its "close knit and close mouthed" nature and the "absence of effective regulation and the ingrained secrecy combine to make transactions conducted through hawala almost impossible to track." An American intelligence official in the region observed that "it was almost impossible to penetrate hawala networks, explaining that the family nature of the businesses made it difficult to get inside cooperation."[13]

The drug trade also "threatens the efforts of the United States and its allies to help the Afghan people bring stability to their country" because "drug money corrupts the government, weakens institutions, and strengthens the Taliban." This prevents Washington from realizing its goal of establishing "an independent, democratic, prosperous Afghanistan."[14] Corruption, the lack of political will and a weak justice system means that building legal cases against government officials "is proving difficult." Even Afghanistan's environment has been blamed, because the "enforcement of narcotics laws is undermined by the vast mountainous terrain."[15]

Afghans are deemed unreliable, which is sometimes used, implicitly, to justify the presence of foreign troops. American officials have voiced skepticism about Afghans' "determination and capacity to carry on counternarcotics programs if and when U.S. Government funding ends" and there is a general view that they will require US and "international support to sustain a credible CN [counternarcotics] effort on their own for the foreseeable future." NATO allies agree that Afghanistan needs a foreign presence to solve narcotics problems, as when a senior German police mentor commented: "We must stay. What are the options?"[16]

The irrationality of locals is another obstacle. For example, a formal assessment noted that illiterate farmers relied on "traditional cultivation methods that made little or no use of insecticides or herbicides. This detracted from any rational discussion of the use of herbicides to destroy poppy." Some blame is leveled at Russia, because peasants' fear of aerial spraying may have something to do with "the history of defoliants applied by the Soviets during occupation of the country," while "Afghans also still remember that the Russians dropped small bombs disguised as toys" and so the "general belief is that bad things come from planes." Public information campaigns have also been organized but have not been effective, due to Afghans' "traditional suspicion of foreigners." The

Afghan government and many others in the international community have opposed aerial eradication, which forced Washington to rely on ground-based eradication, a method it sees as "inefficient, slow and dangerous." According to the United States, the "most effective method for widespread eradication is widely understood to be aerial spraying, the technique used to eliminate huge portions of Colombia's coca crop"—contrary to all evidence.[17] The solutions offered are invariably targeting Afghans and Afghanistan, but rarely consumer countries. The Bush administration developed a "5 Pillar Plan" that guided policy from 2005 to 2009 and involved public information, alternative development to move farmers away from poppy cultivation, elimination and eradication of poppy crops, interdiction (dismantling drug trafficking networks and drug seizures), and law enforcement and justice reform to process drug-related arrests more efficiently. Obama has announced a shift away from eradication and a renewed emphasis on interdiction and rural development, but the spotlight is still on Afghanistan.[18]

The UN Assistance Mission in Afghanistan (UNAMA) put Britain in charge of counternarcotics in the country in the aftermath of the 2001 invasion. The United Kingdom supports the American approach, although it has perhaps put slightly more emphasis on drug use problems since, as the British Foreign and Commonwealth Office observes, over "90% of the heroin on the UK's streets originates from Afghanistan." But the threat remains global, as Catherine Ashton, the EU High Representative for Foreign Affairs and Security Policy, warned that the "problems facing Afghanistan concern the whole world. Violent extremism extends beyond the region. Drugs, grown and produced in Afghanistan find their way to the streets of Europe." Talk of a narco-terrorist nexus and its "destabilizing" effects on the government has also been used to justify the £180 million Britain spent on drug control in Afghanistan from 2004 to 2009.[19] Proposed counternarcotics strategies are similar to those advanced across the Atlantic. For example, Britain specifies three "key priorities": developing strong and effective counternarcotics institutions, targeting traffickers and the top end of the drugs trade, and strengthening and diversifying legal rural livelihood opportunities.[20]

Academic and journalistic accounts have been similar. Criticism is directed towards Afghans; debate is confined to tactics to rein in trafficking, as long as they take place in Afghanistan; the Taliban are the main culprits. For example, Gretchen Peters, who covered the region as a journalist for the Associated Press and ABC News, wrote *Seeds of Terror: How Heroin Is Bankrolling the Taliban and al Qaeda*, in which she recounts that the "more I learned, the more convinced I became that the nexus of smugglers and extremists presented a critical security threat, to both Afghanistan and the West."[21] Her book's first chapter is entitled "The New Axis of Evil," an axis which she argues is constituted by the "union of narco-traffickers, terrorist groups, and the international criminal underworld." Further, in terms of market share, the partnership between Taliban and traffickers "has quickly become dominant: opium produced in southern provinces where the insurgency reaps financial benefits accounted for roughly 80 percent of global supply in 2008." She asserts that "the insurgency is exploding precisely because the opium trade is booming," although she neglects the contribution of the decade-long occupation by coalition forces to fuelling popular and armed opposition.[22]

Also, NATO could soon be attacked by "drug armies" roaming the Afghan countryside and "controlling large areas of territory." And it "doesn't stop at Afghanistan's porous borders. This is a transnational problem ... As insurgent and criminal networks become more deeply intertwined, they will swell in economic and military might, and then what began as a regional headache will become a global security nightmare: the perfect storm." Indeed, in "hotspots around the globe, terrorist and other anti-state groups have forged symbiotic relationships with dope runners and the criminal underworld ... Whether it's the Irish Republican Army moving ecstasy into Northern Ireland, Maoist insurgent groups in Nepal running hash into East Asia, or Sri Lanka's Tamil Tigers moving Burmese heroin to the West."[23]

Peters' proposed solutions set her apart tactically from the Bush administration as she opposes aerial eradication. She nonetheless favors a militaristic approach, recommending "wide-ranging military action against top smugglers," while NATO "should arrest or kill the kingpins and midlevel smugglers" and "chemists able to cook opium into heroin." In addition, warplanes "should bomb heroin labs and launch air strikes against drug convoys," in what looks like an assassination campaign of drug dealers. But what about "collateral" deaths and popular outrage at such actions? Peters minimizes those consequences because drug "convoys don't travel down the highways, so there's less chance of collateral damage and civilian casualties," and in any case, the "kind of campaign I recommend would target 'bad guys,' and not victimize debt-ridden Afghan farmers."[24]

Vanda Felbab-Brown, from the liberal Brookings Institution, wrote a noted book entitled *Shooting Up: Counterinsurgency and the War on Drugs*, which focuses on "the nexus of drugs and insurgency in Afghanistan." Felbab-Brown's purpose is to advise governments "under attack, such as those of Afghanistan and Colombia" on how to "ultimately prevail over both insurgent forces and the illicit economies from which the insurgents derive much of their strength." Although well researched, the book nevertheless accepts conventional assumptions.[25]

Mainstream commentators disagree among themselves about tactics and their debates reflect those within government circles, in particular, between Bush's call for eradication and Obama's preference for interdiction and development. Thomas Schweich, for example, appointed in 2007 by Bush as coordinator for counter-narcotics and justice reform in Afghanistan, argued strongly in favor of eradication.[26] Rachel Ehrenfeld, while claiming that "liberating Afghanistan and Iraq were necessary first steps" in waging a war on terrorism "on all possible fronts," believes that "the most urgent task is to stop terrorist funding—especially that which is derived from the drug trade." She proposes to use mycoherbicides in Afghanistan and South America to "attack and kill" drug plants. Legislation has also been pushed in the US Congress calling for the use of such substances. However, the Drug Policy Alliance reports that mycoherbicides have already been rejected as far too unpredictable and unsafe "by every U.S. government agency that has ever worked with them," including the CIA and DEA, in addition to the Andean Community of Nations and the United Nations, because of their non-selectivity and toxicity on plants and animals. The toxins they produce have even been mass-produced and stockpiled by the major powers for use in chemical warfare. Further, using mycoherbicides in foreign countries "would be perceived globally as biological warfare and considered a violation of the Biological Weapons Convention (BWC), and may increase support for the insurgencies in Colombia and Afghanistan."[27]

Meanwhile, a number of researchers have opposed eradication and supported alternative development to encourage farmers to grow legal crops. For example, Felbab-Brown favors interdiction and a more laissez-faire policy to poppy cultivation because that would not increase the insurgents' "political capital" (the popular support they have). She is arguing against Bush's emphasis on eradication and for Obama's strategy of alternative livelihoods and interdiction, which she deems a "courageous break with [Bush's] ineffective efforts in Afghanistan."[28]

The mass media has also largely followed the same story. The *New York Times*' Thomas Friedman writes from Helmand province, "where mafia and mullah meet. This is where the Taliban harvest the poppies that get turned into heroin that funds their insurgency."[29] In the *Washington Post*, Michèle Alliot-Marie, then French minister of defense, talks about "the links between narcotics, money and terrorism" and proposes "to reinforce the training programs of the Afghan police," as well as "closing down and prohibiting poppy-processing laboratories," increase "counternarcotics operations," encourage crop substitution, and "investigate new markets, such as nuts and grapes," and notes that "several tree nurseries should be renovated" as well.[30] Joel Hafvenstein, an international development consultant, states that the solution to "Afghanistan's drug habit" is to "reform a vital but neglected institution: the local police." American and European drug habits, however, don't get as much consideration.[31] The debate between alternative livelihoods and crop eradication has also received its fair share of attention, along with a number of stories implicitly blaming drugs and the corruption they fuel for Washington's inability to "stabilize" Afghanistan.[32] Thus, the *New York Times* editors state that in "the morass that is Afghanistan, not just the Taliban are flourishing. So too is opium production, which increasingly finances the group's activities," which is a problem because the drug trade "strengthens the extremist forces that American and NATO troops are fighting and dying to defeat" and "undermines the Afghan state they are trying to build."[33] Popular publications agree, such as a recent *National Geographic Magazine* article entitled "Opium Wars," which describes how the Taliban are involved in trafficking while US Marines work hard to foster agricultural development to eliminate poppies.[34]

Finally, there is a right-wing libertarian interpretation which departs somewhat from the mainstream view in that it is opposed to current counternarcotics operations and advocates an end to the prohibition regime, as argued by the CATO Institute's Ted Galen Carpenter. Carpenter is essentially asserting that the US government should not focus on the drug war but on the war on terror, because our "mortal enemy is Al Qaeda and the Taliban regime ... The drug war is a dangerous distraction in the campaign to destroy those forces." Thus, Washington should "look the other way regarding the drug-trafficking activities of friendly warlords" because they help fight the Taliban.[35]

A CRITICAL INTERPRETATION

The remainder of this chapter presents an alternative view. It is argued that American foreign policy is not motivated by concerns to eradicate drugs, being shaped on the contrary by political economic factors. It suggests that drug wars are better seen as rhetorical exercises facilitating intervention overseas, in particular, against groups that challenge US hegemony. This interpretation is shared in whole or in part by others who have described it in relation to other times and places, such as Colombia.[36]

A number of factors have been emphasized in explaining American foreign policy, ranging from economics, politics and military strategy to gender, race, ideology and culture, to name a few.[37] This book conceives of it as shaped primarily by American corporate and political elites and as such largely reflects their global political economic interests. These consist in expanding markets and investment opportunities, ensuring access to needed raw materials and cheap labor, and fundamentally, preserving a global economic and political climate conducive to the implementation of those goals. Those objectives were clearly articulated in the early postwar period, for example in NSC-68, the defining document of the cold war from the US perspective.[38] Because there is bound to be opposition to hegemony—either from rival states, allies, or popular movements—military power has often been needed to counteract it and restore "stability" (meaning conditions favorable to US interests), either through overt intervention, covert operations, or deterrence by maintaining large nuclear arsenals. Territorial control and military positioning in strategic locations are also important to influence developments in key geographical areas, for example in the Middle East and Eurasia. Another important US government need is to maintain "credibility," whereby Washington shows resolve by responding forcefully to challenges to its dominance, militarily or otherwise. The point is to signal to would-be challengers that defiance, disobedience or independence will not be tolerated, as failing to respond decisively could embolden others elsewhere.[39]

Subsequent chapters will illustrate this interpretation with respect to Afghanistan since the late 1970s. But the principles guiding American power have been clearly visible for decades and especially since the end of World War II. The priority was then to rebuild a global economy that would be dominated by the United States, with Germany and Japan acting as regional leaders fuelling the recoveries of Europe and Asia respectively. Washington worked to keep leftist movements out of those arrangements, for example by making Marshall Plan aid conditional on the exclusion of communists from governments in France and Italy.[40] Third World countries were also designated to play a role in the revival of the world economy. For example, Melvyn Leffler carefully reviewed the archival record and showed that key American policymakers "emphasized that the economic recovery and financial stabilization of Europe could not take place if Europe did not have access to markets, raw materials, and foodstuffs in Asia and Africa and if Europe could not earn dollars through overseas investments, especially in Asia."[41] George Kennan, a top US official and the father of cold war "containment" doctrine, proposed the "exploitation" of Africa to that end.[42] American planners thought that Southeast Asia should be organized so that it may "fulfill its major function as a source of raw materials and a market for Japan and Western Europe."[43] Postwar policy towards the Middle East has been remarkably consistent and has sought to allocate the region's energy resources to allies like Japan and European countries and oppose nationalist movements in the region that could reduce US control of its riches through friendly dictatorships. This was both to fuel allies' economies but also to keep some degree of influence over them: James Forrestal, President Truman's Secretary of Defense, noted that "whoever sits on the valve of Middle East oil may control the destiny of Europe," while George Kennan argued that controlling Japan's oil imports would mean a "veto power" over its industrial development.[44] Latin America was to be dominated by the United States, whose objectives there included ensuring "adequate production" and "access" to "raw materials essential to U.S. security." Washington would "encourage" Latin America "by economic assistance and other means... to create a political and economic climate conducive to private investment," including the opportunity for "foreign capital to repatriate a reasonable return."[45]

But opposition to such plans has arisen repeatedly, and Washington has consistently moved to counter it. US elites may perceive that their material interests are directly threatened, or that they must react forcefully to show the world that they mean business and will not tolerate dissent. The postwar diplomatic record contains many references to such concerns. For example, in 1947, the United States was supporting the conservative Greek government in its counterinsurgency campaign against the peasant and worker groups that had fought the Nazis during World War II under Communist leadership. Under Secretary of State Dean Acheson warned Congress that if assistance was not forthcoming, similar "communist" movements would spread to other places. He declared that like "apples in a barrel infected by one rotten one, the corruption of Greece would infect Iran and all to the east."[46] A few years later, when Iran moved to nationalize its oil industry in the early 1950s, Britain and the United States backed a coup that removed the nationalist leader Mosaddeq and brought back the Western-friendly Shah to power in 1953. The *New York Times* then editorialized: "Underdeveloped countries with rich resources now have an object lesson in the heavy cost that must be paid by one of their number which goes berserk with fanatical nationalism."[47] A number of other examples pertaining to Afghanistan will be described in later chapters.

The book differs from mainstream accounts but also from that of critical analysts like Alfred McCoy and Peter Dale Scott, although it shares aspects of their arguments. McCoy in particular has documented more thoroughly than anyone else the CIA's complicity in the global drug trade since World War II through support for local drug lords who proved useful in pursuing American global objectives during and after the cold war. One point of difference arises, however, with regards to the meaning and uses of Washington's drug wars. This book seeks to highlight their rhetorical character. In contrast, McCoy seems to accept that American presidents since Richard Nixon have been waging real wars on drugs, although he asserts that they have been ineffective and self-defeating because those interventions have resulted in an increased global supply by stimulating production worldwide. McCoy argues that overseas counterdrug operations have in the past been carried out "by applying the full coercive resources of the United States government to eradicate narcotics production at its source," but unfortunately this has "unleashed market forces that would ultimately expand the drug trade" elsewhere in the world, as drug production moved to other countries and new consumption markets developed.[48] In the second edition of his landmark book *The Politics of Heroin* (1991), when commenting on President Bush Sr.'s declared war on drugs in Latin America, McCoy even wrote that "Bush invaded Panama" in order to "cut the flow of cocaine northward across the Caribbean." He also opined that with the end of the cold war, "narcotics suppression may become the main aim of U.S. foreign policy in the Third World during this decade" (the 1990s).[49]

McCoy summarizes his conceptualization of the war on drugs by stating that "the U.S. and UN have persisted, for over fifty years, in a Quixotic, self-defeating strategy that defies the dynamics of the global drug market." He explains this by comparing the leaders of America's drug wars as being "rather like Mickey Mouse in the animated Disney film *Fantasia*—a 'sorcerer's apprentice' frantic to stem rising waters by attacking the bucket-carrying brooms with an ax, only to have the chips resurrect as full-grown brooms and the flood turn into a torrent." One problem is that capturing even the biggest drug lords does not alter the global flow of drugs. In fact, if "the downfall of the heroin king is so inconsequential, then the global drug trade may well prove too elusive, too resilient for any repression, even a war on drugs. If so, then the United States and its allies need to admit that drug prohibition might be futile and seek another solution." McCoy concludes by stating that looking back "on this century-long Anglo-American experiment in drug prohibition, we need to entertain the possibility that this effort has failed."[50]

But this is true only if we accept that Washington has indeed been waging real wars on drugs, whose goal has been to reduce drug consumption and production. This book argues that this is very unlikely, because the United States has long supported drug traffickers and pursued a number of other policies supporting or tolerating the global drug trade, in addition to having consistently adopted the counterdrug policies that are well known not to work. In contrast to McCoy, it is thus maintained that it is misleading to assert that the United States has "persisted for over fifty years" and "applied its full coercive resources" to fight drugs. Rather, drug wars are better seen as exercises facilitating intervention overseas and targeting enemies, as will be illustrated in later chapters.[51]

Peter Dale Scott has presented an ambitious thesis about drug wars that claims a high degree of responsibility on the part of the US government in supporting the global narcotics trade. This book's main difference with Scott is in its interpretation of American foreign policy and the latter's relationship with drugs. In plain terms, he conceives of US policy in conspiratorial terms and believes it is significantly influenced by secretive groups that lobby the high levels of government to influence policy in their favor, such as the "China lobby," the "Israel lobby," the "oil companies lobby," and of course what he refers to as the "global CIA-drug connection," a pragmatic alliance between intelligence services and drug proxies. Scott refers to the workings of those secretive forces and their effects as "deep politics," which "can refer to any form of sinister, unacknowledged influence" on government policy.[52] Those secretive forces may even have been responsible for orchestrating events like the 9/11 attacks, according to Scott, who argues that "America's major foreign wars are typically preceded by deep events like the Tonkin Gulf incidents, 9/11, or the 2001 anthrax attacks. This suggests that what I call the war machine in Washington (including but not restricted to elements in the Pentagon and the CIA) may have been behind them." Scott has spent some time "considering whether elements within the U.S. war machine played a part in engineering" 9/11, but so far has found no smoking gun.[53]

Such assumptions lead him to ask: "Did successive crises in the illicit drug traffic induce some drug-trafficking U.S. interest groups and allies to press successfully for U.S. involvement in an Asian war?"[54] He suggests that the US government may have indeed intervened to stimulate the drug trade, perhaps because of lobbying by interested groups. Likewise, he wonders whether Washington intervened in Afghanistan in 2001 or elsewhere previously to protect the drug industry in order to stimulate the American economy. This book contends that available evidence does not support such arguments, as will be seen in chapter 5. The view presented here accepts that interest groups pressure government, but emphasizes that policy is shaped by broad political economic factors. It is unlikely that the CIA or drug traffickers would be able to push government policy in directions that depart fundamentally from elite interests as a whole, which are predominant. When lobby groups are successful, it is often because they share the elite consensus.

3
Rise to Prominence

This chapter surveys CIA support for traffickers in a number of countries since World War II, showing that US government policy has not been driven by a concern for narcotics control. In his authoritative account of the agency's complicity in global trafficking, Alfred McCoy summarizes the record thus: "As our knowledge of the cold war grows, the list of traffickers who served the CIA lengthens to include Corsican syndicates, Nationalist Chinese irregulars, Lao generals, Afghan warlords, Haitian colonels, Panamian generals, Honduran smugglers, and Nicaraguan Contra commanders." Those covert alliances empowered drug lords and boosted the industry in a number of locations around the world, even after the CIA departed. As a result, a "decade after the cold war's end, the CIA's three main covert battlegrounds—Afghanistan, Burma, and Laos—were, in that order, the world's three leading opium producers." (Mexico has recently moved into second place.) Therefore, for decades, CIA operations have been an indirect, but important, cause of addiction in the United States, Europe and the world. For example, at "two key junctures when America's heroin supply and addict population had dropped markedly in the late 1940s and the late 1970s, the CIA's covert alliances contributed to a surge of opium supply that soon revived the U.S. drug trade. Although these alliances represented only a fraction of CIA operations, they had considerable impact on the global heroin trade."[1]

The agency's support for traffickers, and in general the back seat that narcotics control has taken relative to the pursuit of more critical objectives, has been conceded by intelligence officers themselves. For example, Milton Bearden, CIA station chief in Pakistan in 1986–9, said years later while reflecting on the 1980s in an interview: "Did I know there was a drug problem in Afghanistan?... Of course there is, of course there was ... Did we devote our resources to fighting the narcotics problem? No ... it would possibly detract from accomplishing what was an overwhelmingly large mission, that is, driving the Soviet army out of Afghanistan."[2] Douglas Blaufarb, CIA station chief in Laos in the 1960s, noted in his memoirs that "without a doubt" Air America planes [an airline operated by the CIA during the Vietnam War] had then transported opium and that the CIA turned a "blind eye" to its allied Hmong fighters' involvement in drugs. Other former agents have confirmed that Air America "hauled a lot of dope" and that the State Department and the CIA did not give a "rat's ass about smuggling" and protected local "assets" from investigation and arrest. CIA agent Tony Poe (Anthony Poshepny) believed that General Vang Pao, chief of the CIA's Hmong army in Laos, had made "millions" from the drug trade. "You could have a war against Communism or a war against drugs," he said, "but you couldn't have both." Orin DeForest, a chief CIA interrogator, wrote that "South Vietnamese military and political bigwigs" allied with the US "looted the country ruthlessly" and "deposited huge amounts of piasters (Vietnamese currency) in Hong Kong bank accounts," coming partly "from drug sales."[3]

This chapter looks in detail at Afghanistan in the 1980s, when US-backed mujahideen groups fought the Soviets while involving themselves in trafficking. The concluding section discusses the case of the Bank of Credit and Commerce International (BCCI), which laundered drug money in Pakistan and around the world, including the United States. This, however, did not deter the CIA from collaborating with it and the US government seemingly to close its eyes for many years to its narcotics-related activities, while proclaiming to be engaged in a war on drugs.

THE FRENCH CONNECTION

In the 1930s, the heroin consumed in the United States originated mostly from China, with smaller quantities coming from the Corsican syndicates in Marseille, in southern France, as well as from other sources in the Middle East. World War II broke existing trafficking networks: for example, shipping routes in the Mediterranean were disrupted by submarine warfare and the Japanese invasion of China stopped the flow of drugs from there to the United States. The reduction in supply led to decreases in American consumption levels, which reached a low point.

However, soon after the war, trade and addiction increased again, and between 1948 and 1972, the US market was dominated by the Italian mafia and Marseille's Corsican syndicates, known as the "French Connection."[4] How did the renewal of the drug traffic come about? One important cause was American support for key traffickers as allies in the fight against leftists and communists. In the years immediately after World War II, the United States sought to establish a liberal world economic order under its hegemony and revive European and Asian economies to that end. Leftist political movements could potentially disrupt such plans and were thus opposed. Already during the war, intelligence services had formed an alliance with the mafia in Sicily, which helped the Allies invade the island against the Axis powers in 1943; the alliance with the mafia was maintained afterwards, to prevent the Italian Communist Party from growing in strength in Sicily. The invasion was prepared with the help of well-known mobster Charles "Lucky" Luciano. Luciano was a leader of the Italian mafia in the United States who controlled large drug and prostitution networks, for which he was jailed in 1936. However, during World War II, intelligence services (the Office of Naval Intelligence, ONI) sought his help to plan the invasion of Sicily, due to Luciano's contacts with the mafia there. In 1946, he was freed by US authorities on the grounds that he had helped the war effort. He went to Italy, from where he soon organized an international heroin trafficking network. Supplies were taken in the Middle East, refined in Europe, and distributed in the United States, which saw its number of addicts grow from 20,000 at the end of World War II to 150,000 by 1965.[5]

The Corsican syndicates in Marseille were also key players in the traffic and acted in coordination with Luciano and the Italian mafia to ship heroin to the United States. But first, their power and hold over Marseille had to be established, which was achieved with CIA help. "From 1948 to 1950, the CIA allied with the Corsican underworld to fight the French Communist Party for control over the strategic Mediterranean port of Marseille. With CIA support, the Corsicans won control of the waterfront and used it, for the next quarter-century, to export heroin to the U.S. market."[6] In Marseille, the CIA supported the Corsicans to reduce the power of the Communist Party over the city government and to break two strikes in the docks which threatened shipping in 1947 and 1950. This was important for Washington because much of Marshall Plan aid, itself delivered by the United States on the condition that communists be excluded from the national government, arrived at Marseille's docks. For example, when 80,000 workers went on strike in Marseille in 1947, the CIA sent agents and a psychological warfare team who dealt directly with Corsican leaders in an effort to break the strikes. The agency supplied weapons and money to the Corsican gangs, who used the supplies to murder a number of striking workers, assault Communist picket lines and harass union officials. Food aid was used as a weapon, as when the American government threatened to ship back to the United States 65,000 sacks of flour supposed to alleviate hunger in the city if dock workers did not unload them immediately. The workers yielded, and the strike eventually ended. In 1950, workers on the docks decided to boycott shipments of weapons for the war in Indochina, which was unpopular among Marseille's leftist unions. The action spread to other industries and regions of France as well, but the CIA intervened again and sent $2 million which was used to hire scab workers from Italy to work on the docks to replace the strikers. Some tough gangsters were also hired to break the picket lines. The operation was done in collaboration with Corsican leaders, and eventually was successful in breaking the work stoppage.[7]

In sum, US intelligence services supported and collaborated with the criminal underworld, including drug traffickers, to weaken communists and leftists. In a pattern that would repeat itself more than once during the cold war, one consequence was an increased global supply of narcotics, with some of it making its way to the United States. The Corsicans, having been empowered financially and politically thanks to CIA aid, acquired the capacity to establish themselves more firmly in Marseille, control its docks, and use the city as a base to refine and ship heroin to the United States and other markets. For the next 20 years, together with the Italian mafia, their business flourished.

BURMA

In 1949 in China the Communists defeated the Nationalist Chinese (Kuomintang, or KMT) government and proceeded with a drastic anti-drug campaign in the country that proved very effective at reducing production and consumption.[8] Poppy cultivation shifted to neighboring Burma, Laos, and Thailand, and KMT remnants in those areas became involved in the opium trade. In 1951, the CIA started supporting the KMT based in Burma in an anti-Communist campaign seeking to assist it in regaining a foothold in China's Yunnan province, unsuccessfully as it turned out. The KMT financed its operations by forcing local hill tribes to produce opium, which led to a significant increase in poppy cultivation on Burma's Shan Plateau, from less than 20 tons in 1958 to 500 tons in 1970. The CIA's fleet of aircraft, Civil Air Transport (CAT, later renamed Air America), supplied the KMT in the Shan States of Burma with weapons and supplies, and from there sometimes reloaded the planes with KMT opium, which they flew back to Bangkok. In Thailand, the national police chief, General Phao Siyanan, another CIA ally, oversaw exports and local distribution.[9]

The result was the opening of a Shan State–Bangkok corridor which took opium cultivated in Burma to Thailand, and on to the world market. In effect, the CIA had planted the seeds for increased opium production in the Golden Triangle, the region of Southeast Asia covering parts of Laos, Thailand and Burma that became the world's largest opiate supplier before Afghanistan took over in the 1990s. CIA support for the KMT in Burma and General Phao in Thailand set the stage for a recurring pattern consisting in the agency backing local warlords and strongmen involved in drugs, resulting in a flourishing narcotics traffic. Drug revenues mean a supplemental income useful to finance local groups' operations, as well as a line of funding independent of official sources, which helps keep the operations secret. Support for drug traffickers is instrumental in pursuing broader objectives of foreign policy, and in Burma, this meant opposing Communist China, in line with cold war strategy. For example, in 1950, the US Joint Chiefs of Staff suggested the implementation of a "program of special covert operations designed to interfere with Communist activities in Southeast Asia."[10] A byproduct was the expansion of the drug traffic and the rise of the Golden Triangle as global production center, since even after the CIA stopped supporting the KMT, the latter continued expanding its activities. By 1973, it controlled nearly one-third of global illicit opium supply.[11]

SOUTHEAST ASIA

During the first Indochina war (1946–54), the French military and intelligence services, in order to raise funds for covert operations against local communists and nationalists, involved themselves in various aspects of Indochina's opium trade, from poppy cultivation in Laos to transport and distribution in Vietnam. Those secret activities were referred to as Operation X, which ran from 1946 to 1954. The French bought the opium from Hmong and Yao hill tribes and sold it in Vietnam, and even to the Corsican syndicates in Marseille. Colonel Edward G. Lansdale from the CIA visited Indochina in 1953 on a mission and learned about the operation. He later claimed that he reported this back to the United States but received the following response from Washington: "Don't you have anything else to do? We don't want you to open up this keg of worms since it will be a major embarrassment to a friendly government. So drop your investigation."[12]

In the 1960s and early 1970s, the United States supported drug proxies in Southeast Asia, within the context of the Vietnam War, contributing to the rising importance of the Golden Triangle in opium production. At that time, the heroin from the Golden Triangle was exported to the world via two routes. As seen above, one was the Burma–Thailand corridor, and the other was the Laos–South Vietnam corridor. The CIA role in the establishment of the latter (which closed after the end of the Vietnam War in 1975) was similar to that in the former. During the Vietnam War, the CIA relied on Hmong tribes led by General Vang Pao in Laos to fight local communists (the Pathet Lao). In exchange, CIA agents would help transport (with Air America, for example) the Hmong's opium from their villages to heroin refineries, from which the heroin could then be sold on the market. This arrangement provided cash to support the Hmong tribes and guerrillas. At the same time, Washington supported various allies in the government, police, and military officials in Southeast Asia who were involved in trafficking, even if some of the drugs were consumed by American soldiers in Vietnam. US protection allowed the officials to raise illicit funds to strengthen their position, resulting in a significant expansion of the traffic. For example, the Nguyen Van Thieu-Nguyen Cao Ky government of South Vietnam in power in the 1960s and 1970s, along with the South Vietnamese military, police and customs, were all involved in protecting the industry. In Laos, General Phoumi Nosavan and General Ouane Rattikone also oversaw the trade. In short, American allies in the Vietnam War were trafficking in drugs, and part of this traffic, originating in the Golden Triangle, was slowly making its way to the United States.[13]

Support for local drug proxies was instrumental to the pursuit of broader objectives. US intervention in Indochina was initially motivated by its importance for the economic recovery of Europe and Japan after World War II. American planners assigned Southeast Asia the important role of providing Japan with food and raw materials, while the region could also send dollars to Europe to fill its "dollar gap," in addition to providing a market for manufactured goods. If leftist movements took power in Southeast Asia, such plans could be disturbed. Thus, Washington felt it had to intervene to support puppet governments in Vietnam against nationalist resistance.[14]

LATIN AMERICA

In the 1980s, the Contras, irregular forces backed by Washington in their attacks on Nicaragua's leftist Sandinista government, were involved in cocaine trafficking from the Colombian Medellín cartel into the United States. Senator John Kerry launched an investigation of "Contra drug links" that lasted over two years, and which concluded: "it is clear that individuals who provided support for the Contras were involved in drug trafficking, the supply network of the Contras was used by drug trafficking organizations, and elements of the Contras themselves knowingly received financial and material assistance from drug traffickers." Moreover, the State Department made payments of over $806,000 to known drug traffickers to deliver supplies to the Contras. In several cases, the payments were made even after the traffickers had been indicted on drug charges by US federal prosecutors. Assistance to the Contras by traffickers included "cash, weapons, planes, pilots, air supply services and other materials." For example, weapons came on small planes carrying drugs. The planes unloaded the weapons and then headed to the United States with the drugs for the American market. The pilots also used the Contra airstrips to refuel their planes even when there were no arms to unload. The traffickers "knew that the authorities would not check the airstrips because the war was 'protected.'"[15] Thus, the relationship was mutually beneficial: the Contras gained much needed support supplementing their limited resources, while the traffickers gained cover and protection for their criminal activities. Following the usual pattern, the fact that the CIA conducted operations in Central America made it an "enforcement-free zone" where authorities turned a blind eye toward traffickers. Once again, this was a case of "tolerance for drug dealing by the [CIA's] local assets and concealment of their criminal activity to protect its covert operation."[16]

In Colombia, although mainstream commentary has focused on the links between drugs and the FARC rebels, which are real, right-wing paramilitaries have also been significantly involved in trafficking. President Bill Clinton's Plan Colombia was ostensibly a war on drugs package, but in fact it neglected the paramilitaries' role in narcotics. Carlos Castaño, who was the leader of the paramilitary group AUC (United Self-Defence Forces of Colombia) before his death in 2004, once stated that 70 percent of his organization's operations was financed by drug trafficking and traffickers. Plan Colombia also ignored the trafficking networks "run, protected and sustained by Colombia's narco-mafia and their paramilitary armies." Meanwhile, the United States has for a long time been a strong supporter of the Colombian government and military, and indirectly of the paramilitaries collaborating with the Colombian armed forces, in order to "pacify" rebels and make Colombia's resources and markets accessible on profitable terms.[17]

In Mexico, the state has historically set the rules of the game in drug trafficking, while receiving strong support from Washington. During its seven decades in power, the PRI (Partido Revolucionario Institucional), until it lost power to the PAN (Partido Acción Nacional) in 2000, oversaw an informal system whereby every key actor, from the military, police, traffickers and local and national political officials, took a cut from drug trafficking. Narco-violence was kept to relatively low levels and every group had an incentive to conduct its business in a relatively predictable and stable manner. But Washington mostly looked the other way because the Mexican government was an anti-communist ally during the cold war. Today, the state does not preside over a smoothly regulated traffic anymore—hence the violence due to fighting among cartels and the authorities—but sectors of the Mexican government and security forces are still associated with it.[18]

AFGHANISTAN

Until the late 1970s, Afghan opium was traded regionally, within Asia. Afghan and Pakistani farmers produced limited quantities consumed, for example, by Iran's addicts. However, during the 1980s, Afghanistan became a major producer, and the Pakistani border area became an important source of heroin globally. One significant factor behind this transformation was the CIA's covert warfare operations, which gave traffickers the protection needed to expand their production, so that during the 1980s, the "covert war in Afghanistan transformed Central Asia from a self-contained opium zone into a major supplier of heroin for the world market."[19]

Other circumstances abetted the growth of the Afghan narcotics industry, including the 1978–1980 drought in the Golden Triangle, which reduced opium production there from 700 tons in 1971 to 225 in 1980.[20] Also, the 1979 Iranian revolution brought a theocratic regime to power that cracked down on drug use and production. Although ineffectual in many ways, the Iranian ban appears to have reduced poppy cultivation from about 33,000 hectares in 1979 to 3,500 hectares by 1993. Nevertheless, consumption continued to increase and Iran remained a large absorber of opiates regionally, while transforming itself as an important transit country for Afghan narcotics.[21] Finally, in 1979, Pakistan's General Zia ul-Haq implemented a poppy ban that caused much of the cultivation simply to move across the border into Afghanistan.[22]

What was the role of the United States in Afghanistan's transformation from regional to leading global producer? In 1978, leftist factions in the Afghan army toppled President Mohammed Daud and set up a pro-Soviet regime in Kabul. The new leaders advocated modernization reforms that alienated the traditional tribal order in the countryside, energizing a nascent insurgency that would soon be exploited by the United States and Pakistan to destabilize the Afghan government. Groups based in Pakistan and opposed to the new regime began to send armed guerrillas across the border to capitalize on the growing popular discontent.[23] According to Robert Gates, US support for the mujahideen started months before the Soviet invasion of December 1979. In early 1979, the Carter administration began exploring possibilities to assist the rebels covertly and in March 1979 the CIA proposed several options to this end. Senior American officials deliberated at that time on whether "there was value in keeping the Afghan insurgency going, 'sucking the Soviets into a Vietnamese quagmire.'" American intelligence pointed out that an advantage of covert support to the insurgents would be to "raise the costs to the Soviets and inflame Moslem opinion against them in many countries." A National Security Archive review stated that in April 1979, the American embassy in Islamabad asked Pakistani military officials to recommend a group of rebels towards which US aid could be directed. In May 1979, a CIA official was thus introduced to Gulbuddin Hekmatyar, a radical Islamist and anti-American who headed "the most militant and organized rebel group, the Hizb-i Islami (Hekmatyar)." Finally, in July 1979, Jimmy Carter approved covert assistance to the insurgents—six months before the Soviet invasion. The initial authorized support included psychological operations in Afghanistan and the provision of cash and nonmilitary supplies. At first, a little more than half a million dollars was allocated to those operations.[24]

Zbigniew Brzezinski, Jimmy Carter's National Security advisor, declared in 1998 that by initiating covert operations before the Russians invaded, "we knowingly increased the probability that they would" invade. One important motivation for American involvement was to give the Russians their Vietnam war; the conflict in Afghanistan led to some one million Afghans dead. When asked if he regretted the decision, Brzezinski responded:

> Regret what? That secret operation was an excellent idea. It had the effect of drawing the Russians into the Afghan trap and you want me to regret it? The day that the Soviets officially crossed the border, I wrote to President Carter: We now have the opportunity of giving to the USSR its Vietnam war. Indeed, for almost 10 years, Moscow had to carry on a war unsupportable by the government, a conflict that brought about the demoralization and finally the breakup of the Soviet empire.

When asked if he regretted having supported, armed and advised future Islamic terrorists, he replied: "What is most important to the history of the world? The Taliban or the collapse of the Soviet empire? Some stirred-up Moslems or the liberation of Central Europe and the end of the cold war?"[25]

The Soviet invasion led to increased American support: within a year, tens of millions of dollars were allocated to clandestine operations, along with the provision of weapons. For example, in January and February 1980, Brzezinski went to Egypt, Pakistan, and Saudi Arabia to discuss the expanded covert action program. President Sadat of Egypt recalled the meeting as the Americans asking: "'Please open your stores for us so that we can give the Afghanis the armaments they need to fight,' and I gave them the armaments." Secretary of Defense Harold Brown flew to China to agree on Chinese arms shipments. The Saudis consented to give $25 million in aid to the Afghan insurgents. The CIA purchased foreign weaponry in order to "plausibly deny" American involvement in case the operation was exposed. Throughout the war, the CIA bought Soviet-designed weapons from Egypt, China, and other countries and shipped them to Pakistan; Kalashnikov rifles and anti-aircraft missiles arrived as early as 1980. The level of aid received by the insurgents was modest until 1984 and increased thereafter. Over the 1980s, the CIA supplied the mujahideen with some $3 billion in military aid and Saudi Arabia added at least another $2 billion. Pakistani intelligence was in charge of distributing the funds and equipment to the rebels.[26]

The setting up of covert operations in Afghanistan took place against the backdrop of American policymakers' worries about "stability" in the region. In the 1970s, President Nixon chose to rely on regional proxies to police the Middle East, such as the Shah of Iran, who was provided with massive amounts of weaponry. Therefore, the 1979 Islamic revolution that removed him from power was a serious setback for American power, especially given Iran's large energy reserves and strategic location. When 52 American hostages were taken at the US embassy in November 1979, this added to the humiliation and raised concerns about US credibility in the region, while a botched rescue attempt in April 1980 compounded the gravity of the situation. It was the kind of indigenous radicalism that had always worried Washington. Zbigniew Brzezinski talked of an "arc of crisis" in the region where the "resulting political chaos could well be filled by elements hostile to our values and sympathetic to our adversaries." The arc spread from Bangladesh through Pakistan through Yemen, including Afghanistan, "where a pro-Soviet junta that seized power last year is trying to rule over one of the world's most ungovernable tribal societies." When Afghanistan was invaded, Brzezinski said that the "Soviet Union has chosen both to exploit that turbulence and to project its power into it. This is likely to be highly destabilizing for all of the neighbors of Afghanistan."[27]

In the wake of the invasion, the Carter Doctrine was proclaimed in January 1980 and called for a more aggressive US posture globally, and in particular in the Middle East. Carter's speech made reference to the Soviet invasion and the Iranian revolution and hostage crisis. He declared:

> The region which is now threatened by Soviet troops in Afghanistan is of great strategic importance: It contains more than two-thirds of the world's exportable oil ... The Soviet Union is now attempting to consolidate a strategic position, therefore, that poses a grave threat to the free movement of Middle East oil ... Let our position be absolutely clear: An attempt by any outside force to gain control of the Persian Gulf region will be regarded as an assault on the vital interests of the United States of America, and such an assault will be repelled by any means necessary, including military force.[28]

The Soviet invasion was also used as an official rationale for Carter's rearmament program:

> It's imperative that Congress approve this strong defense budget for 1981, encompassing a 5-percent real growth in authorizations, without any reduction ... We are also improving our capability to

deploy U.S. military forces rapidly to distant areas. We've helped to strengthen NATO and our other alliances.[29]

But in fact, the invasion and the Iranian revolution acted as catalysts to push forward plans already in the making for a Rapid Deployment Force (RDF) to be dispatched to the Middle East and elsewhere, along with the establishment of a regional security framework including American access to ports, bases and joint military exercises. Already in August 1977, Carter had signed Presidential Directive no. 18 (PD-18) on "US National Strategy" which instructed the military to establish a "deployment force of light divisions with strategic mobility ... designed for use against both local forces and forces projected by the USSR ... in the Middle East, the Persian Gulf, or Korea." In January 1978, Harold Brown, Carter's secretary of defense, directed the US military to plan for a rapid deployment force of up to 100,000 men, ready to intervene in the Persian Gulf or elsewhere.[30]

Although it is the alleged threat posed by the USSR to the Persian Gulf that was emphasized in public pronouncements, the main threat was that posed by nationalist movements that could challenge friendly dictators in the energy-rich region and hence threaten US dominance over the world economy. This has been a recurring pattern for decades. For example, when Egypt's Nasser nationalized the British-controlled Suez Canal company in 1956, Britain and France, in collaboration with Israel, attacked Egypt. Washington did not like Nasser either: President Eisenhower noted in 1956 that "the growing ambition of Nasser" is a fundamental problem, although it could be overcome by "build[ing] up some other individual as a prospective leader of the Arab world ... My own choice of such a rival is King Saud." On his part, John Foster Dulles, Eisenhower's secretary of state, opined in 1958 that Nasser was an "extremely dangerous fanatic" who was "moved by a dream of pan-Arabism, something like Hitler's pan-Germanism."[31]

Similarly, in the aftermath of the Soviet invasion of Afghanistan, as Melvyn Leffler has documented, "Carter's defense officials were not primarily concerned with Soviet military strength in the Persian Gulf area. Soviet capabilities for power projection, although growing, were not overwhelming, even in the gulf. Indeed the threat of outright Soviet invasion was not considered a likely contingency." On the contrary, Robert Komer, one of the architects of the RDF and under-secretary of defense for policy under Carter, testified before Congress after the Soviet invasion that "the most likely use of the

RDF was not to resist a Soviet attack but to deal with indigenous and regional unrest within the Persian Gulf region."[32] Moreover, the head of the CIA, Stansfield Turner, wrote in January 1980 that it "is unlikely that the Soviet occupation is a preplanned first step in the implementation of a highly articulated grand design for the rapid establishment of hegemonic control over all of southwest Asia."[33] Nevertheless, under President Reagan, the RDF and its successor CENTCOM (US Central Command) would grow to cover 19 countries in Southwest Asia and the Horn of Africa.[34]

SUPPORTING DRUG PRODUCTION

The Reagan administration adopted a hardline policy toward Afghanistan and sought to make support for the mujahideen an important element of the "Reagan Doctrine" in order to hurt the Soviets. Pakistan was key to this objective. Within days of the invasion, Carter offered General Zia hundreds of millions of dollars in aid in exchange for cooperation in supporting the rebels. It is the Reagan administration however that cemented the relationship by giving Zia a six-year economic and military aid package that made Pakistan the third largest US foreign aid recipient. Although Zia was going ahead with his nuclear weapons program and didn't seem interested in ever holding elections, he had now become a fellow "freedom fighter."[35]

The insurgency against the Russians was composed of seven Islamist mujahideen groups based in Pakistan's refugee camps.[36] Those groups received the bulk of American, Pakistani and Saudi funding through Pakistan's Inter-Service Intelligence (ISI). The ISI was able to maintain control over the mujahideen thanks to the large amounts of cash and supplies it dispensed to them. However, it is important to note that there were alternative resistance groups which were more broadly representative and not fundamentalist. For example, within days of the Soviet invasion, on 4 January 1980, Mohammed Omar Babrakzai, a tribal leader and former judge of the Kabul High Court, convened a "National Council" designed to organize and plan the resistance to the invasion. After a number of meetings, the group called a popular assembly (Loya Jirga) that gathered 916 delegates from all of Afghanistan's provinces, and included all major Pashtun tribes as well as all non-Pashtun ethnic groups. The meetings' purpose was to organize formally resistance activities, as much political as military, and possibly set up a government-in-exile until the Russians would leave the country.

But precisely because of its inclusive and representative character, the movement was seen as a threat by the seven mujahideen groups and the ISI. The Loya Jirga sharply rejected fundamentalist doctrine and called for a form of Islam acceptable to all persuasions in the country. It also rejected a centralized Islamic state and favored a decentralized form of national government, respecting regional and tribal autonomy. Internationally, it called for nonalignment and coexistence, in contrast with the fundamentalists' message that Islamic countries and the Soviet Union were irreconcilable enemies.[37]

Predictably, the apparent initial momentum in setting up an alternative resistance movement led the ISI and the mujahideen to undermine the newly created "National Commission." The *Christian Science Monitor* reported that some mujahideen were "doing everything possible to subvert the proceedings" and some of them "venomously attack the loya jirga," calling it "illegal." But in fact, "support for the loya jirga is far greater than most of the [mujahideen] parties would like to admit." Although the parties claimed "to be the true representative of the Afghan people," it seemed that "their influence does not substantially spread beyond the refugee camps in Pakistan and the frontier Afghan provinces." Selig Harrison wrote that "numerous accounts of this campaign were reported to me during a Peshawar visit in late June" 1980. Groups walked out of the Commission under threat by the ISI that the limited economic and military aid on which they subsisted would be cut off, and soon enough the Commission collapsed. Although a number of local resistance groups sprung up during the 1980s to fight the Russians, the alternative of a non-fundamentalist and unified resistance movement that could have offered a more stable and peaceful government in the wake of the Soviet withdrawal, was nipped in the bud: by late 1980, the National Commission had virtually ceased to exist.[38] Other organizations could also have been supported instead of the mujahideen parties, such as RAWA (Revolutionary Association of the Women of Afghanistan), a secular women's rights group still active today that encouraged Afghans "to unite and fight for the independence of our beloved country" against the Russian occupation. RAWA's goal was "to build a society in which oppression, torture, execution, and injustices must be replaced by democracy and social justice."[39]

However, the CIA and ISI favorite was Gulbuddin Hekmatyar, who got more than half the CIA's total covert aid for Afghanistan. Hekmatyar was one of the most violent fundamentalists among the rebels and he became one of Afghanistan's key drug lords. In the

1970s, he reportedly organized attacks on women by throwing acid in their faces if they refused to wear the veil. Journalist Tim Weiner reported that "CIA and State Department officials I have spoken with call him 'scary,' 'vicious,' 'a fascist,' 'definite dictatorship material.' A democrat he is not. If Hekmatyar becomes the king of Afghanistan, he will ascend upon bodies of countrymen he has killed with the CIA's weapons." As Sonali Kolhatkar and James Ingalls suggest, it is plausible that those are the very qualities that made him appealing to Washington's objective of bleeding the Russians, for which less extremist and more representative groups calling for coexistence and nonalignment like the National Commission, would have been less suited. Hekmatyar was also favored by the ISI because he was anti-nationalist and bitterly anti-communist. That is to say, he preferred allying himself with President Zia rather than call for an independent homeland for the Pashtuns who lived in Pakistan's North-West Frontier Province (NWFP).[40] In short, for both the United States and Pakistan, supporting him and other similar mujahideen factions while rejecting more democratic resistance groups can be seen as a logical choice in line with their own geopolitical interests. If Washington had had serious concerns for human rights, development, or drug control, the choices would surely have been entirely different.

The mujahideen ordered peasants living in the areas they captured to grow poppies, and they then smuggled the opium across the border to Pakistan where they sold it to refiners who transformed it into heroin. There was thus a "double pipeline" linking Afghanistan, Pakistan and the world: one moving drugs from Afghanistan to Pakistan and to the global market, and the other funneling weapons and equipment to the insurgents from various supporting countries to Afghanistan via Pakistan. Sometimes the same Pakistani army trucks were used to first bring weapons to Afghanistan, unload them, and then reload the vehicles with opium en route back to Pakistan, protected along the way by the ISI from police searches. Precise numbers on drug production in Pakistan are not available and vary from one author to another, but by 1988, estimates put at 100 to 200 the number of heroin refineries in the Khyber district of Pakistan's NWFP alone. The drug trade was reportedly under the protection of General Fazle Haq, NWFP governor and Zia's associate. Hekmatyar himself reportedly controlled six heroin laboratories in Pakistan's Baluchistan province. Pakistan's heroin production, using opium grown locally or imported from Afghanistan, increased from 40 tons in 1984–85 to 200 tons in 1987–88. One result, apart from increasing the supply of drugs to the West, was a heroin epidemic in the 1980s: some have estimated the number of Pakistani addicts to have zoomed from 5,000 in 1980 to over 1.3 million in 1985.[41]

In addition to protecting mujahideen involved in the narcotics traffic, Washington also sustained the trade indirectly by supporting Islamabad as a strong ally even though it knew that Pakistan had become "the prime opium source for U.S. heroin," in the words of Dominick DiCarlo, the assistant secretary of state for narcotics, supplying more than half the heroin used by America's 500,000 addicts. US officials argued that Pakistan was an ally on drug control because "President Zia and NWFP governor Haq restated Pakistan's commitment to its opium poppy ban." Similarly, Charles Greenleaf, a senior USAID official, commended President Zia for his "noteworthy progress in reducing opium production." But Pakistan was awash with drugs, leading to drastic increases in addiction and to the corruption of the political process, which became particularly apparent in the 1990s: Zia had, in a way, prepared the ground for the transformation of Pakistan into a narco-state.[42] For example, in 1983, ISI director General Akhtar Abdul Rahman was reportedly forced to remove a number of ISI staff in Quetta because of their links with the narcotics trade.[43] In 1986, Army major Zahooruddin Afridi was reportedly caught transporting 220 kilograms of heroin from Peshawar to Karachi, and two months later an air force officer was caught with another 220 kilograms of heroin on the same route. Both officers were jailed but escaped in mysterious circumstances.[44] After the covert war against the Russians was over, former CIA officials admitted that they had turned a blind eye to trafficking. For example, as Charles Cogan, former CIA director of the operation in Afghanistan, explained: "Our main mission was to do as much damage as possible to the Soviets. We didn't really have the resources or the time to devote to an investigation of the drug trade ... I don't think we need to apologize for this. Every situation has its fallout ... There was fallout in terms of drugs, yes. But the main objective was accomplished. The Soviets left Afghanistan."[45]

Washington's lack of concern for drug control was further demonstrated by the inaction of its DEA office in Islamabad, Pakistan. During the 1980s, the office achieved very little: it wrote detailed reports identifying "forty significant narcotics syndicates in Pakistan," but no investigations or arrests were carried out. The US Government Accountability Office (GAO) noted in 1988 that "not a single significant international Pakistani trafficker is known to have been imprisoned prior to 1984" and those who were put in jail after that date "were quietly released after serving a few months" only. The fact that CIA interests took priority over the DEA's led several DEA agents to ask for transfers to other locations, while at least one resigned, because they were prevented from carrying out their duties.[46]

The media didn't cover the drug involvement of US-backed guerrillas during the years of covert warfare. "Even as Pakistani heroin had flooded Europe and America in the early 1980s, there had been a curious silence about the origins of this new narcotics supply," downplaying negative reporting about American allies. After the Soviets withdrew and the mujahideen became less valuable to Washington, the press started publishing stories of the rebels' involvement in narcotics.[47] For example, in the 1980s, the American media put a positive spin on Hekmatyar, but in 1990, having lost his usefulness, the *Washington Post* stated, in a passage worth quoting at length, that the

> U.S. government has for several years received, but declined to investigate, reports of heroin trafficking by some Afghan guerrillas and Pakistani military officers with whom it cooperates in the war against Soviet influence in Afghanistan ... Afghans, including mujaheddin guerrillas, have given U.S. officials firsthand accounts of heroin smuggling by commanders under Gulbuddin Hekmatyar ... Officers of Pakistan's military intelligence agency, Inter-Services Intelligence (ISI), protect and participate in the trafficking ... Nevertheless, according to U.S. officials, the United States has failed to investigate or take action against some of those suspected in part because of its desire not to offend a strategic ally, Pakistan's military establishment. Also, since the Soviet invasion of Afghanistan in 1979, U.S. narcotics policy in Afghanistan has been subordinated to the war against Soviet influence there, especially under the Reagan administration.[48]

Hopes that the end of the war and the prospect of Soviet withdrawal and termination of CIA support for the rebels would reduce opium production were quickly dashed. On the contrary, the size of the narcotics traffic continued to increase as mujahideen commanders rushed to control and cultivate opium land. For example, in Nangarhar province in the east of Afghanistan, 80 percent of arable land around the city of Jalalabad was rapidly converted to opium production by 1992. In Helmand province in the south, blessed with very fertile land, mullah Nasim Akhundzada, a great rival of Hekmatyar's, controlled some of the best irrigated lands and ordered a significant proportion of them to be planted with poppies, even though the region had once been Afghanistan's main food production area. He was believed to kill or castrate any landowner who did not follow his directives, and eventually was able to appropriate most of the 250 tons of opium produced in Helmand, making him one of the most powerful warlords in the country, and giving meaning to his nickname the "King of Heroin." Mullah Nasim's brother explained to a *New York Times* journalist in 1986 that we "must grow and sell opium to fight our holy war against the Russian nonbelievers." Two months before, the US embassy in Islamabad had denied formally that Afghan rebels "have been involved in narcotics activities as a matter of policy to finance their operations." Just across the border, in Pakistan, Hekmatyar, anticipating in 1988 that the Soviets would soon withdraw and CIA support would dry up, directed his commanders to increase poppy cultivation and made investments in a half-dozen heroin refineries with Pakistani traffickers. Drugs were only gaining in importance, and the mujahideen sometimes fought each other for its proceeds, as when the forces of Mullah Nasim and Hekmatyar came to blows in 1989 for control of an opium area in Helmand province, with heavy casualties.[49]

BCCI AND DRUG MONEY LAUNDERING

BCCI existed from 1972 to 1991, and was reportedly nicknamed by Robert Gates the "Bank of Crooks and Criminals." It was founded and directed by Agha Hasan Abedi, a Pakistani businessman, who rapidly expanded its operations to 400 branches in 73 countries. The bank was owned by Arab capital from the Persian Gulf (the controlling shareholder of the bank was the multibillionaire president of the United Arab Emirates, sheikh Zayed bin Sultan al Nahyan). In the late 1980s and early 1990s, BCCI got caught in scandals that led to its forced closure by regulators around the world. It was involved in drug money laundering, used by many countries' intelligence agencies to finance their covert operations, and provided its services to arms dealers and other criminals. In the words of Peter Truell and Larry Gurwin, who wrote a well-received book on the subject, "BCCI was a criminal enterprise that catered to some of the most notorious villains of the late twentieth century, including Saddam Hussein, the blood-thirsty ruler of Iraq; leaders of the Medellín drug cartel, which controls the bulk of the world's cocaine trade; Khun Sa, the warlord who dominates heroin trafficking in Asia's Golden Triangle; Abu Nidal, the head of one of the world's leading terrorist organizations; and Manuel Antonio Noriega, the drug-dealing former dictator of Panama."[50]

The CIA held accounts with BCCI, through which it financed its covert operations, including funneling money to the mujahideen fighting the Soviets in Afghanistan. At the same time, the financial institution laundered some of the mujahideen's and traffickers' narcotics money: in 1983, General Zia reportedly authorized Pakistani traffickers to deposit their drug funds in BCCI accounts. The bank was important in facilitating the drug money transfers which reached $4 billion in Pakistan by 1989, an amount larger than the country's legal exports. According to internal documents, BCCI also "acted as a collection agency for war matériel and even for the mujaheddins' pack animals." A popular center to launder drug money from Afghanistan and Pakistan was the United Arab Emirates, where BCCI was the most important foreign bank.[51]

BCCI was also involved in laundering narcotics money from Latin America. It established branches in Colombia and saw impressive growth in the country, with its assets reaching a value of $213 million. The drug trade was one of the main reasons why it went to Colombia. Abdur Sakhia, the top BCCI official who ran its operations in the United States, said: "We knew that the money that we would be getting in Colombia would be drug money." BCCI "aggressively solicited deposits" from drug kingpins and provided them with advice on "how to invest and cover the money." A US investigator stated that the bank "absolutely and specifically sought out narco money." Panama was another growth center, where it collected tens of millions of dollars from Manuel Noriega, among others. One source of his funds was the drug trade, something that was known to US officials. In 1988, in Tampa, Florida, a federal grand jury indicted BCCI on drug money laundering charges. In 1990, the institution pleaded guilty, but received no stiff sanctions: it remained open and forfeited only $14 million. It would not be the only occasion on which the US government adopted a lenient approach towards banks involved in drug money laundering.[52]

Senator John Kerry led an investigation of the bank's activities and produced a report entitled *The BCCI Affair*, which made the following points. First, the US government dragged its feet and was not firm in prosecuting the bank, even while and after it was investigated and indicted on drug money laundering charges in 1988 in Tampa: "The Justice Department, along with the U.S.

Customs Service and Treasury Departments, failed to provide adequate support and assistance to investigators and prosecutors working on the case against BCCI in 1988 and 1989," which led the chief undercover agent in the sting against the bank to quit the Customs Service. US authorities even acted in a way "discouraging BCCI's officials from telling the U.S. what they knew about BCCI's larger criminality." Second, the Kerry investigation documented the nature and extent of the CIA's relationship with the bank. The report stated that after "the CIA knew that BCCI was as an institution a fundamentally corrupt criminal enterprise, it continued to use both BCCI and First American, BCCI's secretly held U.S. subsidiary, for CIA operations." In other words, the CIA was not bothered by the fact that it was maintaining close links with a drug money laundering institution, as long as this allowed the spy agency to pursue its activities. Moreover, the CIA was averse to cooperating with Kerry's investigation, providing it with "untrue" and "incomplete" information and refusing to provide "a 'full' account about its knowledge of BCCI until almost a year after the initial requests for the information."[53]

No matter what was the precise involvement of the CIA with BCCI, it is clear, as the Kerry report stated, that it collaborated with it while it knew it to be involved in criminal activities, including drug money laundering. Indeed, it was eventually revealed that the US government had received hundreds of warnings about the nature of BCCI's activities in the decade before it was finally tackled by federal authorities. Reports and memos from various government agencies were filed as far back as 1978, and plenty were produced and circulated throughout the 1980s. In fact, the CIA itself had been reporting on the bank's criminal activities and drug money laundering to the US government "since the early '80s," as later admitted by CIA Deputy Director Richard Kerr. Kerr also said that BCCI, "from the early '80s—it was quite obvious—was involved in illegal activities such as money laundering, narcotics and terrorism." Other warnings, among many, came in 1984 and 1985 when the Internal Revenue Service (IRS) learned on three separate occasions that BCCI was possibly a center for money laundering.[54]

Thus, it is clear that Washington never pursued the numerous leads and warnings it received on BCCI for about a decade and did nothing until the late 1980s, when it started moving against it, slowly. This is in spite of the fact that the government had professed to be conducting a war on drugs all along. As the *Washington Post* accurately noted: "Throughout the 1980s various federal enforcement agencies collected literally hundreds of reports of illegal activities on the part of BCCI ... the Drug Enforcement Agency's files alone show 379 references to BCCI involving 134 cases going back to 1978. Despite the Reagan and Bush administrations' repeated fierce declarations of war on drugs, BCCI was not prosecuted on any drug charge until late 1988, and it was not shut down and kicked out of the country until last year [in 1991]."[55]

As Alexander Cockburn noted at the time, due to the secret nature of their work, there is a natural association between intelligence agencies like the CIA and the banking underworld: "To do their dirty business, spy agencies like the CIA need dirty money and the services of dirty banks, which is why we find the Central Intelligence Agency using the same institution as did Abu Nidal, Manuel Noriega, the Contras and the Medellin cartel." However, when the relationship ceases to be useful, revelations and prosecutions may follow: "The CIA used BCCI to move money around, and its officials, when queried about the probity of BCCI and the nature of their relationship with it, were noncommittal until BCCI outlived its usefulness."[56]

4
From Forgotten State to Rogue State

The period from the Soviet withdrawal in 1989 until 9/11 can be divided roughly into two phases. In both, American policy was not determined by concerns over drugs (or human rights), but by economic and strategic factors and credibility concerns.

In the first half of the 1990s, civil war raged as competing mujahideen factions fought for power. During those years, the United States effectively disengaged from Afghanistan. Drug production almost tripled between 1989 and 1994, rising from 1,200 tons to over 3,100 tons, amidst a host of human rights abuses committed by all warring groups.[1] It is easy to see that Washington's attitude was not motivated by drug control, as it turned away from Afghanistan.

In the second phase, from 1996 until 2001, the Taliban were able to gain control over most of the country and impose a certain degree of stability. American policy toward the new regime shifted from an initial cautious welcome in 1996 to attempts at isolating the "rogue state" from 1998 onwards. Many commentators assert that concerns over drugs, human and women's rights played an important role in motivating the shift. But this chapter argues that such matters were quite incidental. It is maintained that the American policy of engagement was motivated by the prospect of laying pipelines across Afghanistan, while the shift toward isolation in 1998 was determined first and foremost by the Taliban's refusal to expel Osama bin Laden in the wake of the US embassy bombings in Africa. The Taliban implemented a successful narcotics ban in 2000–01. If drug control had been a key American concern, a warming of relations with the regime would have been expected. On the contrary, Washington reacted by slapping more sanctions on Afghanistan.

CIVIL WAR AND US DISENGAGEMENT

The Soviets completed their withdrawal in February 1989—while the CIA celebrated—but this did not bring peace. Even if Amnesty International called on the Soviet Union, the United States, Pakistan and the United Nations "to use all international facilities at their disposal to ensure that international humanitarian and human rights principles were observed throughout Afghanistan," the appeals were largely ignored.[2] For the next three years, Washington and Moscow exacerbated the crisis by supporting proxy forces in the civil war militarily, financially and diplomatically, as they had done since 1979. Russia funded the Najibullah government and the United States—together with Pakistan, Saudi Arabia, and Iran—the mujahideen. The superpowers knew very well that their local allies "were committing gross and widespread human rights abuses," but that didn't trouble them. As Amnesty International stated, the "message they sent was clear: do what you like, as long as you win."[3] By 1992, out of a total population of 23 million, the war had left 1.5 million Afghans dead, 5 million disabled, 4.5 million refugees and 10 million land mines.[4]

The superpowers terminated their military aid to warring factions in late 1991.[5] But the country was still in for more destruction. As Afghanistan expert Barnett Rubin observed, "when the Soviet Union withdrew and then dissolved, and the United States disengaged, Afghanistan was left with no legitimate state, no national leadership, multiple armed groups in every locality, a devastated economy, and a people dispersed throughout the region, indeed the world."[6] In April 1992, the mujahideen captured Kabul and the Najibullah regime fell. However, almost immediately, the rebels started fighting each other for the control of the capital and Afghanistan. The result was a dirty civil war from 1992 to 1996, which left at least 25,000 dead in Kabul alone, large parts of which were destroyed by the fighting, according to the Red Cross.[7] The *New York Times* reported in 1995 that "Kabul lies largely in ruins ... whole neighborhoods look like Hamburg or Dresden after World War II bombing raids."[8] After Najibullah's fall, Washington rapidly lost interest in the deepening crisis. In the words of two well-informed analysts, the "truth is that the Bush [Sr.] administration didn't care anymore what happened in Afghanistan."[9] And as an American expert on Afghanistan told the *New York Times'* Thomas Friedman at the time,

> most people in the U.S. Government have long since come to the conclusion that our objectives for Afghanistan are pretty limited ... What we basically want is an Afghanistan that does not destabilize its neighbors, like Pakistan and the Central Asian republics, where we really do have important interests. We don't

want a boiling Afghanistan exporting radicalism to the Central Asian republics when they are just coming of age.[10]

During the civil war, sovereignty over the country was divided up among warring groups and commanders. Territorial control and alliances shifted constantly and fighting raged in Kabul and other cities. As a result, "Afghanistan became, in the lingo of the time, a 'failed state,' where Afghans suffered from a 'humanitarian emergency.'" World powers neglected the country and regional powers, "especially Pakistan, but also private networks— smugglers, drug dealers, and terrorists—treated it as an open field for manipulation and exploitation."[11]

Although Russia and the United States had stopped delivering weapons to their Afghan clients, the latter continued receiving support from regional powers and US allies, perpetuating the violence. Four main armed groups fought each other to gain power in Kabul, and each supported itself through a variety of sources, which could include the drug trade, foreign allies' funding, as well as taxes and customs collections in areas under their control. Rashid Dostum led a mostly Uzbek group in the north and received support from Uzbekistan (and perhaps from Russia); Ahmad Shah Massoud and Barhanuddin Rabbani led mainly Tajiks in the northeast and received financial aid and fuel from Saudi Arabia; Gulbuddin Hekmatyar was the leader of a mostly Pashtun group and although he lacked a firm territorial base, received support from Arab radicals and Pakistan; finally, the Hizb-i Wahdat group was based in the Hazarajat in the center of the country and organized the Shia in Kabul, and was armed by Iran.[12] Human rights organizations have documented a catalog of abuses committed by warring factions during those years, ranging from rape to abduction to torture to murder. For example, Amnesty International reported that during "a rare lull in the bombardment of Kabul in 1994, a woman left her home to find food. Two Mujahideen guards grabbed her and took her to a house, where 22 men raped her for three days. When she was allowed to go home, she found her three children had died of hypothermia."[13] By 1995, tens of thousands of civilians had been "killed in deliberate or indiscriminate artillery attacks on residential areas by all factions in the civil war. These killings have been carried out with arms and ammunition supplied to the political groups by outside powers ... The use of cluster bombs on residential areas has been a common feature of attacks by most of the rival factions."[14]

It is clear that Washington was not concerned about protecting human rights or women's rights. But neither did it care about drugs, even if the industry's size expanded considerably during the civil war, as rival warlords' factions used narcotics trafficking to finance their operations. From 1979 to 1989, opium production had grown from 250 tons to 1,200 tons, and it reached 3,100 tons in 1994.[15] What did the international community do? Nothing.

The Afghan economy was progressively shifting toward one based significantly on drugs, "transformed from a diverse agricultural system—with herding, orchards, and sixty-two field crops—into the world's first opium monocrop."[16] Before the Soviet invasion, the Afghan countryside survived on subsistence agriculture. But Russia's counterinsurgency campaign destroyed the rural economy and food production decreased by as much as two-thirds. The withdrawal led to the monetization of the economy because the Soviet-supported Najibullah government presided over a policy of "national reconciliation" which consisted in increased spending for such things as local security forces and subsidies to military commanders. But at the same time, Soviet aid declined, just like natural gas revenues, due to poor infrastructure maintenance and the departure of Russian troops and technicians who worked on the gas fields. The resulting deficit was financed by printing money, which led to inflation: for example, food prices rose five to ten times between the late 1980s and early 1990s. Because the agricultural sector and trading networks had been destroyed by the war, Afghans now faced a food deficit and often had to rely on cash purchases to feed themselves at the new high prices. This state of affairs led many to devote themselves to occupations generating cash, in particular, smuggling and opium production.[17]

Poppy cultivation is well suited to raising cash because there is a strong global demand for drugs, while transportation costs are relatively low given the compact nature of the product and the fact that traders come directly to farmers to buy it. Opium production in Afghanistan is also labor intensive, generating employment for many and allowing farmers to access credit from traders and traffickers to make ends meet. Ignored by the international community and with no aid forthcoming to rebuild their livelihoods, farmers often simply gravitated towards harvesting opium to survive. As one of them explained: "In 1991, I returned to my village to farm. I planted 5 percent of my land with this filth (opium). This year, my family has returned from Pakistan to join me, and so I had to plant 25 percent this year." The United Nations reported in late 1991 that because they were anticipating a cut in CIA funding, Afghan guerrillas were wasting no time in increasing the size of their opium plantations to make up for the drop in external financing. For example, in Nangarhar province, which had seen a lot of fighting during the 1980s, villages were destroyed and depopulated by the end of the decade. But in the first half of the 1990s, opium revived the economy with annual harvests reaching 1,500 tons and heroin production created additional employment.[18]

A CAUTIOUS WELCOME: THE TALIBAN AND PIPELINES

The Taliban were formed in 1994, composed in part of religious students who had fought the Soviets in the 1980s together with the mujahideen and spent time in Islamic seminaries (madrassas) in Pakistan.[19] They sought to stabilize Afghanistan and rid the country of the fighting and warlordism that afflicted it since the Soviet withdrawal. They made their mark as a new military and political force by capturing Kandahar in November 1994. Better organized than the warring mujahideen factions, by February 1995, they controlled almost a third of Afghanistan's 30 provinces and were on their way to occupying Kabul. Pakistan provided them with much support throughout the 1990s, including millions of dollars, weapons, food, and "trucks and buses full of adolescent mujahid crossing the frontier shouting 'Allahu Akbar' [God is Greater] and going into the line with a day or two of weapons training," which, according to the US ambassador to Pakistan, Thomas Simons, "was Pakistan's real aid" to the Taliban.[20] Initially, Islamabad had supported Hekmatyar as their leading mujahideen, but reportedly, when he proved unable to assert his control over Afghanistan, Pakistan turned to the Taliban as their new proxy force. Pakistan hoped to gain "strategic depth" in Afghanistan against India by installing a friendly regime in power. The latter could also make roads safe for commerce by disarming strongmen and ending illegal "toll" collections. Reducing lawlessness would also make possible a Trans-Afghan pipeline (TAP, see below) bringing gas from Turkmenistan to Pakistan. Lastly, the Taliban would help Pakistan by tempering Pashtun nationalist claims over the country.[21] In Barnett Rubin's words, "Pakistan ultimately sought to create a corridor to Central Asia by bringing the fragmented Pashtuns under the control of the Taliban, a purely religious leadership that did not support nationalist demands, that would not ally with non-Muslim powers, and that depended on Pakistan through a variety of networks that had developed over twenty years of war and dispersion."[22] Saudi Arabia also gave them support, given its rivalry with Iran, its strategic cooperation with Pakistan, similar religious ideology, and because some Saudi companies and individuals had interests in the pipeline proposals.[23]

Initially, the Taliban were "generally welcomed by the Afghan people, long wearied of war and the continued fighting between Afghan factions," the State Department noted.[24] But notwithstanding the relative stability they brought, they soon implemented harsh policies on the population and women in particular. When they took over Kabul in September 1996, they caught Najibullah, the former president, tortured him and hanged him in public view. As will be seen below, they also legalized the drug trade, whose size increased dramatically under their rule.

Drugs, human rights and the mistreatment of women were often invoked by Washington when dealing with Afghanistan under the Taliban, but in fact, such concerns did not shape attitudes toward the regime. Rather, two main factors were prominent: energy resources and Osama bin Laden's presence in Afghanistan and his relationship with the Taliban. Overall, US policy moved from one of cautious engagement in the mid-1990s to one of clear antagonism by the late 1990s. Around the time the Taliban assumed power in Kabul in 1996, Washington essentially sought to determine whether the new regime would be friendly to its interests and the diplomatic mood was exploratory. American officials saw potential areas of cooperation on pipelines and to neutralize or extradite bin Laden, but were also aware that the Taliban could at some point decide to adopt an independent or confrontational stance.[25]

As noted by Milton Bearden, by 1996, the "West fleetingly saw the Taliban as the source of a new order and a possible tool in yet another replay of the Great Game—the race for the energy riches of Central Asia." As such, during the first Clinton administration, Washington made some supportive pronouncements toward the new regime, such as exploring engagement and suggesting that it might reopen the American Embassy in Kabul.[26] In September 1996, the day after the Taliban captured the capital, the State Department sent instructions to the American embassy in Pakistan on how to deal with them. It stated: "We wish to engage the new Taliban 'interim government' at an early stage to demonstrate USG [US Government] willingness to deal with them as the new authorities in Kabul; seek information about their plans, programs, and policies." Bin Laden was already an issue, as diplomats were told to ask the Taliban: "Do you know the location of ex-Saudi financier and radical Islamist Osama bin Laden?... His continued presence here would not, we believe, serve Afghanistan's interests."[27]

Washington wanted to see if it could find "moderate" Taliban, meaning friendly to its interests. This exploratory attitude toward a new regime coming to power was standard procedure, as stated in a cable sent from the American embassy in Pakistan exploring ideas on how "the US could proceed on 'moderating and modernizing' the Taliban." It stated that the

> type of problem that the U.S. faces in a Taliban-dominated Afghanistan is not a new one in our diplomatic history. We faced similar problems in dealing with the French revolution ... the Bolshevik revolution, and most recently, the Iranian revolution (remember trying to find the Iranian moderates?). The basic issue is how the U.S. should react to the rise of radical movements ... The question boils down to whether to engage, and if the choice is to engage, how to do it and maintain U.S. credibility.

One problem was that the group had a "troubling record," for example, "they have continued to grant sanctuary to Osama bin Ladin"; however, "on the plus side," they "have restored security and a rough form of law and order in their areas of control," which could prove useful to build pipelines. Therefore, US diplomats recommended a policy of "restrained engagement" rather than "all-out engagement," the latter being too premature because "it could leave the U.S. closely associated with a movement we find repugnant." Thus, "a policy of limited engagement to try to 'moderate and modernize' the Taliban" is more appropriate, that is, trying to convince them that good relations can be established if they toe the US line. How should this be done? By "ratcheting up public diplomacy," meaning that "we should continue to highlight the stark differences the U.S. has with the Taliban over the issues [of] support for terrorism, narcotics, intolerance, and human rights abuses. By doing this, we will be able to continue to apply pressure on the Taliban to change its ways." As argued here, narcotics, intolerance and human rights abuses are not serious concerns and were invoked to keep pressure on the new regime. The goal was to convince them to go along with American objectives on what really mattered, namely, Osama bin Laden, whom the United States should make an "all-out effort to press the Taliban to expel."[28]

American interests in the Caspian basin's energy resources were not significant before the collapse of the Soviet Union in 1991. But since then, with US diplomatic and military assistance, private energy companies have moved to capture those resources. One important objective has been to steer the Central Asian republics away from Russia, the region's traditional master, from Iran, which has challenged US hegemony in the region, and from China, which is also interested in accessing the reserves. The strategy has remained virtually unchanged up to this day, although the pretexts have varied, notably since 9/11, as the threat of terrorism has been invoked to justify intervention.[29]

Growing interest in Caspian resources was first motivated by exaggerated estimates of their size, assessed at around 200 billion barrels of oil, or ten times the North Sea reserves, although they were later reduced to 30 billion barrels.[30] Nevertheless, the early estimates contributed to magnifying the region's perceived importance in diversifying energy sources away from the Persian Gulf. As Dick Cheney said to oil executives when he was CEO of Halliburton in 1998: "I can't think of a time when we've had a region emerge as suddenly to become as strategically significant as the Caspian."[31]

In February 1998, the House of Representatives held hearings entitled "U.S. interests in the Central Asian republics," during which Representative Doug Bereuter outlined American objectives succinctly: "Stated U.S. policy goals regarding energy resources in this region include fostering the independence of the States and their ties to the West; breaking Russia's monopoly over oil and gas transport routes; promoting Western energy security through diversified suppliers; encouraging the construction of east–west pipelines that do not transit Iran; and denying Iran dangerous leverage over the Central Asian economies." Robert Gee, the assistant secretary for policy in the Department of Energy, added: "We also have an interest in maximizing commercial opportunities for U.S. firms and for U.S. and other foreign investment in the region's energy development … Accordingly, our government has promoted the development of multiple pipelines and diversified infrastructure networks to open and integrate these countries into the global market." He underlined the important aim of isolating Tehran: "The U.S. Government opposes pipelines through Iran. Development of Iran's oil and gas industry and pipelines from the Caspian Basin south through Iran will seriously undercut the development of east–west infrastructure, and give Iran improper leverage over the economies of the Caucasus and Central Asian States."[32]

US company Unocal had plans that conformed to Clinton's "multiple pipelines" policy to drain the Caspian's energy reserves: it proposed one oil and one gas pipeline to go from Turkmenistan to Pakistan, via the western and southern parts of Afghanistan. Robert Gee said that the "Unocal pipeline is among those pipelines that would receive our support."[33] However, as analyst Michael Klare noted, no other pipeline was "more fraught with hazard" given the war conditions in Afghanistan.[34]

So, at around the time that the Taliban captured Kabul, Washington saw them as a force that could unify the country and permit pipelines to cross it safely. US officials actively promoted Unocal's project with Niyazov, Turkmenistan's president, while trying to convince Pakistan to adopt Unocal's planned project instead of that of the rival Argentine company, Bridas. Unocal found Sheila Heslin, director of energy issues at the National Security Council, "responsive, full of information and ideas, and very supportive of Unocal's agenda in Afghanistan," and Robin Raphel, the assistant secretary of state for South Asia in charge of Afghanistan, "very helpful." In short, the White House had become "engaged in a hardheaded synthesis of American commercial interests and national security goals": the private ambitions of Unocal would help Washington isolate Iran and take Central Asian resources away from Russia.[35] As a result, when the Taliban announced new laws against women's rights and civil liberties to be enforced by their religious police, Washington voiced little protest. Even if female government employees were now ordered to stay at home and the new regime declared that jail terms would apply to tailors who took women's body measurements, American diplomats, when meeting with Taliban officials, were instructed to "demonstrate USG willingness to deal with them as the new authorities in Kabul."[36] As one official said, despite some concerns, Washington was willing to "give the Taliban a chance."[37]

However, American support for the Taliban at that time should not be exaggerated.[38] Although they could potentially bring stability to the country on their own, according to the declassified internal record, State Department officials always seem to have kept in mind that a settlement in which a number of warring factions would share power, perhaps negotiated through the United Nations, could be a viable option as well. For example, Secretary of State Warren Christopher instructed diplomats in September 1996 that the "USG fully supports the proposal for gas and oil pipelines from Turkmenistan to Pakistan via Afghanistan," but that there was a need to make sure the political settlement in Afghanistan included all major factions, otherwise this could only generate more instability down the line and jeopardize pipeline projects: "It is true that the Taliban currently control the entire pipeline route... However, others have the military capability to interfere with pipeline construction and operation, and it stands to reason that in the absence of a negotiated peace settlement that allows pipeline benefits to be shared, those left out could be tempted to disrupt the pipeline." Unocal itself also maintained contacts with all Afghan factions, hedging its bets in the face of uncertain outcomes.[39] In November 1996, the US ambassador to Pakistan, Thomas Simons, met with Taliban acting foreign minister Ghaus and told him that all warring factions had to recognize "that one group cannot control the whole country" and called for "renunciation of the 'winner-take-all' approach to the conflict."[40] Finally, Washington never recognized the Taliban government officially (only Saudi Arabia, Pakistan, and the United Arab Emirates did so), and as far as is known, there is no evidence that either the United States or Unocal ever provided the regime with direct material support.[41]

ROGUE TALIBAN

The US position evolved from one of cautious engagement to one of antagonism, with the main turning point being the 1998 US embassy bombings in Kenya and Tanzania and subsequent Taliban refusal to expel bin Laden. The shift in Washington's attitude is well illustrated by Zalmay Khalilzad's views before and after the embassy bombing (Khalilzad, an American citizen born in Afghanistan who joined the government under the Reagan administration, would later become ambassador to Afghanistan from 2003 to 2005). In October 1996, he called on the United States to "reengage" Afghanistan. He said that the "Taliban does not practice the anti-U.S. style of fundamentalism practiced by Iran—it is closer to the Saudi model" and saw a "common interest" between them and the United States in seeking the "departure of Osama bin Laden." However, in 1999, he wrote another article in which he now labeled Afghanistan a "rogue state." "Protecting U.S. interests and stopping the spread of 'Talibanism' require confronting the Taliban"—"engagement ... is not likely to work [and] could even backfire, encouraging Taliban radicalism." "Washington must weaken" the regime and "should offer existing foes of the Taliban assistance."[42]

Afghanistan became al-Qaeda's main base when bin Laden returned to the country from Sudan in May 1996. At that time, he tended to be considered a threat mainly confined to the Middle East, and the Taliban promised Saudi Arabia that they would not allow him to carry out acts of terrorism abroad. Nevertheless, in Washington's eyes, his presence in Afghanistan was always a warning sign that the Taliban were not reliable allies. This became even clearer after the August 1998 embassy bombings in Africa, which killed over 200 people, including twelve Americans. The fact that the regime continued to defend bin Laden after this event and denounced the ensuing American missile strikes on their country increased US concerns and ruled out diplomatic recognition and oil and gas pipeline projects.[43] From at least that point onwards, as Milton Bearden stated, "the hunt for bin Ladin has been the driving force behind U.S. policy toward Afghanistan."[44] Likewise, the US ambassador to Pakistan, William Milam, said in October 1998 that "our paramount interest in Afghanistan at the present time was to secure the immediate extradition of bin Laden from the country."[45] Steve Coll reports that in the wake of the bombings, "White House officials feared" that if bin Laden kept attacking American targets he "might seriously weaken the power and prestige of the United States."[46] Saudi Arabia followed the United States: by the summer of 1998, Riyadh reduced financial assistance to the Taliban, having seemingly lost trust in their willingness to curb bin Laden's activities. With the embassy bombings following in August 1998, the Saudis terminated assistance and diplomatic relations, upset by the Taliban's refusal to hand him over.[47]

Of course, bin Laden's presence in Afghanistan before the embassy bombings preoccupied Washington, but not as much as after the attacks. A State Department report noted that between 1996 and summer 2001, the United States pressed the Taliban to expel bin Laden over 30 times. For example, they were told that harboring him "greatly hurt prospects for Afghanistan rejoining the world community" (December 1996) and that this has "alienated the U.S. and the international community" (January 1997). When bin Laden issued a statement calling on all Muslims to wage a holy war on Americans, Secretary of State Madeleine Albright instructed diplomats to convey to the Taliban "at the earliest opportunity" that Washington finds statements such as bin Laden's "outrageous and unacceptable" and that "the Taleban must share responsibility for Usama bin Laden's terrorist actions and inflammatory statements as long as he remains a guest in Qandahar" (February and March 1998).[48] But two weeks after the embassy bombings, Washington responded much more forcefully by launching Tomahawk cruise missiles on Afghanistan and Sudan (75 and 13 missiles respectively, according to Steve Coll). The targets in Afghanistan were training camps near Khost, where a number of "terrorist leaders," including bin Laden, were allegedly gathering at the time of the strikes. The 9/11 Commission report stated that the "strike's purpose was to kill Bin Ladin and his chief lieutenants," but he apparently had left the camps hours before the missiles hit, although 21 people were reportedly killed and 53 wounded. President Clinton also authorized the CIA to use lethal force to capture bin Laden and his top aides "within days" of the embassy bombings.[49]

The missile strikes were a show of force, and Madeleine Albright explained that "this is our way of making very clear that we will not be intimidated and that when our national interests are threatened, that we will respond unilaterally." President Clinton added: "Let our actions today send this message loud and clear: There are no expendable American targets; there will be no sanctuary for terrorists." One concern was that others could be emboldened, as Thomas Friedman explained while questioning Clinton's toughness: "when people think they can attack the U.S. with impunity, they will be tempted to try again." Perhaps the Los Angeles Times editors best summed up the American attitude when they stated that "we strongly support Clinton's determination to demonstrate that terrorists can have no sanctuary" because the missile strikes "do serve notice to countries that are friendly to terrorists, as both Sudan and Afghanistan are, that their support is not cost-free. The attacks were necessary and appropriate—timely evidence that the military reach of the United States is long and that its knowledge of terrorist hiding places and activities can be exact and devastating."[50]

A few months after the strikes, Washington slapped sanctions on the Taliban, unilaterally in July 1999, then through the UN Security Council in October 1999 (resolution 1267) and December 2000 (resolution 1333). The purpose was to retaliate for their failure to obey and extradite bin Laden (the 2000 sanctions were also prompted by the bombing of the US Navy warship USS Cole while it was refueling in Aden harbor, Yemen, killing 17 American sailors). The sanctions precluded American oil companies from taking their pipeline projects further. President Clinton declared that the "message to the Taliban is unmistakable: bin Ladin's training camps must be closed; the threats and operational activity must cease, and bin Ladin must answer for his crimes." He stated that it "is time for the Taliban to heed the will of the United Nations" and that the sanctions will "demonstrate the need to conform to accepted norms of international behavior."[51] This effectively meant that Afghanistan needed "to heed the will of the United States" and "conform to US orders." US Ambassador to the United Nations Nancy Soderberg emphasized that the sanctions "will send a direct message to Usama bin Laden, and terrorists everywhere: 'You can run, you can hide, but you will be brought to justice.'" The measures were cosponsored by Russia, which also opposed the rulers of Afghanistan, fearing they would embolden Islamic militants in the former Soviet republics of Central Asia and destabilize regimes friendly to Moscow.[52]

The sanctions show that US policy toward the Taliban regime was driven primarily by credibility concerns, not by drugs (or human rights). Their purpose was to isolate and shame the Taliban for failing to expel bin Laden, not to address the atrocities and dire humanitarian situation faced by the population, nor to address drug problems (see next section). They imposed an arms embargo on the Taliban, but not on the factions fighting them—calling themselves the "United Front" or "Northern Alliance" and composed of old mujahideen groups under the command of Abdul Rashid Dostum, Ahmad Shah Massoud, Ismail Khan and others—even though "all have committed severe abuses and none is making a serious effort to bring perpetrators to justice." Human Rights Watch deplored this emphasis and called on the Security Council "to impose an arms embargo on all warring factions," not just a "one-sided embargo unconnected to the human rights of the Afghan people."[53] A similar one-sidedness characterized the clauses concerning drug production in Afghanistan, as will be seen below. Human rights organizations have documented the sanctions' negative impact on the Afghan population. A report by the Office of the UN Coordinator for Afghanistan concluded that they contributed "to worsening poverty and vulnerability amongst the general population," and the study only considered the impact of the first round of sanctions, before the second round intensified them. International humanitarian organizations "were unanimous in the opposition" to sanctions, and Oxfam warned that their implementation "threatens to deepen this already desperate humanitarian crisis" in which many Afghans "face starvation in the coming months."[54]

THE TALIBAN AND DRUGS

Conventional interpretations assert that concerns over drugs played an important role in motivating the American policy shift toward isolation of the Taliban. For example, Richard Mackenzie writes that one reason why relations deteriorated was because "the hope that the Taliban would put an end to the cultivation of the opium poppy in Afghanistan predictably proved to be an illusion. Far from being partners in a 'war against drugs,' the Taliban were revealed to be the beneficiaries of the poppy."[55] Also, UNODC states that the "international isolation of the Taliban regime over its violations of human rights, support of terrorism and increasing opium production led to the Security Council imposing sanctions on Afghanistan in October 1999."[56] This section downplays the role of narcotics in shaping American policy.

The Taliban brought relative stability to the countryside and security on the roads, leading to a moderate economic recovery in areas where the fighting had ceased during their first years in power. Agricultural and horticultural production benefited and livestock herd numbers rose.[57] As a farmer told journalist Ahmed Rashid: "We cannot be more grateful ... The Taliban have brought us security so we can grow our poppy in peace. I need the poppy crop so I can support my 14 family members."[58] One consequence of the Taliban ban on the formal employment and education of women was that a large, cheap work force became available to work in the informal opium industry. UNODC reported that in northern and eastern Afghanistan, women played "a fundamental role in the cultivation of the opium poppy" in tasks ranging from planting and weeding to harvesting and cooking for other laborers.[59]

The regime had originally planned to clamp down on opium production, but once in power, only prohibited cannabis production, realizing that the income from opium would be needed and that banning its production would anger the rural population. The drug trade became de facto legal, making it largely "peaceful and competitive." Between 1996 and 1999, opium production doubled, reaching over 4,000 tons a year and generating important revenues for the state as poppy farmers paid an agricultural tax (*ushr*) of 10 percent and drug traders paid a 20 percent tax (*zakat*). It has been estimated that in 1999, the Taliban raised roughly $45 million through those taxes (other estimates put the annual revenue at some $75–100 million). Heroin refining also expanded: for example, in Jalalabad, in Nangarhar province, hundreds of refineries were tolerated and taxed. But the Taliban were not the only faction to control opium territories. Northeast Afghanistan, where Ahmad Shah Massoud's group was based, produced about 3 percent of the national opium harvest (Taliban-controlled areas produced 97 percent). Commanders in the northeast also levied ushr on farmers, and traders were also taxed by some local authorities. Although Massoud received more income from the gem trade, there were nevertheless a number of heroin refineries on his territory.[60]

Pakistan, on its part, eradicated poppy cultivation and shut down heroin labs in the mid-1990s, under some American pressure. As Ahmed Rashid observed, it "was only after the Soviet withdrawal from Afghanistan that US and Western pressure began to mount on Islamabad to curtail the production of opium in Pakistan."[61] But on balance, Islamabad's moves against poppy cultivation and heroin refineries changed nothing because they simply moved across the border into Afghanistan. The so-called "balloon effect" increased the size of the Afghan narcotics industry and by the same token, the Taliban's tax revenue. The balloon effect refers to the fact that when poppy or coca plants are eradicated in one country, their cultivation will soon emerge somewhere else if global demand remains constant, just like a balloon pressed at one end expands at the other end. Moreover, Pakistan still acted as an important transit country for Afghan heroin exports to the world market. During the 1990s, the country's politics became corrupted by drugs, a consequence of its important role as drug transit and refining country in the previous decade. Narcotics money now flooded the political system and the annual earnings from the industry were estimated at $8 to $10 billion, a sum much greater than the government's budget and about a quarter of its GDP. A 1993 UNODC report observed that the main traffickers had put in place a "parallel government" to protect their interests, while some of them were able to get elected in the national assembly. Elements of the governments of Benazir Bhutto and Nawaz Sharif, which alternated in power in the 1990s, were both perceived by many to have formed alliances with drug traffickers while accusing the other of doing the same.[62]

In July 2000, the Taliban banned poppy cultivation (but not trade in opium). The ban was implemented through regional governors who met with provincial authorities, local administrators and tribal elders to inform them of the new regulations, while mixing "persuasion, negotiation and enforcement." Some farmers who cultivated poppies were imprisoned, although they were usually released after a few days if they promised to eradicate their crops. The regime's precise motivations for the ban have been debated, but probably included a bid to gain international recognition. Some observers have pointed to the fact that the Taliban could profit from selling their opium at the higher prices that would result from a contraction in supply.[63]

The ban was issued in time for the planting season in October 2000 and resulted in a drastic decrease in opium production during the spring 2001 harvest, which was less than 200 tons, and most of it was in areas controlled by the Northern Alliance. This meant that the Taliban had virtually eliminated opium production from the country, no small feat for the world leader. Reports in early 2001 confirmed that the measures were being enforced systematically: a UNODC survey reported in February 2001 that "cultivation of opium poppy appeared to have been eliminated" and in May 2001, an investigative mission reported that it had been "effectively eliminated."[64] In October 2001, UNODC's Annual Opium Poppy Survey for 2001 confirmed in detail "the near total success of the ban in eliminating poppy cultivation in Taleban controlled areas." For example, "Helmand Province, the highest cultivating province last year with 42,853 Ha [hectares], recorded no poppy cultivation in the 2001 season. Nangarhar, the second highest cultivating province last year with 19,747 Ha is reported to have 218 Ha this year." Moreover, the survey stated that 80 percent of Afghanistan's total 185 tons of opium harvest came from areas controlled by the Northern Alliance. For example, in "Badakhshan, there has been an increase from 2,458 Ha to 6,342 Ha compared to last year."[65] In short, opium production fell by 94 percent in 2001, down to the levels of the early 1980s before it started to expand under CIA protection. One analyst commented that by the spring of 2001, the ban's effectiveness "was already confirmed beyond any doubt," with the result that it "astonished the international community."[66]

However, Washington reacted by intensifying sanctions on the Taliban through the Security Council. Clearly, concerns about refusal to expel bin Laden took precedence over drug control. In December 2000, resolution 1333 was adopted, followed by resolution 1363 in July 2001 (the latter was enacted to monitor and enforce the implementation of previous resolutions 1267 and 1333). Even when drug control was mentioned, the objective was more to isolate the regime than to address drug problems. For example, resolution 1333 ordered all states to prevent the sale or transfer of acetic anhydride (a key chemical precursor to make heroin) to the Taliban, but seemingly not to the Northern Alliance, whose drug revenues tripled between 1999 and 2001: it stated that the chemical could not be sold "to any person in the territory of Afghanistan under Taliban control." Other clauses were similarly clearly directed at the Taliban but vague on Northern Alliance activities, as when the Security Council noted "that the Taliban benefits directly from the cultivation of illicit opium by imposing a tax on its production and indirectly benefits from the processing and trafficking of such opium, and *recogniz[es]* that these substantial resources strengthen the Taliban's capacity to harbour terrorists," and as such "*demands* that the Taliban, as well as others, halt all illegal drugs activities and work to virtually eliminate the illicit cultivation of opium poppy, the proceeds of which finance Taliban terrorist activities." At the United Nations, Nancy Soderberg said that the United States was "disturbed by the significant rise in illicit opium production under areas of Taliban control," neglecting to mention the areas under Northern Alliance control.[67]

The international community, through UNODC, also turned its back on the regime's anti-drug efforts. In October 1997, Pino Arlacchi, the organization's director, announced a deal with the Taliban: in exchange for eradicating poppies, they would receive $25 million per year during ten years to fund alternative development programs. In September 1999, following a bumper harvest of 4,565 tons, the regime directed that cultivation area in the country be reduced by a third (the actual result turned out to be a 10 percent decrease in cultivation area but a 28 percent drop in opium production).[68] However, this didn't influence the Security Council: the following month, in October 1999, it adopted the first round of sanctions (1267) on Afghanistan. Later, when the 2000–01 ban was successfully implemented, instead of acting on his promises, Arlacchi announced in September 2000 that UNODC was closing down its anti-poppy cultivation operations in the country. The Taliban were angry and the director of their High Commission for Drug Control, Abdel Hamid Akhundzada, declared: "We are wondering how the [UN] can step out of its programme on the pretence of not having the funding. We have fulfilled our obligations. We demand that the agreement we made should be fulfilled up to the end." But Arlacchi had not been able to obtain enough funding from the international community, which was bent on confrontation with the regime. The bin Laden issue took priority over drug control. This was business as usual, as between 1993 and 1997, UNODC had asked for $16.4 million for drug control programs in Afghanistan from international donors, but received only half the requested funds. The United States contributed $3.2 million over five years, out of an annual drug war budget of about $14 billion.[69]

It is true that the Bush administration gave $43 million in humanitarian aid to Afghanistan in May 2001, to show appreciation for the effectiveness of the ban. Two American officials were also sent to the country as part of an international mission to assess the situation and explore ways to help farmers living in poverty, while Colin Powell said to Kofi Annan in April 2001 that "the United States is prepared to fund a United Nations International Drug Control Program proposal in Afghanistan to assist former poppy cultivators hard hit by the ban."[70] This has led some observers to suggest that the Bush administration was initially more open to exploring diplomatic contacts with the regime, perhaps signaling "an important shift in U.S. policy."[71] One can only speculate on the direction the Bush administration would have taken had 9/11 not happened, but arguably, the apparent shift was likely a minor one. Crucially, sanctions were never lifted, and a new round was even approved in July 2001 (resolution 1363). *Inter Press Service* reported Kofi Annan as saying that "the General Assembly has already urged international financial institutions and regional development banks to provide funding for alternative crops ... But U.N. sanctions bar such assistance to Afghanistan. The only U.N. funding is for humanitarian assistance," which had in any case been neglected by world powers: despite Annan's repeated appeals for $275 million in humanitarian aid to Afghanistan, only $46 million were received.[72]

Moreover, before and after the Bush administration announced the $43 million aid package, US officials continued to work to isolate Afghanistan internationally. For example, in June and July 2001, Bush signed an executive order maintaining economic sanctions as well as the "National Emergency" with respect to the regime because it "continues to allow territory under its control in Afghanistan to be used as a safe haven and base of operations for Usama bin Laden and the al-Qaida organization."[73] Further, the humanitarian aid offered was welcome, but not so exceptional: the $43 million in aid brought the total US contribution for the year to $124 million, but Washington had also contributed a total of $114 million the preceding year.[74] Such aid made the United States the leading provider of humanitarian assistance to Afghanistan, but this does not lead to the conclusion that American policy was motivated by humanitarian concerns. The same applies to narcotics and policy toward the Taliban: it had essentially not changed—Washington was still not concerned with drug control to any significant extent, and bin Laden was still the most important issue.

WOMEN'S RIGHTS CONCERNS?

A number of analysts have argued that the shift in American attitude toward Afghanistan in the second half of the 1990s was triggered by a concern for the Taliban's gender policies. For example, Richard Mackenzie believes that "probably most importantly," it was "the Taliban's treatment of women" that motivated moves to isolate the regime, because such disrespect for women "was an affront to key values for which the United States avowedly stood."[75] Likewise, William Maley writes that "the main consideration which thwarted the efforts of the Taliban to secure international recognition and legitimacy was their treatment of women."[76] A related factor is alleged to be the replacement of Warren Christopher by Madeleine Albright as secretary of state. Albright's November 1997 statement that the Taliban were "despicable" for their attitude toward women is often cited in this regard. For example, Ahmed Rashid writes that the "shift in US policy was also because of major changes in Washington. The dour, hapless Warren Christopher was replaced by Albright as Secretary of State in early 1997. Her own experiences as a child in Central Europe ensured that human rights would figure prominently on her agenda." Rashid also suggests that the "US rejection of the Taliban was largely because of the pressure exerted by the feminist movement at home."[77]

But it is very doubtful that US policy was influenced by concerns for women's rights. Moreover, staff changes in the political establishment are incidental to the broad outlines of policymaking, as long as the structures of power remain unchanged. Thus, one would be hard put to find significant instances of human rights concerns driving American foreign policy over the years. Washington has supported Saudi Arabia for decades, where women have very limited rights. We can also pass on the alleged humanizing impact of Albright's experiences as a child in Central Europe. When asked on US television in 1996 if she thought the reported deaths of half a million children because of sanctions on Iraq was a price worth paying, she said: "I think this is a very hard choice, but the price— we think the price is worth it."[78] Moreover, just a few years before Albright said the Taliban were "despicable," Afghan individuals and groups as harsh on women as the Taliban—such as Gulbuddin Hekmatyar's Hizb-i Islami—"were funded with few qualms by the US Administration," notes a Council on Foreign Relations report. During the civil war years of 1992–96, the "Ministry for the Promotion of Virtue and Prevention of Vice" was formed by the

Rabbani government. The Ministry became well known during the Taliban regime for curtailing human rights and civil liberties, but its origins go back to the civil war years, and at that time, Afghanistan had faded away from the US agenda, and there was no outrage.[79]

It could still be claimed that although Washington was not concerned with women's rights, feminist groups were able to pressure the US government and force it to modify its policies. It is true that an important movement developed in Europe and North America denouncing the Taliban's attitude towards women. Some have claimed that the fact that the regime failed to receive recognition as the government of Afghanistan or to secure the country's General Assembly seat at the United Nations "reflected in part the effective lobbying" of women's rights group. In the United States, organizations like the Feminist Majority Foundation, led by Eleanor Smeal, were active in this respect and received the support of celebrities such as Mavis Leno (talk show host Jay Leno's wife) and singer Lionel Richie. Their cause was bolstered in August 1998 when the Physicians for Human Rights released a report entitled *The Taliban's War on Women*, which documented a series of abuses.[80]

But the role of pressure by women's groups in shaping policy should not be exaggerated; it seems more probable that such groups were able to generate momentum and publicity in the media because the Clinton administration happened to be in the process of shifting its views on the Taliban due to the embassy bombings in Africa and their refusal to expel bin Laden. This made acceptable in mainstream discourse a variety of criticisms of the regime, related to narcotics, women's rights, and human rights. In 1999, the *Washington Post* ran a story about the Feminist Majority's campaign to raise awareness about the Taliban's treatment of women based on an interview with Mavis Leno that substantiates this interpretation. It stated that from January 1998 to August 1998—the first eight months of Mavis Leno's involvement—the campaign made no significant progress. Indeed, by August 1998 the women of the Feminist Majority "were utterly miserable" because those eight months of hard work had gotten "no real action." For the first eight months of her involvement, Leno "came close to popping a blood vessel," she said: "I couldn't get anything rolling." There were small accomplishments, but by and large, she recalled: "Nothing. Zip. No interest. No nothing." The media was not interested: "The silence of the media delayed any action," Leno said. "I couldn't get this into a single paper or radio station. Not even NPR (National Public Radio) was interested." When she testified before a congressional committee, only "one media outlet, Afghan radio, showed up. Stories would air on shows like '20/20,' and there would be no bounce." "No one could get anyone to raise the visibility of this one-eighth of an inch," Leno said.

However, from August 1998 onwards, things started to change. The *Washington Post* article and Leno attribute this to better organizational skills and a $100,000 donation from her husband, Jay Leno, to explain why interest picked up and celebrities joined in greater numbers. This might have played a role, but the fact that the turnaround happened just in the wake of the August 1998 embassy bombings and missile response by the United States provides a more likely explanation: from that time on, the US government clearly rejected the Taliban, and a space was created in the media for all sorts of criticisms of their regime. Indeed, when the Feminist Majority held a press conference scheduled coincidentally just one day after the Clinton administration launched missiles on bin Laden's camps, "the media showed up this time." Two months later, in October 1998, the "Lenos hosted a briefing for insiders at their home. The media showed up in force at their news conference ... Even President Clinton got on board ... he spent an hour talking with a Feminist Majority delegation about the plight of Afghan women." As a surprised Mavis Leno said: "At the beginning we thought, 'If we get two or three celebrities on board'—and I don't even know what happened. All of a sudden it just blew up." Indeed, it quickly became apparent that "the Taliban's 'war on women' has become the latest cause celebre in Hollywood. Tibet is out. Afghanistan is in."[81]

In other words, one important reason why certain lobby groups are able to get their message through in mainstream discourse while others aren't is that their interests happen to coincide with elite interests, or at least do not threaten them. The women's rights lobby's campaign against the Taliban fulfilled this condition. This is also what William Maley suggests when he writes that "there were no compelling reasons for the [Western] governments to ignore this domestic pressure" from women's rights groups asking to withhold acceptance of the Taliban internationally, "in contrast to what might have been the case had the rulers of a resource-rich state such as Saudi Arabia been under fire."[82] In the latter case, strategic interests have always trumped concerns for women and human rights. Mavis Leno herself explained that when she started the campaign with the Feminist Majority, it would not have been feasible to focus on Saudi Arabia, because, she said: "As we know, there are other countries,

such as Saudi Arabia, where women undergo similar abuse, but …
they are not places where effort would yield any effect." A Feminist
Majority official also said in an interview for this book that the
reason why her organization had chosen to focus on Afghanistan
but not Saudi Arabia was that "Saudi Arabia is a strong US ally,
and because of oil!" In short, policy is shaped by political economic
factors, while drugs and rights mostly serve a rhetorical function.[83]

5
To Afghanistan

This chapter outlines the likely reasons why the United States attacked Afghanistan after 9/11 as well as the broad outlines of Washington's attempts at recreating the Afghan polity in the ensuing years. The next chapter will build on this discussion and examine in detail the drug industry since 2001.

It is argued that Washington's principal motivation for the attack was to hit al-Qaeda hard to show that challenges such as happened on 9/11 would not be tolerated. There were also additional benefits that could be reaped if a friendly government could be installed successfully in Afghanistan, given the country's strategic location in the heart of Eurasia and near the Persian Gulf's and Caspian basin's energy resources. However, the claim that the United States allegedly invaded Afghanistan to prop up the drug trade in order to secure the financial benefits it provides to the global banking system will be refuted.

The chapter continues the line of argument presented for the decade of the 1990s. US policy toward Afghanistan has not been shaped by concerns for drugs (or human rights), which have been routinely mentioned by commentators. The American strategy of supporting Afghan warlords since 2001 corroborates this view, as will be seen in the last section below.

MAINTAINING CREDIBILITY

Hegemons do not tolerate dissent, much less overt assaults as on 9/11. For this reason, Washington reacted swiftly and forcefully by attacking Afghanistan and warning that all states needed to join the "war on terror" or else. The target offered a few important advantages. It was militarily weak and had been devastated by years of war, hence should have been an easy victory. Also, the Taliban was a harsh regime and would not be difficult to demonize to rally public opinion behind the campaign.[1]

A few days after 9/11, President Bush announced that the United States "will pursue nations that provide aid or safe haven to terrorism. Every nation, in every region, now has a decision to make: Either you are with us, or you are with the terrorists. From this day forward, any nation that continues to harbor or support terrorism will be regarded by the United States as a hostile regime."[2] His administration was "planning a broad and sustained campaign" against "opponents who believe they are invisible. Yet, they are mistaken. They will be exposed, and they will discover what others in the past have learned: Those who make war against the United States have chosen their own destruction."[3] Washington would do as it pleases, with no necessary consultation with others. Before the bombing started, Cofer Black, director of the CIA's Counterterrorism Centre, flew to Moscow and told the Russians: "We're in a war. We're coming. Regardless of what you do, we're coming anyway."[4]

Charles Krauthammer, a cheerleader for retaliation and militarism, laid out the rationale in explicit terms:

Success does, however, mean demonstrating that the United States has the will and power to enforce the Bush doctrine that governments will be held accountable for the terrorists they harbor. Success therefore requires making an example of the Taliban. Getting Osama is not the immediate goal. Everyone understands that it is hard, even for a superpower, to go on a cave-to-cave manhunt. Toppling regimes is another matter. For the Taliban to hold off the United States is an astounding triumph. Every day that they remain in place is a rebuke to American power. Indeed, as the war drags on, their renown, particularly in the Islamic world, will only grow. After September 11, the world awaited the show of American might. If that show fails, then the list of countries lining up on the other side of the new divide will grow.[5]

Bush and his advisers held the same attitude, believing that previous US responses to bin Laden, under Clinton, "had been so weak as to be provocative, a virtual invitation to hit the United States again," reports Bob Woodward in his chronicle of the administration's reaction to 9/11. Referring to Clinton's cruise missile strikes on Afghanistan in 1998 following the US embassy bombings in Africa, Bush said:

The antiseptic notion of launching a cruise missile into some guy's, you know, tent, really is a joke. I mean, people viewed that as the impotent America ... a flaccid, you know, kind of technologically competent but not very tough country that was willing to launch a cruise missile out of a submarine and that'd be it. I do believe that there is the image of America out there that ... we wouldn't fight back. It was clear that bin Laden felt emboldened and didn't feel threatened by the United States.[6]

Others used clearer metaphors, such as Cofer Black, who described the strategy in Afghanistan thus: "We're going to kill them. We're going to put their heads on sticks. We're going to rock their world."[7]

It is debatable to what extent such perceptions conform to the reality, but there is certainly a sizable grain of truth in this way of thinking: challenges to power that are allowed to survive for a certain time will possibly embolden others elsewhere to take action, as seen recently when the Occupy Wall Street movement spread around the world and the Arab Spring in the Middle East cascaded from one country to another, which many authoritarian leaders in the region and elsewhere certainly wish could have been nipped in the bud.

Bush seemed aware of this potential snowball effect when he told his advisers at a meeting to plan the war: "Tell the Afghans to round up al Qaeda. Let's see them, or we'll hit them hard. We're going to hurt them bad so that everyone in the world sees, don't deal with bin Laden."[8] There would be no pity for those who disobey. On September 17, Bush ordered Colin Powell to issue an ultimatum to the Taliban

warning them to turn over bin Laden and his al Qaeda or they will suffer the consequences. If they don't comply, we'll attack them... Let's hit them hard. We want to signal this is a change from the past. We want to cause other countries like Syria and Iran to change their views. We want to hit as soon as possible... I want to have them quaking in their boots.[9]

Note that this is a straightforward case of terrorism, but conducted by Washington. The US Department of Defense, for example, defines terrorism as the "unlawful use of violence or threat of violence to instill fear and coerce governments or societies. Terrorism is often motivated by religious, political, or other ideological beliefs and committed in the pursuit of goals that are usually political."[10] Washington explicitly wanted to have the Taliban "quaking in their boots" to convince them to act in certain ways, in the pursuit of

political goals. Another example of state terrorism was given a
month later, as the bombing was proceeding. Admiral Sir Michael
Boyce, the chief of the British Defence Staff, announced that the
US-British attack on Afghanistan would continue "until the people
of the country themselves recognize that this is going to go on until
they get the leadership changed."[11]

According to recently declassified documents, after 9/11, the
United States had no inclination to enter into negotiation or
dialogue with the Taliban to investigate the possibility that bin
Laden might have been involved in the attacks, and perhaps organize
to extradite him. On 13 September 2001, the US ambassador to
Pakistan, Wendy Chamberlin, "bluntly" told Pakistani President
Musharraf that there was "absolutely no inclination in Washington
to enter into a dialogue with the Taliban. The time for dialog was
finished as of September 11."[12] But Pakistan disagreed and tried to
move Washington towards diplomacy, unsuccessfully as it turned
out. ISI Director Mahmud Ahmed told Chamberlin "not to act in
anger. Real victory will come in negotiations." He thought that
we "should get the Afghans to do this job for us. Reasoning with
them to get rid of terrorism will be better than the use of brute
force. If the strategic objective is Al Quaida and UBL [Usama bin
Laden], it is better for the Afghans to do it. We could avoid the
fallout." He added that a military "strike will produce thousands of
frustrated young Muslim men. It will be an incubator of anger that
will explode two or three years from now," a prescient observation.
But Washington was proceeding apace with the military option no
matter what. Chamberlin said that Pakistan's attempts at dialog
should not interfere, telling Mahmud: "We are on a tight schedule
and your efforts should not impede any of the military planning
we are engaged in today."[13]

The United States also brushed aside Taliban offers to extradite
bin Laden or proceed with a trial before the bombing started on 7
October 2001, as well as offers in the following days. The details
of such proposals remain murky, and one can only speculate as to
where they would have led, because they were not explored seriously.
One sticking point was that the Taliban wanted proof of bin Laden's
involvement in 9/11 before proceeding with a trial or extradition—a
sensible request from the point of view of international law—but
Washington kept telling them to hand in bin Laden immediately.
On 17 September 2001, Pakistan's General Mahmud met with
the Taliban leadership and presented American demands to them,
including to hand over bin Laden and his top associates, as well as

to close all terrorist camps in Afghanistan. Mahmud then reported to the United States that the Taliban's "response was not negative on all these points" and that they were now engaged in "deep introspection" about their decisions.[14] Later, other reported Taliban offers to hand over bin Laden to a neutral country were rejected. For example, on 14 October 2001, it was reported that "US warplanes pounded Taliban frontline targets Sunday as President George W. Bush rejected the ruling Afghan militia's conditional offer to hand over Osama bin Laden for trial in a neutral country." ABC News related on the same day that "President Bush firmly rejected the Taliban's offer to discuss turning Osama bin Laden over to a neutral country for trial ... Taliban officials said today they would hand bin Laden over if the US ends its air strikes and provides proof of his guilt." But Bush said that they "must have not heard. There's no negotiation. This is non-negotiable."[15]

GEOPOLITICS, ENERGY AND MILITARY BASES

Other advantages could be derived from the establishment of a friendly regime in the country. Although of little value in itself to the United States, Afghanistan occupies a strategic location in Eurasia and would allow Washington to position itself near the heart of the continent and close to the Persian Gulf. Moreover, military bases could be established next to Iran, a declared enemy. Zbigniew Brzezinski had already highlighted the importance of the Eurasian landmass in US grand strategy in his 1997 book, *The Grand Chessboard*.[16]

The outlines of American policy toward the Caspian region since 2001 have followed the direction taken in the second half of the 1990s. Clinton's objective of diversifying energy sources was adopted by Dick Cheney's *National Energy Policy* in the early Bush years, which stated: "Growing levels of conventional and heavy oil production and exports from the Western Hemisphere, the Caspian, and Africa are important factors that can lessen the impact of a supply disruption on the U.S. and world economies. Overall U.S. policies in each of these high-priority regions will focus on improving the investment climate and facilitating the flow of needed investment and technology." In the Caspian region in particular, foreign "investors and technology are critical to rapid development of new commercially viable export routes. Such development will ensure that rising Caspian oil production is effectively integrated into world oil trade. U.S.-supported East–West pipeline routes will add substantial new oil transportation capacity to allow continued expansion of production and exports."[17] In fact, there has been a greater effort under Bush and Obama to assert control over the region and develop its energy resources, a strategy implemented within the context of the war on terror and the operations in Afghanistan. As a recent US Senate report recommends: "The U.S. role in Afghanistan is changing, but Washington should repeatedly stress that its engagement is not ending ... The United States must keep working to change the narrative by making it clear that we will protect our long-term interests in the region."[18]

Asian powers, led by Russia and China, have taken important steps toward continental integration, through organizations like the Shanghai Cooperation Organization (SCO) and the Collective Security Treaty Organization (CSTO). For example, at the 2006 SCO summit, Russian president Vladimir Putin proposed that the organization should create an "energy club," and moves have been made toward the establishment of an "Asian energy grid" that would share and distribute the continent's resources.[19] Because this would strengthen Asian independence, it is opposed by Washington, which has tried to position itself on and around the continent to counteract those developments.[20] For example, Western and Asian powers have sponsored a series of competing pipelines across Eurasia in an ongoing struggle to determine who will control its resources. Russia seeks to dominate the marketing of Caspian oil and gas by having regional leaders use its own pipeline system. Washington has attempted to thwart those plans by sponsoring alternative routes that bypass Russian territory, such as the Baku-Tbilisi-Ceyhan pipeline (BTC), while Beijing is trying to connect western China to the Caspian area. The European Union, on its part, hopes to build the Nabucco gas pipeline from Azerbaijan through Turkey to Austria, while Russia is pushing for an alternative one called South Stream.[21] The Pentagon has played an important role in assisting private capital in penetrating the region. Between 1997 and 2001, the Caspian states received $84 million in military assistance from the United States, an amount that zoomed to almost $900 million between 2001 and 2006. This was justified by reference to the war in Afghanistan, although it belied broader geopolitical considerations related to natural resources. Military assistance has been used to attempt to pull the region's militaries away from Russia and towards Western alliances such as NATO.[22]

Washington has built or leased a number of military bases in Afghanistan and the region. Colonel Wayne Shanks, an ISAF spokesman, recently stated that there were "nearly 400 U.S. and coalition bases in Afghanistan, including camps, forward operating bases, and combat outposts." Some are "mega-bases that resemble small American towns," like Kandahar Airfield and Bagram Air Base, "complete with Burger King and Popeyes outlets," among other facilities.[23] Active duty US military personnel are also deployed in all of Central Asia's former Soviet republics.[24] For example, in 2001, troops arrived at former Soviet facilities in Kyrgyzstan and Uzbekistan, while Tajikistan made available its airfields to American aircraft and Kazakhstan, Tajikistan, and Turkmenistan provided the United States and NATO with overflight rights over their territories. As a SIPRI report remarked, these "steps heralded the building of a broad US military infrastructure in the region." But Russia has sought to revive its political and military relationships with Central Asia, as demonstrated by the formation of the CSTO in 2002–03. The years since then have witnessed the competition between Western and Eurasian powers to carve spheres of influence by attempting to convince regional powers to conclude basing agreements with them. The United States and NATO were allowed to use facilities in Kyrgyzstan and Uzbekistan in 2001, but forced to leave the latter in 2005, while in Kyrgyzstan, rights to the Manas installation have had to be renegotiated periodically, with reported Russian pressure to end American access.[25]

It has been suggested that the United States attacked Afghanistan to build Unocal's pipeline across the country. For example, Wayne Madsen wrote that "there is simply too much evidence that the War in Afghanistan was primarily about building UNOCAL's pipeline, not about fighting terrorism."[26] The argument is as follows: President Hamid Karzai is "a former employee of US oil company Unocal," and therefore, the fact that he was installed by Washington as Afghan president in the wake of the invasion shows that the intention was to have a leader that would be able to implement Unocal's plans for building the TAP pipeline.[27]

However, according to veteran Pakistani journalist Ahmed Rashid, President Karzai was never employed by Unocal. Rashid said that he had "investigated this Unocal allegation very closely" and that "Unocal, when they were active in Afghanistan in the mid-1990s, met with all sorts of Afghans. And certainly he [Karzai] met with them, along with other Afghans. But he was never on their pay roll. He was not involved with them closely."[28] Zalmay Khalilzad, the US ambassador to Afghanistan in 2003–05, had on his part worked as a consultant on a project funded by Unocal in the mid-1990s, but not directly for Unocal. Khalilzad said: "I was asked, not by Unocal but by Cambridge Energy Research Associates, a research company, if I would do a cost-benefit analysis of building pipelines across Afghanistan. And from then it evolved, but I always went through Cambridge."[29]

Nevertheless, the more important point is that even if Karzai had been a Unocal employee, and even if a pipeline eventually gets built across Afghanistan, and even if Unocal is then involved in the project, it would not mean that the United States invaded Afghanistan primarily to build a pipeline. The region's energy resources are of course a clear motivation for Washington to position itself in Afghanistan and Eurasia. But it is very difficult to believe that a war would be launched for the sake of one pipeline, especially one related to Caspian basin resources, which are not at all on a par with those of the Persian Gulf, the most important ones globally. There are many other pipelines in Eurasia, some planned and some built, and they all compete in one way or another with Russian and Chinese projects. There would have been many more armed conflicts if such pipelines inevitably led the United States to war.

INTERVENTION TO SUSTAIN THE DRUG ECONOMY?

It has been advanced that the United States might have intervened in Afghanistan in order to revive its drug industry. The argument has taken a number of forms. For example, economist Michel Chossudovsky, in an article entitled "Washington's Hidden Agenda: Restore the Drug Trade," states: "One of the 'hidden' objectives of the war was precisely to restore the CIA sponsored drug trade to its historical levels and exert direct control over the drug routes. Immediately following the October 2001 invasion, opium markets were restored." Chossudovsky notes that the Taliban had been able to reduce drug production by 94 percent but that what "this war has achieved is to restore a compliant narco-State, headed by a US appointed puppet."[30] The broader point is that there "are powerful business and financial interests behind narcotics. From this standpoint, geopolitical and military control over the drug routes is as strategic as oil and oil pipelines."[31]

Professor Peter Dale Scott also suggests that Washington might have intervened in Afghanistan in 2001 or elsewhere previously to protect the drug industry, perhaps in order to stimulate the American economy. He talks of a "sustained pattern of intervention in support of drug economies" in US foreign policy, and writes that the "global drug traffic itself will continue to benefit from the protracted conflict … in Afghanistan, and some of the beneficiaries may have been secretly lobbying for it." He has also insinuated that Washington attempts to control the global drug traffic in order to stimulate the American economy, as the "consistent U.S. recourse to actions that have built up the global drug traffic raises an analogous question: Did the United States seek to maintain control over the global drug economy to ensure that its riches would strengthen the U.S. economy and to deny them to communist enemies?" Finally, he states that with respect to drugs, "the United States must end those repressive policies whose result (and often intention) is to maintain the high drug prices that strengthen and enrich the international drug traffic."[32]

In short, what those authors are claiming is that the United States invaded Afghanistan to ensure that the drug trade did not vanish because it benefits Western banks and other elites, whose interests were endangered by the successful Taliban ban. Or something like that: Scott and Chossudovsky provide little elaboration on their claims, one reason being that it is difficult to articulate precisely such rationales since in fact, there is no evidence to support them, as Scott himself concedes when he writes: "I have no evidence that the U.S. government intervened militarily as a conscious means of maintaining control over the global drug traffic."[33]

One important reason why such explanations should be discarded is that there are much more obvious reasons for the invasion related to credibility, geopolitics and energy resources, as seen above. But even on its own, the argument makes little sense. It is estimated that the global financial system launders about $220 billion of drug money annually. Let's assume therefore that global drug trafficking generates $220 billion in extra bank deposits.[34] The contribution of Afghan drugs to this sum is unknown, but assuming that about two-thirds ($40 billion) of their total street value ($60 billion) is laundered by the banking system, it is difficult to imagine how banks would care that much about those drug monies. Even assuming that all the drug money from Afghanistan ends up in banks located in the United States—which is clearly exaggerated because much of the money would actually be laundered in Europe and in other locations—this would still constitute a small fraction of US banks' total deposits, which amounted to about $4,560 billion in 2001 and $8,755 billion in 2011.[35] In any case, if the global drug trade disappeared from the face of the earth, would the $220 billion also disappear? In simple terms, no, because all the money spent on drugs would be spent on other goods and services, and would eventually also make its way into the banking system. It is unclear, therefore, how maintaining the size of the Afghan drug traffic could be seen as so important from the banks' perspective.

Moreover, the ban's potential to wipe out the drug industry permanently was thin. Indeed, it is unlikely that it could have been maintained for long because it cut off a vital means of survival for farmers in the countryside—it was effectively "an act of economic suicide" that created popular resentment against the regime, which is one reason why the latter imploded rapidly in the wake of the US attack, since in "banning opium, the Taliban destroyed the country's only major industry." David Macdonald, who has worked as a drugs advisor for a number of years with UNODC in Afghanistan and the Ministry of Counter Narcotics in Kabul, reported that the ban "was initiated by the Taliban in the knowledge, at least by some ranking Talib, that it could be no more than a temporary, and unsustainable, measure"; the ban put many farmers in debt, and "if the Taliban had continued with the ban they would have run the risk of a revolt from many of the farming communities left more debt-ridden because of the ban."[36] As UNODC explained, the Taliban offered no alternatives to farmers while enforcing the ban, which "caused extreme hardship to a significant number of farmers in a year in which Afghanistan was experiencing a severe drought and thus very poor yields for other crops. Overall crop production was more than halved and livestock herds were heavily depleted, erasing the gains made since the mid 1990s. The ban in combination with the ongoing drought meant that malnutrition worsened and cases of starvation deaths were reported." After the Taliban were dislodged from power, the Interim Administration issued a new ban on poppy cultivation in January 2002, but it was too late. Farmers had already sown their fields just after the Taliban regime had collapsed, and the 2002 opium harvest reached the same level as before the ban (3,400 tons).[37] Furthermore, even if the Taliban had been able to wipe out all drug production in Afghanistan permanently, new production would most likely have emerged in other countries to meet world demand for narcotics, preserving the size of the global drug trade (balloon effect).

Finally, to claim that US control over the drug traffic is "as strategic as oil and oil pipelines" is incorrect. Oil has a strategic value for the world and American economies because it fulfills the concrete function of fuelling economic activity. Hence the United

States has sought for decades to control the Persian Gulf's energy resources. However, drugs have no such strategic value.

THE WARLORD STRATEGY

This section sets the stage for the next chapter's discussion of the Afghan drug trade by describing a central aspect of US policy in Afghanistan since 2001: the empowerment of warlords, regional strongmen and their militias first as proxies on the ground in the initial attack, and then to maintain "stability" throughout the country up to this day. The problem with such individuals, however, is that they already had a clear record of involvement in narcotics and human rights abuses prior to 2001, to which they have only added since then. The selected warlords are anti-democratic, fundamentalist, violent, or a combination thereof. Democratic-minded groups and individuals with no such history could have been supported, but this alternative was never considered. There is nothing irrational about this strategy from the perspective of US power, as democratizing Afghanistan is not an objective— attempting to install a friendly government is, and the warlords have been deemed useful in this respect.

During the Taliban regime (1996–2001), the opposition groups in the northern parts of Afghanistan formed the Northern Alliance. Led by commanders Ahmad Shah Massoud, Ismail Khan, Abdul Rashid Dostum, and Karim Khalili, they received support from Russia, Iran and India. Before 9/11, the CIA also collaborated with Massoud in an effort to obtain intelligence on bin Laden.[38] Therefore, in the wake of 9/11, with connections between the United States and the Northern Alliance already established, the CIA was able to increase its support for the group and provide commanders with millions of dollars in cash in addition to weapons and political support, which allowed them to act as proxy forces and position themselves to take power once the Taliban fell, as they did. The *New York Times* summarized the situation succinctly in late 2001:

As warlords have carved out chunks of Afghanistan after the fall of the Taliban, the lawlessness that gave rise to the strict Islamic movement in the mid-1990's has begun to spread, once again, across this country. The United States-led military campaign ... has returned to power nearly all of the same warlords who had misruled the country in the days before the Taliban.[39]

Many of the individuals brought back into government had a tainted past, having been commanders during the early 1990s' civil war, and have also involved themselves in similar abuses since 2001—they are thus "repeat offenders." In 2009, Human Rights Watch noted that one of its reports entitled "Blood Stained Hands: Past Atrocities in Kabul and Afghanistan's Legacy of Impunity" had

> documented the involvement of some highly influential figures in the current Afghan government and legislature in war crimes during brutal fighting that killed or displaced hundreds of thousands of Afghans in the early 1990s—and precipitated the rise of the Taliban. Prominent among this group are Abdul Rabb al Rasul Sayyaf, Burhanuddin Rabbani, Minister of Energy Ismail Khan, Army Chief of Staff Abdul Rashid Dostum, and Vice President Karim Khalili, all of whom continue to misuse positions of power. Despite the findings in this report and other reliable accounts, no action has been taken by the Afghan government or international community to sideline or prosecute the individuals responsible.[40]

American support allowed the warlords and commanders to divide the country into personal fiefdoms early on. According to Ahmed Rashid's account, in the north, General Rashid Dostum's soldiers engaged in widespread looting and made it impossible for humanitarian relief to start. General Mohammed Atta was one of Dostum's rivals in the north, and was also armed by the United States. General Daud, on his part, took control of Kunduz and three northeastern provinces. In the east, the governor of Nangarhar province, Abdul Qadir, received generous funding from the CIA, just like Hazrat Ali, who "was given so much money by the CIA that he quickly created an eighteen-thousand-strong militia." Those two competed fiercely for the control of the four eastern provinces of Nangarhar, Laghman, Nuristan, and Kunar. In the southeast, the CIA paid former Taliban commanders while US ally Gul Agha Sherzai was also supported. In the west, Ismail Khan was the dominant figure, while in the center of the country, Karim Khalili, Syed Akbari, and Mohammed Mohaqiq took control. The United States saw the warlords as "a cheap and beneficial way to retain U.S. allies in the field." Showering them with millions was considered by Bush "one of the biggest 'bargains' of all time."[41]

A number of reports from human rights organizations described the negative consequences. For example, in 2003, "the U.S., Iran, and

Pakistan all actively supported local warlords in various regions of the country," and in particular "the United States, United Kingdom, and other coalition partners supplied warlords with cash, weapons, uniforms, and satellite telephones" with the result that individuals "with records of human rights abuses, for instance Ismail Khan, Muhammad Karim Khalili, and Rashid Dostum, all strengthened their grip on local power outside of Kabul."[42]

In particular, the political process following the fall of the Taliban and designed to establish a new government and constitution has been "subverted," "infiltrated and manipulated" by warlords, which have entrenched their power over the country and sidelined civil society, resulting in them maintaining their "stranglehold on Afghan politics." "[O]rdinary Afghans are increasingly terrorized by the rule of local and regional military commanders," Human Rights Watch reported. Throughout the country, strongmen "continue to cement their hold on political power at the local level, using force, threats, and corruption ... Voters in many rural areas have already been told by warlords and regional commanders how to vote ... Women, both as voters and as political actors, remain marginalized." One problem is that the United States is "cooperating and even supporting warlord leaders like Hazrat Ali in Jalalabad, General Dostum and Commander Atta in Mazar-e Sharif, and General Fahim in Kabul."[43]

Therefore, unsurprisingly, the parliament elected in 2005 was packed with unsavory characters. The deputy head of the Afghan Independent Human Rights Commission estimated that "more than 80 percent of winning candidates in the provinces and more than 60 percent in the capital Kabul have links to armed groups." Another analysis determined that the national assembly included "40 commanders still associated with armed groups, 24 members who belong to criminal gangs, 17 drug traffickers, and 19 members who face serious allegations of war crimes and human rights violations." It is not without reason that many Afghans referred to the parliament as a "chamber for warlords."[44]

The empowerment of strongmen by the United States and NATO continues up to this day. They hold positions in government, the police, the army and in business. Though they have largely relinquished their tanks and heavy artillery, most have maintained their militias in the form of private security companies, political parties or loose business networks, exerting control through a mafia-like system. For example, the *Wall Street Journal* reported that warlords cooperating with the United States included Gul Agha Sherzai, Ismail Khan, and Atta Mohammed Noor, among others.

The parliament elected in 2010 still "contains a gallery of former 'mujahedeen' warlords and guerrilla commanders who've been held responsible for the deaths of thousands of civilians."[45] When Hamid Karzai appointed his two vice-presidents, Mohammed Qasim Fahim and Karim Khalili, Kenneth Roth, the head of Human Rights Watch, was "appalled" by Karzai's selection of Fahim, calling him a "disastrous choice." Brad Adams, Asia director of Human Rights Watch, said that Fahim "is one of the most notorious warlords in the country, with the blood of many Afghans on his hands from the civil war" of the 1990s.[46]

But there were alternatives. For example, some of the better known progressive ones include RAWA and Malalai Joya. Malalai Joya is a former elected member of parliament who has been very vocal in opposing commanders and fundamentalists. RAWA has been active in Afghanistan and Pakistan since 1977 and is one of the most important women's organizations there. It has opposed strongmen, the Taliban and the NATO occupation, fought for women's rights, worked with Afghan refugees, and provided Afghans with health care and education. But RAWA has never been offered any aid from the US government (or any other government), while warlords have received millions of dollars.[47]

The reason is simple: supporting a more democratic Afghanistan as opposed to friendly authoritarian figures would have reduced US control over the country. There would likely have been more serious moves against impunity for human rights abusers. Afghans could have called more forcefully for the withdrawal of foreign troops, more development aid, and perhaps peacekeepers to maintain security, among other things. In short, many decisions would have been outside US control, and the actions of many American allies, as well as of Washington itself, could have been investigated, perhaps leading to prosecutions for their crimes. For example, Human Rights Watch stated that although

> war crimes tribunals or truth commissions are politically sensitive, inaction is driven more by the vested interests of politicians than public opinion, which is strongly in favor of holding war criminals and human rights abusers accountable. Civil society organizations are becoming actively engaged in documentation work and a range of victims' groups are demonstrating Afghans' desire for open discussion about war crimes. Most Afghans would welcome moves by their government to hold war criminals to account, as long as it was shown to be even-handed.[48]

6
Washington and the Afghan Drug Trade since 2001

Opium production in Afghanistan skyrocketed from 185 tons to 8,200 tons between 2001 and 2007.[1] Most commentary glosses over Washington's large share of responsibility for this dramatic expansion while magnifying the Taliban's role, which available data indicates is relatively minor. Also, identifying drugs as a main cause behind the growth of the insurgency absolves the United States and NATO of their own role in fomenting it: the very presence of foreign troops in the country as well as their destructive attacks on civilians are significant factors behind increases in popular support for, or tolerance of, the Taliban. In fact, as a recent UNODC report notes, reducing drug production would have only a "minimal impact on the insurgency's strategic threat," because the Taliban receive "significant funding from private donors all over the world," a contribution that "dwarfs" drug money.[2]

This chapter discusses the role of the United States and NATO in sustaining the Afghan drug trade at a number of levels. It demonstrates that drug control is not one of Washington's concerns, a point also illustrated by the last section's discussion of American counterdrug policy since 2001.

THE TALIBAN'S ROLE

A UNODC report entitled *Addiction, Crime and Insurgency: The Transnational Threat of Afghan Opium* provides a good example of the conventional view of the Taliban's role in drug trafficking. It claims that they draw some $125 million annually from narcotics, resulting in the "perfect storm" of drugs and terrorism heading toward Central Asia and endangering its energy resources. UNODC maintains that when they were in power in the second half of the 1990s, the Taliban earned about $75–100 million per year from drugs, but since 2005 this figure has risen to $125 million. Although this is presented as a significant increase, the Taliban play a lesser role in the opium economy than the report would have us believe

81

as they capture only a small share of its total value. Moreover, drug money is likely a secondary source of funding for them: UNODC itself estimates that only 10 percent to 15 percent of Taliban funding is drawn from drugs and 85 percent comes from "non-opium sources" such as private donations.[3]

The total revenue generated by opiates within Afghanistan is about $3 billion per year. According to UNODC data, the Taliban get only about 5 percent of this sum. Farmers selling their opium harvest to traffickers get 20 percent.[4] And the remaining 75 percent? Al-Qaeda? No: the report specifies that it "does not appear to have a direct role in the Afghan opiates trade," although it may participate in "low-level drugs and/or arms smuggling" along the Pakistani border.[5] Instead, the remaining 75 percent is captured by traffickers, government officials, the police, and local and regional power brokers—in short, many of the groups now supported or tolerated by the United States and NATO are important actors in the drug trade (although this does not mean that US allies capture 75 percent of drug revenues, because some individuals are rather independent, as will be seen shortly). Such analysis has been corroborated by others. For example, leading drug policy researchers have written that in "the popular and American political imaginations, the Taliban are thought to be the big winners" in Afghanistan's drug industry. However, the "Taliban's take is subject to debate, with responsible estimates varying from $70 million to $500 million—but either way it's not a big slice of the pie. The Taliban take 2 to 12 percent of a $4 billion industry; farmers, traffickers, smugglers, and corrupt officials collectively earn much more."[6]

Therefore, claims that "Taliban insurgents are earning astonishingly large profits off the opium trade" are misleading. Nevertheless, UNODC insists on the Taliban-drugs connection but pays less attention to individuals and groups supported or tolerated by Washington. The agency seems to be acting as an enabler of coalition policies in Afghanistan: when asked what percentage of total drug income in Afghanistan is captured by government officials, the UNODC official who supervised the above report quickly replied: "We don't do that, I don't know."[7]

The share of total drug money in Afghanistan captured by the various players involved in the trade can only be roughly estimated.[8] One report claimed that "Afghan government officials are involved in at least 70 percent of the traffic," although precise numbers are impossible to obtain.[9] One reason is the lack of data due to the illicit nature of the activity, including uncertainty regarding

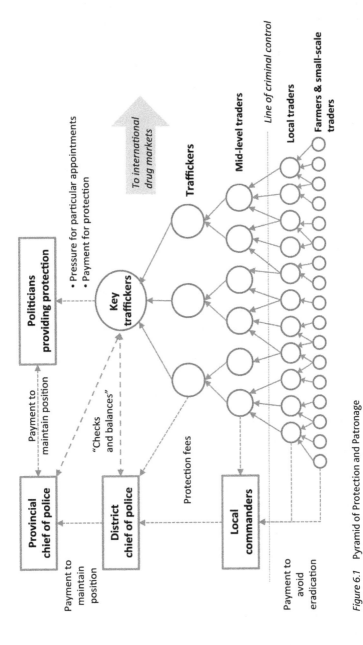

Figure 6.1 Pyramid of Protection and Patronage

Source: Mark Shaw and Walter Kemp, *Spotting the Spoilers: A Guide to Analyzing Organized Crime in Fragile States* (New York: International Peace Institute, 2012), p. 23.

the networks and actors that constitute the industry, which is composed of "pyramids of protection and patronage, effectively providing state protection to criminal trafficking activities." Mark Shaw has provided a useful sketch of the structure of the industry (Figure 6.1). The figure shows that at the bottom of the pyramid are about 350,000 families of farmers involved in poppy cultivation and harvesting of opium. Farmers may enter or leave poppy cultivation from year to year depending on a variety of factors like the enforcement of cultivation bans and changing prices for opium and other crops. Credit and seeds are usually provided by the traffickers themselves. Farmers sell directly their opium harvest to small-scale traders, mostly local shopkeepers or general traders with whom they have established a relation of trust. Small-scale traders sell to middle-scale traders, who in turn sell to traffickers, of which there are about 200–250 countrywide. Traffickers sell their drugs to contacts outside Afghanistan (for example across the border in Pakistan), which may be opium, morphine or heroin depending on the level of refinement it has undergone. They are the ones in charge of moving the drugs and are comparatively wealthy. At the top of the pyramid are about 25–30 key traffickers, very wealthy individuals who supervise the trade without getting directly involved. They have a number of political connections at high levels in the Afghan government, ensuring that their shipments are protected.

From the bottom to the top of the pyramid, protection payments lubricate the trade and ensure that many actors at different levels of political power take a cut. Farmers first pay local officials (the police or local commanders) in cash or in drugs to prevent eradication of their fields. Small and middle-scale traders also pay local authorities to be able to continue trading, and in areas where the Taliban are the authorities in power, they receive such payments. Traffickers pay the district chief of police in order to be able to trade freely. The district chief of police in turn makes payments to his superiors in the police force who also make payments to their political superiors in government. If someone in the pyramid does not play his role properly, meaning that he does not make the necessary payments to his higher-ups and keeps too much money for himself, players above him may simply replace or kill him. Also, traffickers can exert pressure on political officials or police chiefs to appoint subordinates seen as more favorable to their business.

It is easy to see how corruption pervades the system and how the drug industry has become such an integral part of the economy because so many people from the bottom to the top of society benefit from it. As an official in the Afghan Finance Ministry declared: "We all eat corruption and drug money, albeit in different quantities."[10] Afghan governors and customs and police officials are known to be making large amounts of money by offering protection to traffickers. This is why positions like police chief in certain districts can be auctioned off to the highest bidder, and a six-month appointment to such a privileged position can go for as much as $100,000.[11] An Afghan judicial official remarked that the "people at the very top are high-level; they cannot be touched," and a judge agreed: "The top drug dealers are beyond the law—no one can touch them. Small-scale traffickers and smugglers are sometimes brought to the court—it gives me shame to sentence them as none of the big traffickers are arrested—they cannot be stopped, their hand is law." Tom Schweich opined that "Karzai had Taliban enemies who profited from drugs, but he had even more supporters who did."[12]

Returning to the discussion on the distribution of drug income, an additional difficulty in describing precisely the allocation of revenues is that many players fit in more than one category. For example, a number of traffickers are also police officers: should they be classified as "traffickers" or "government actors"? Similarly, many traffickers are simultaneously allied with the insurgents, government-backed militias, and the police: should they be considered on the government's side or the Taliban's? This would determine how drug money is allocated between "the insurgents and their allies" versus "the US-backed government and allies." Further, other militants tap into the drug trade, in particular, the Haqqani network and the group led by Gulbuddin Hekmatyar. The UNODC report did not consider these groups; had they been included, the portion of drug money captured by insurgents could have been larger. Or maybe not: because they are based partly in Pakistan, a portion of their drug money income would not be taken out of the $3 billion Afghan drug trade, but out of the $1 billion Pakistani drug trade. This factor would need to be included in the equation, along with the proportion of drug money trickling up to Pakistani officials.[13]

US ally Pakistan indeed plays an important role in trafficking. For example, the State Department recently reported that "Pakistan is a major transit country for opiates and hashish for markets around the world, especially for narcotics originating in Afghanistan. Pakistan also is a major transit country for precursor chemicals illegally smuggled into Afghanistan where they are used to process heroin." Moreover, the country is "a producer of opiates from approximately 1700 hectares of illicit poppy." Drug traffickers "smuggle approximately 150 tons of heroin and 80 tons of opium across the border [with Afghanistan] annually." The "sheer volume of drugs transiting this country... fuels a significant domestic drug addiction problem. The country's enforcement and judicial structures are weak, underfinanced, and fail to cooperate among themselves. Corruption in Pakistan is widespread."[14] A senior American official in the region remarked that "major traffickers cross the border from Afghanistan and operate with impunity in Quetta and other Pakistani cities."[15]

Further, while it is true that the Taliban have benefitted from the drug trade, especially since 2005, they have other sources of revenue. When the movement was rebuilding itself from 2002 to 2004, Mullah Omar reportedly organized the raising of funds through a "wide and varied Islamic network—Karachi businessmen, Peshawar goldsmiths, Saudi oil men, Kuwaiti traders and jihadi sympathizers within the Pakistani military and intelligence ranks," in addition to profits from smuggling legal goods across the Pakistani border. The fact that such countries are allies means that Washington could use its leverage over them to attempt to reduce the flow of donations to the Taliban. Today, the latter also rely on taxation of whatever economic activities take place in areas under their control, as well as gem smuggling, illegal logging, trade in wildlife, and ransoms from kidnapping. Moreover, the insurgents reportedly receive support from Pakistan's ISI, ranging from financial, medical and intelligence support.[16] American taxpayers' money also seems to be making its way to the Taliban: US government funds used to pay transport contractors to carry goods to troops in Afghanistan are reportedly used to bribe the Taliban to ensure safe passage. As a NATO official in Kabul who believed millions of dollars were making their way to the Taliban said: "We're funding both sides of the war."[17]

In short, the Taliban appear to be, in relative terms, minor actors in the drug trade in terms of the income they derive from it. However, this does not necessarily mean that the groups actively supported by the coalition capture all the money not appropriated by the Taliban, as more or less independent traffickers, militias, warlords, and strongmen also capture a portion of the funds. Nevertheless, foreign troops do not target such groups to the same extent as the insurgents, if at all. It may be appropriate to conclude this section with one of Gretchen Peters's findings—buried deep in her book, since it weakens her central argument associating the drug trade with the insurgents: "The Taliban and their allies may be earning hundreds of millions from the drug trade, but one thing almost everyone interviewed for this project agreed on was that crooked members of Hamid Karzai's administration are earning even more." This assessment is corroborated by the fieldwork of David Mansfield, who reports that among Afghans, "there is a growing belief in the south that those working for the government are more actively involved in the trade in narcotics than the Taliban... farmers in some of the most rural areas often claim that it is only those in positions of power in their area that can trade illegal drugs."[18]

THE UNITED STATES' ROLE

Mainstream commentary blames the size of the narcotics industry and much of what goes wrong in Afghanistan partly on corruption. But to focus on bad apples in the Afghan government and police misses the systemic responsibility of the United States and NATO for the dramatic expansion of opiates production since 2001 and for their support of numerous corrupt individuals in power. The United States attacked Afghanistan in association with Northern Alliance warlords and drug lords and showered them with weapons, millions of dollars, and diplomatic support. The empowerment and enrichment of those individuals enabled them to tax and protect opium traffickers, leading to the quick resumption of narcotics production after the hiatus of the 2000–2001 Taliban ban, as many observers have documented. Ahmed Rashid has written that the whole Afghan Interior Ministry "became a major protector of drug traffickers, and Karzai refused to clean it out. As warlord militias were demobilized and disarmed by the UN, commanders found new positions in the Interior Ministry and continued to provide protection to drug traffickers." The United States was not interested in cleaning Afghanistan of drug traffickers either.[19] Thus, to blame "corruption" and "criminals" for the current state of affairs is to ignore the direct and predictable effects of US policies, which have followed a historical pattern of toleration and protection of strongmen involved in narcotics.

As seen in chapter 5, impunity and support for drug lords and warlords has been the norm since 2001, and a number of them have made their way into government. "Diplomats and well-informed Afghans believe that up to a quarter" of the members of parliament are involved in drug production and trafficking.[20] A 2009 US Senate report noted that no major trafficker had been arrested in Afghanistan since 2006, and that successful prosecutions are often overturned by a simple bribe or protection from higher officials, revealing counternarcotics efforts to be deficient at best, notwithstanding Washington's allocation of $383 million between 2005 and 2009 to "rule of law" and "justice reform" in Afghanistan.[21] Tom Schweich wrote that the United States is well aware of the degree to which the Afghan government is pervaded by drugs: "A lot of intelligence... indicated that senior Afghan officials were deeply involved in the narcotics trade. Narco-traffickers were buying off hundreds of police chiefs, judges and other officials. Narco-corruption went to the top of the Afghan government. The attorney general, Abdul Jabbar Sabit... told me and other American officials that he had a list of more than 20 senior Afghan officials who were deeply corrupt—some tied to the narcotics trade."[22]

True, important figures such as Haji Bashir Noorzai have been arrested, but they are exceptions. Moreover, before his arrest in New York in 2005, Noorzai, nicknamed the "Pablo Escobar of Afghanistan" by DEA agents, had collaborated with and served as an asset to the US government, even if his record as a drug dealer was known.[23] Why was he taken into custody and eventually sentenced to life in prison in 2009? Although the case is somewhat murky, it seems that the benefits of arresting him had become greater than the benefits he could provide to the United States. Gretchen Peters provides a plausible explanation. She says that in 2004, poppy production was booming in Afghanistan and the insurgency was regaining in strength. Therefore, to "demonstrate it was getting tough on drugs, Washington needed a high-profile arrest." Eventually, diplomats and drug control agents "came up with a target everybody could agree on." An informed official told Peters that Zalmay Khalilzad, then US ambassador in Afghanistan, "wanted to find a superficial solution that was high-profile and made everyone happy. That ended up being the arrest of Haji Bashir Noorzai." Noorzai's links with the Taliban were underlined by prosecutors and the media, helping to cast him in a negative light.[24]

Another individual arrested by American officials is Haji Juma Khan, who has been described by federal prosecutors as perhaps Afghanistan's biggest and most dangerous drug trafficker. According to a *New York Times* investigation, Juma Khan had collaborated with the CIA and DEA for some years, notwithstanding reports of his narcotics activities. In 2001, shortly after the attack on Afghanistan, he was briefly detained by US forces, even though officials knew he was a trafficker. However, he was quickly released because at that time, the military was not interested in counternarcotics. After that, he met with the DEA and CIA, for example in Washington, DC in 2006, according to American officials (his lawyer denied he has ever worked for the CIA). The Americans were reportedly interested in Juma Khan's knowledge of the Taliban and drug networks. Juma Khan is believed to have received as much as $2 million in payments from the CIA or US military, even though he controlled drug routes in southern Afghanistan. It is not known exactly why US authorities eventually shifted their stance on him from ally to enemy. Some say he did not provide good information. In any case, he seems to have ceased to be useful, which would explain his arrest in 2008.[25]

Drug control is generally overridden by more important objectives, as when the DEA reportedly found nine tons of opiates in the offices of the governor of Helmand, Sher Mohammed Akhundzada, in 2005. President Karzai removed him from the governorship but soon after appointed him a member of parliament. Akhundzada's case has never been investigated, and he has never faced charges. The US military was not interested in counternarcotics, and the *New York Times* reported that the DEA had been "thwarted in their attempts to stem drug corruption" and "blocked from taking any action against the governor, who had close ties to American and British military, intelligence and diplomatic officials."[26]

Also, in 2007, Hamid Karzai appointed his childhood friend Izzatullah Wasifi as Afghanistan's anticorruption chief, with responsibility for narcotics, with a staff of 84 employees. The problem is that Wasifi had earlier been arrested in 1987 for attempting to sell heroin worth $2 million on the streets to an undercover agent in Las Vegas, for which he served nearly four years in a Nevada state prison.[27]

More recently, the *New York Times* reported, based on American officials' accounts, that Ahmed Wali Karzai, the brother of President Hamid Karzai killed in July 2011, had been receiving "regular payments" from the CIA since 2001. The agency paid him for a variety of services that he offered as the political leader of southern Afghanistan, and in particular to recruit an Afghan paramilitary force, the Kandahar Strike Force, operating under CIA direction in and around Kandahar. But Wali Karzai was also reportedly involved in trafficking. The exact extent of his involvement is difficult to tell, but as a senior American military official in Kabul said: "Hundreds of millions of dollars in drug money are flowing through the southern region, and nothing happens in southern Afghanistan without the regional leadership knowing about it." A number of stories have been reported describing Wali Karzai's links to narcotics. In 2004, Afghan forces found an enormous cache of heroin in a truck near Kandahar, but both Wali Karzai and an aide to President Karzai called the commander of the group that had made the discovery to tell him to release the drugs and the truck. Two years later, American and Afghan counternarcotics forces seized more than 110 pounds of heroin near Kabul, which US investigators said were linked to Wali Karzai. But Wali Karzai was only the tip of the iceberg, as a former CIA officer asserted that virtually "every significant Afghan figure has had brushes with the drug trade." In private, American officials acknowledge ties with drug-linked Afghan figures. A Wikileaks cable recounting US officials' meetings with Wali Karzai in September 2009 and February 2010 stated that while "we must deal with AWK [Ahmed Wali Karzai] as the head of the Provincial Council, he is widely understood to be corrupt and a narcotics trafficker." But in public, the ties are denied. As Senator John Kerry, chairman of the Senate Foreign Relations Committee, said: "We should not condemn Ahmed Wali Karzai or damage our critical relations with his brother, President Karzai, on the basis of newspaper articles or rumors."[28]

President Karzai's vice-president and former defense minister, Marshal Muhammad Qasim Fahim, is also suspected of involvement in the drug trade (although the Afghan ambassador to the United States, Said Tayeb Jawad, said such allegations were "politically motivated"). Fahim is one of the most influential figures around Karzai, who has "surrounded himself with checkered figures who could bring him votes: warlords suspected of war crimes, corruption and trafficking in the country's lucrative poppy crop." But Washington has chosen to "look the other way," for obvious reasons. Fahim was a key American ally during the 2001 invasion as the Northern Alliance's military commander. He had a close collaboration with the CIA and received funds from the United States. He became defense minister under the Karzai government and Washington's objective of building an Afghan army "meant sending millions of dollars in aid to General Fahim and his ministry." This is even if "by 2002, C.I.A. intelligence reports flowing into the Bush administration included evidence that Marshal Fahim was involved in Afghanistan's lucrative drug trade," in addition to the fact that he "had a history of narcotics trafficking before the invasion." The reports even contained allegations "that he was still involved after regaining power and becoming defense minister. He now had a Soviet-made cargo plane at his disposal that was making flights north to transport heroin through Russia, returning laden with cash," according to US officials.[29]

NATO forces also support traffickers. A recent New York University report documented the widespread use by coalition troops of private security companies and militias that "are frequently run by former military commanders responsible for human rights abuses or involved in the illegal narcotics and black market economies." For example, in Badakhshan Province, General Nazri Mahmad, a warlord who controls "a significant portion of the province's lucrative opium industry," had the contract to provide security for the German Provincial Reconstruction Team.[30]

Another ISAF ally is Abdul Razik, the leader of a tribal militia operating in Kandahar and Helmand, in the heart of the country's poppy fields. A warlord only in his thirties, he became the "master of Spin Boldak," a town in southern Afghanistan next to the Pakistani border. His story, as told by journalist Matthieu Aikins, is typical, being "a former child refugee who scrambled to power during the post-9/11 chaos, his rise abetted by a ring of crooked officials in Kabul and Kandahar" and by "NATO commanders who found his control over a key border town useful in their war against the Taliban." According to Aikins, Razik quickly moved to expand his militia's "involvement in the enormous opium traffic pouring through the region, and in the process would grow powerful enough to defy even his own tribal elders." ISAF supported him as regional power broker. When asked about Razik's alleged involvement in drug trafficking, Brigadier General Jonathan Vance, the Canadian commander of ISAF forces in Kandahar Province, said: "Yes. We are completely aware that there are a number of illicit activities being run out of that border station." But in Kandahar, "it's hard to find that paragon of civic virtue." Razik denies all charges.[31]

FLOWERS vs. MONEY

Poppy growing has in recent years been concentrated in Afghanistan's south, where the Taliban presence is most extensive. The geographical coincidence of cultivation and insurgency areas is clearly highlighted in conventional accounts such as UNODC reports, which underline that 98 percent of opium poppy cultivation takes place in the country's south and west, the least secure regions. Maps are used to illustrate how drugs and insurgency overlap spatially by pointing to the superimposition of areas of cultivation and areas of insecurity— and how this contrasts with the "poppy-free" areas of the north,

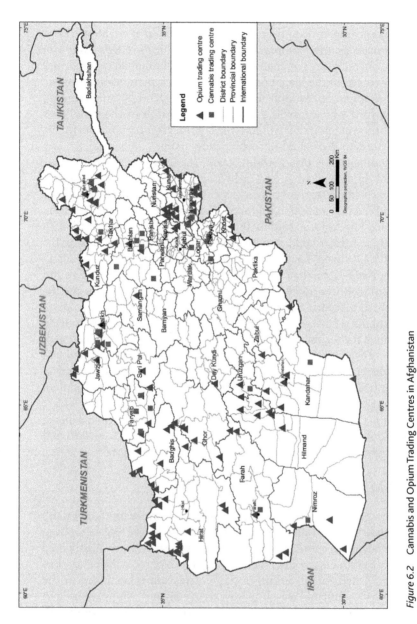

Figure 6.2 Cannabis and Opium Trading Centres in Afghanistan

Source: UNODC, Afghanistan Cannabis Survey 2009 (Vienna: UNODC), p. 36.

where there is less militant activity.[32] For instance, UNODC states that the "continued concentration of poppies and processing in the south are good illustrations of links between insurgents and the drug trade."[33]

It is true that cultivation is concentrated in the south, where there is less government control and more insecurity. However, there is plenty of drug money in the north and elsewhere—regions over which the Afghan government and foreign troops have more control. Geographically, the fact that narcotics money and trafficking have spread to almost all areas of Afghanistan can be seen from a map of drug trading centers, which are scattered all over the country (Figure 6.2). For instance, Barnett Rubin once noted that Balkh province in the north "may be poppy-free, but its center, Mazar-i Sharif, is awash in drug money." Some Western officials suggest that political elites in northern Afghanistan are engaging in successful counternarcotics operations while the southern drug economy expands, implying that it is the Taliban who are fuelling the drug trade and that if they could only be eliminated, drugs would go away. But the fact is that although the commanders who control the north may have eliminated cultivation, few if any have moved against trafficking. Most of them, it is widely believed, continue to profit from it, and some are thought to have become millionaires.[34]

Nevertheless, a case could still be made that there is a relative concentration of drug activities in the south. For example, Mark Shaw estimated a few years ago that more than half the 20 to 30 largest traffickers in Afghanistan were based in the south. He describes the south as the "gateway" for smuggling and the place where criminal groups have consolidated. However, he emphasizes that a key aspect of the trade is "the strong connections between southern traffickers and opium cultivation and trade in the north."[35] Similarly, the largest heroin laboratories appear to be located in the south, although such facilities exist throughout the country, both in government- and insurgent-controlled areas: in Nangarhar in the east and Badakhshan in the northeast, and in the south and west of the country. In any case, there is no evidence that insurgents themselves manage the processing labs, whose total number is estimated to be between 100 and 500.[36]

CHEMICAL PRECURSORS

Precursors are the chemicals used to transform opium into morphine and heroin. Today, most opium is transformed into heroin within

Afghanistan before it is exported, and it has been estimated that as many as 13,000 tons of chemical precursors are required annually to this end. The chemicals needed include both common, licit ones and internationally controlled ones, such as ammonium chloride, hydrochloric acid, acetone, lime and sodium bicarbonate, but the most important one is acetic anhydride. UNODC estimates that 475 tons of the latter is needed annually for heroin production, but seizure rates remain very low. None of the key precursors is produced in Afghanistan and thus they need to be smuggled in by more or less the same networks, individuals and transport routes used for opiates, but in the opposite direction. As such, one major precursor trade route goes from Europe to Afghanistan via the Balkans, Turkey and Iran.[37] The total value of the Afghan precursor trade is unknown but available data suggest that the retail value of acetic anhydride alone was about $450 million in 2009.[38]

Some commentators have pointed to the possible involvement of Taliban networks in precursor trafficking, a claim reinforcing the view that insurgents dominate the drug industry.[39] This assertion needs to be put in perspective, however. Even if the Taliban take a cut, Western countries and their allies also share a part of responsibility. For instance, UNODC reports that "Europe and East Asia are the main regions of origin of the acetic anhydride trafficked into Afghanistan."[40] The International Narcotics Control Board (INCB) stated that "control measures applied to internal trade in the European Union appear to be insufficient to prevent the diversion of the substance [acetic anhydride]," and because traffickers "have continued to target the European Union and East and West Asia to source acetic anhydride for the illicit manufacture of heroin in Afghanistan," the "Board calls upon the European Commission to adopt comprehensive and effective control measures to prevent the continuing diversion of acetic anhydride as expediently as possible." Moreover, it also noted that the "Republic of Korea was identified in 2008 as a major source and diversion point of acetic anhydride seized in West Asia en route to Afghanistan."[41] For example, 220 liters of acetic anhydride were intercepted in 2009 at Kabul airport on a flight arriving from India, apparently after having been diverted from a company in France, while Afghan authorities have reported that some precursors found in Afghan morphine laboratories were from South Korea.[42] Yet, Western chemical corporations do not receive as much criticism as the Taliban, nor are their factories raided. Tighter safeguards should be implemented. Finally, although Pakistan does not manufacture acetic anhydride, it "is a major transit country for precursor chemicals illegally smuggled to Afghanistan." "The largest precursor flows arrive at Karachi or other seaports on Balochistan's coast, in recent years often from or via the Republic of Korea."[43]

MONEY LAUNDERING

The conventional view notes that the informal banking network operating in Afghanistan and neighboring countries, called hawala, makes it easy for insurgents to launder their criminal proceeds. It is estimated that there are about 900 significant hawala shops in Afghanistan. For example, Gretchen Peters argues that we need to bring "transparency" to this unregulated system to clean it of narcotics money.[44] However, the need to regulate and clean up the formal Western banking system is much greater. Indeed, of the annual $65 billion global market for opiates, only 5 to 10 percent ($3 to $5 billion) is estimated to be laundered by informal banking systems, while two-thirds ($40 to $45 billion) is available for laundering through the formal banking system.[45] A recent UNODC report estimated that about $220 billion of drug money is laundered annually through the financial system. However, only about 0.2 percent of all laundered criminal money is seized and frozen, as governments have other priorities than regulating the banking industry, which benefits from this extra liquidity.[46]

There is nothing new in this state of affairs. Chapter 3 discussed the case of BCCI, which laundered narcotics money before it was closed in 1991. Turning to Latin America, in 1976, the US Treasury Department detected a currency surplus of $1.5 billion in Florida banks and "connected it to the large scale laundering of drug receipts." After several years of delay during which "no concerted action was taken against drug bankers," Operation Greenback was launched in 1979, but failed to clean up the banking system. President Reagan eased rather than tightened financial regulations and froze hiring for the operation, limiting its investigative powers. The operation's chief prosecutor, Charles Blau, declared that George H.W. Bush, who led the anti-drugs effort, "wasn't really too interested in financial prosecution." Under his watch, Operation Greenback was immediately downgraded administratively from a high-level committee in Washington, DC to a lesser unit in Miami. Bush Sr.'s drug czar, Bill Bennett, showed that the war on drugs is more a war against the underclass than against bankers. When the Federal Reserve Bank in Washington reported a currency surplus of $8 billion in Miami and Los Angeles banks, he did not ask the Fed which banks had received it. Instead, he moved to evict "sixty low-income, mostly black, residents of public housing projects in southeast Washington. Drug use had been reported in their apartments." As Jefferson Morley rightly observed at the time, in "Bennett's 'national strategy,' state coercion must be visited on poor drug consumers before rich drug financiers."[47]

President Obama recently declared that his administration is "putting unprecedented pressure on [Mexican] cartels and their finances here in the United States."[48] In fact, light regulation has been the norm for decades. It was recently reported that in 2010, Wachovia (now part of Wells Fargo) had to forfeit $110 million to US authorities for having allowed drug-related financial transactions, in addition to $50 million for failure to monitor funds used to ship 22 tons of cocaine. The bank was sanctioned for not applying anti-money laundering procedures to the transfer of $378.4 billion into dollar accounts from Mexican *casas de cambio* (currency exchange houses). Jeffrey Sloman, the federal prosecutor, said that "Wachovia's blatant disregard for our banking laws gave international cocaine cartels a virtual carte blanche to finance their operations." Yet the banking sector is powerful enough so that serious regulation is not applied: Wachovia's total fine was less than two percent of its $12.3 billion profit for 2009, and it was decided that there would be no criminal trial. And this was not because the bank did not know: "As early as 2004," the court settlement stated, "Wachovia understood the risk that was associated with doing business with the Mexican CDCs [casas de cambio] ... Wachovia was aware that other large US banks were exiting the CDC business based on [anti-money laundering] concerns ... despite these warnings, Wachovia remained in business."[49]

An earlier case had Antonio Giraldi and Maria Lourdes Reategui, two American Express Bank executives, convicted in 1994 of laundering $33 million for Mexico's Gulf Cartel, in what was at the time the largest money-laundering case involving a US bank. They were sentenced to ten and three years in jail respectively, and the bank was sentenced to pay $7 million in civil penalties.[50] Also, in the early 1990s, Citibank helped Raúl Salinas, the brother of Mexico's President Carlos Salinas (1988–94), to transfer secretly about $100 million from Mexico to Europe. A GAO report stated that "Citibank actions assisted Mr Salinas with these transfers and effectively disguised the funds' source and destination, thus breaking the funds' paper trail." Raúl Salinas has claimed that the money was simply part of an investment fund, but it is unlikely that none of the money was related to drugs. A Swiss police investigation reported that he was a key player in Mexico's cocaine trade, collecting large bribes to protect the traffic into the United States.[51]

US COUNTERNARCOTICS POLICY

Until about 2005, American policy in Afghanistan was, by and large, not concerned with drugs. General Tommy Franks, who led the initial attack, declared in 2002 that US troops would stay clear of drug interdiction and that resolving narcotics problems was up to Afghans and civilians. When Donald Rumsfeld was asked in 2003 what the United States was doing about narcotics in Helmand, he replied: "You ask what we're going to do and the answer is, I don't really know." A US military spokesman at Bagram base, Sergeant Major Harrison Sarles, stated: "We're not a drug task force. That's not part of our mission." Ahmed Rashid recounts that a "frustrated" US Special Operations Forces colonel in charge of the Provincial Reconstruction Team in Helmand told him "how he watched convoys of opium travelling past his camp every morning but did not have orders to stop them. His rules of engagement stated that if he discovered drug shipments he *could* destroy them, but there was no order saying he *must* destroy them or that he *must* interdict drug convoys." Moreover, the DEA had only two agents in Afghanistan in 2003 and didn't open an office in the country until 2004.[52]

Nonetheless, there is one counternarcotics scheme to mention in this early period, but its short life confirms that such projects were not a priority. In 2002, the State Department's Bureau of International Narcotics and Law Enforcement Affairs drafted a strategy with the United Kingdom, designated as lead country on drug control. It combined interdiction and compensated eradication, which consisted in paying farmers to steer them away from poppies and toward legal crops. In 2002–03, about $70 million were distributed to growers as rewards for eradicating their fields. However, the scheme soon faced several problems and was quickly abandoned. The money was often pocketed by local officials while a number of farmers who had cleared their fields never received compensation. Local officials asked for bribes to protect crops from eradication, resulting in those who could not afford to pay bearing the brunt of the campaign. Results were not always verified and thus money could be received while cultivation kept expanding. In short, the

British scheme enriched local commanders while failing to decrease cultivation. In fact, it even increased it in some areas because farmers decided to grow more in order to receive larger sums. Furthermore, the strategy generated much popular opposition. For example, in Nangarhar, 10,000 farmers attacked eradication teams and police with stones and blocked roads in protest, and tribes decided to join forces to resist the campaign. The fact that the Pentagon had no desire to participate, sticking to its laissez-faire approach, did not help. The US military reportedly refused to share intelligence with the British on key traffickers, leading Tony Blair to raise the issue with Bush.[53]

Several reasons explain the early opposition to counternarcotics on the part of the White House and the military.

First, Afghanistan was attacked to show that Washington should not be challenged, and destroying poppy crops and heroin labs contributes nothing in this respect. Therefore, there is no reason why any effort should have been directed toward that task. A US military official explained that resources were limited and had to be directed toward the real mission, not drugs: top Pentagon officials "just don't want to mess with that stuff ... We don't have enough resources now to kill the bad guys," so how could drug control be carried out simultaneously?[54] In late 2005, Lt. Gen. Karl Eikenberry, then commander of US forces in Afghanistan, made it clear that "drugs are bad, but his orders were that drugs were not a priority of the U.S. military in Afghanistan." He said that "the Pentagon strategy was 'sequencing'—defeat the Taliban, then have someone else clean up the drug business."[55] Furthermore, Washington's most important target at that time was Iraq, whose oil resources and strategic location in the Persian Gulf region ensured that it would take priority.

Second, many of the United States' local Afghan allies were involved in trafficking, from which they drew money and power. Destroying drug labs and poppy fields would have been, in effect, a direct blow to American operations and proxy fighters on the ground. As Western diplomats conceded at the time, "without money from drugs, our friendly warlords can't pay their militias. It's as simple as that." According to James Risen, this explains why the Pentagon and the White House refused to bomb the 25 or so drug facilities that the CIA had identified on its maps in 2001. Similarly, in 2005, the Pentagon denied all but 3 of 26 DEA requests for airlifts. Barnett Rubin summarized the US attitude well when he wrote in 2004 that when "he visits Afghanistan,

Defense Secretary Donald Rumsfeld meets military commanders whom Afghans know as the godfathers of drug trafficking. The message has been clear: Help fight the Taliban and no one will interfere with your trafficking."[56] As a result, US military officials closed their eyes to the trade. An Army Green Beret said he was "specifically ordered to ignore heroin and opium when he and his unit discovered them on patrol." A US Senate report mentioned that "congressional committees received reports that U.S. forces were refusing to disrupt drug sales and shipments and rebuffing requests from the Drug Enforcement Administration for reinforcements to go after major drug kingpins."[57]

This state of affairs resulted from the American military strategy which initially consisted in using a small number of troops and local proxy forces, mainly from the Northern Alliance, as seen in chapter 5. For example, only about 110 CIA officers and 316 Special Forces were used in the invasion and in 2001–02, there were no more than 8,000 American troops in Afghanistan. The CIA and US Special Forces distributed $70 million in $100 bills to strongmen in various parts of the country, in order to gather intelligence and fight al-Qaeda and the Taliban. The country was partitioned geographically in spheres of influence controlled by dominant warlords, for example, Ismail Khan in the west, Hazrat Ali in the east, and Abdul Rashid Dostum, Mohammed Fahim, and Mohammed Atta in the north.[58] Many commanders controlling regional and local territories were involved in trafficking. US support and protection resulted in the consolidation of their power and an increase in the scale of the industry.[59]

Third, the Department of Defense thought that eradicating crops would upset farmers and hurt attempts at winning Afghan hearts and minds. Indeed, since 2001, the Taliban have sought to capitalize on resentment caused by eradication schemes. For example, in Helmand "they appear to have offered protection to the farmers targeted by eradication" and in Kandahar "they were even reported to have offered financial assistance to farmers whose fields were being eradicated, in exchange for support in fighting against the government."[60] Thus, it is far from certain that eliminating drugs would weaken the insurgency. In fact, the opposite is more likely, as it would only add to the opposition already generated by NATO operations in the country, as noted by a well-informed analyst: "As the conflict progressed, victims of abuses by both Afghan and foreign troops and of the side-effects of US reliance on air power began to represent another important source of recruits for the Taliban."[61]

From 2004, counternarcotics started slowly moving up the US agenda. In 2005, Washington developed its first counternarcotics strategy for Afghanistan, composed of five pillars: elimination/ eradication, interdiction, justice reform, public information, and alternative livelihoods (although the pillars were not weighted equally: alternative development was relatively neglected, while eradication/ elimination was the priority). The Afghan government incorporated this strategy into its own 2006 National Drug Control Strategy, which was later updated and integrated into its National Development Strategy in 2008.[62] Around 2005, counternarcotics operations were still relatively isolated from the broader counterinsurgency strategy. Nevertheless, the Pentagon started to consider the possibility of getting involved in counterdrug missions and issued new guidelines authorizing the military to "move antidrug agents by helicopters and cargo planes and assist in planning missions and uncovering targets," among other things.[63] A number of counternarcotics units were set up, such as Task Force 333 (a covert squad of special agents) and the Central Poppy Eradication Force, an Afghan team trained by the American private contractor Dyncorp at a cost of $50 million and supervised by the United States through the Afghan Ministry of the Interior, where Washington's main contact was Lieutenant General Mohammed Daoud. It didn't seem to be a problem that Daoud was "an ex-warlord from the north who was reputed to have major connections with the drug trade."[64]

Since that time, debates have taken place among policymakers regarding what counterdrug strategies should be adopted, but the discussion has revolved almost exclusively around actions in Afghanistan. For example, in November 2004, Robert Charles proposed an aggressive aerial eradication campaign referred to as "Plan Afghanistan" because it was modeled on Plan Colombia, even if, as a Transnational Institute report noted, "the Plan Colombia spray programme by one key measure of success—the price, purity and availability of cocaine in the US—has failed utterly." At a congressional hearing entitled "Afghanistan: are British counternarcotics efforts going wobbly?" he said the British were squeamish because they favored manual eradication combined with alternative livelihoods.[65]

Tom Schweich argued strongly in favor of tough methods. He recounted how while in Afghanistan, he "continued to press for aerial eradication" even though Afghan resistance constrained him to use only the ground-based version, which he saw as "inefficient, costly, dangerous and more subject to corrupt dealings among local officials" than spraying. But he was reassured by White House officials that Bush continued to be "a big fan of aerial eradication." Nevertheless, he faced international opposition, writing that "the truth was that many of our allies in the International Security Assistance Force were lukewarm on antidrug operations, and most were openly hostile to aerial eradication." For example, Britain opposed spraying crops and British forces "issued leaflets and bought radio advertisements telling the local criminals that the British military was not part of the anti-poppy effort."[66] Bush's National Security Council authorized aerial spraying in late 2007, ostensibly aiming to weaken the Taliban by cutting their profits. The *Washington Post* reported that "Bush was passionate about spraying" and declared "I'm a spray man myself." Nonetheless, the policy was shelved for fear that it would generate popular opposition: Karzai told Bush that "the sight of spray planes would 'look like chemical warfare' to the Afghan people."[67]

Another hardliner was William Wood, the US ambassador to Afghanistan from 2007 to 2009, nicknamed "Chemical Bill" by NATO officers. He had previously been ambassador to Colombia, and this perhaps influenced his views, as he first called for "a massive aerial-eradication program that would wipe out 80,000 hectares of poppies in Helmand Province, delivering a fatal blow to the root of the narcotics problem." He said that if "there is no poppy, there is nothing to traffic." Moreover, "he didn't really care whether the farmers were poor or rich," because there are "a lot of poor people in the drug trade in the U.S.A.—people mixing meth in their trailers in rural areas and people selling crack in the inner cities—and we put them in jail," so why not in Afghanistan too?[68] Counterterrorism expert David Kilcullen also recommended aggressive tactics, such as "mobile courts that had the authority to execute drug kingpins in their own provinces." Tom Schweich noted that "[y]ou could have heard a pin drop when he first made that suggestion at a large meeting of diplomats."[69]

At the other end of the narrow spectrum, Vanda Felbab-Brown argues in favor of interdiction and a more laissez-faire policy to cultivation because that does not increase the insurgents' "political capital," or the popular support they have. She opposes the Bush administration's emphasis on eradication and supports Obama's strategy of alternative livelihoods and interdiction, which she deems a "courageous break with [Bush's] ineffective efforts in Afghanistan."[70] Similarly, Barnett Rubin and Jake Sherman call for rural development that "must precede coerced reduction in cultivation or eradication," along with "enhanced interdiction efforts, including the removal of high officials who receive any narcotics money."[71] Obama's envoy to Afghanistan and Pakistan, Richard Holbrooke, agreed and described Bush's tactics as "the most wasteful and ineffective program I have seen in 40 years." Organizations such as the Afghanistan Research and Evaluation Unit (AREU) have also published reports favorable to alternative livelihoods projects.[72]

Since 2007, the United States has intensified its counternarcotics efforts and sought to integrate them more closely with the counterinsurgency campaign. In particular, in late 2008, the Pentagon changed its rules of engagement to permit US troops to target traffickers allied with insurgents and terrorists, and soldiers were allowed to accompany and protect counternarcotics operations run by Americans and Afghans. This shift was also adopted by NATO, whose members were allowed to participate in interdiction missions.[73]

Since 2009, the Obama administration's strategy has deemphasized eradication by ending support for the Afghan central eradication force while focusing on interdiction and the destruction of heroin labs, based on the reasoning that this "would more precisely target the drug-insurgency nexus." A focus on rural development has also been announced because, as Richard Holbrooke declared, eradication is a "waste of money," it alienates farmers, and it "might destroy some acreage, but it didn't reduce the amount of money the Taliban got by one dollar. It just helped the Taliban."[74] The number of permanent DEA agents in Afghanistan has increased from 13 to over 80 in 2011 and the Pentagon has established a Combined Joint Interagency Task Force-Nexus in Kandahar to provide coordination support and intelligence for DEA interdiction missions and ISAF counterinsurgency operations that target insurgents with links to the drug trade.[75]

Overall, an interesting question is to explain the emergence, intensification and militarization of US counternarcotics operations in Afghanistan. Although such a discussion remains somewhat speculative, what follows discusses possible reasons that may account for the evolution of the anti-drug strategy over time.

Some have pointed to the resignation of Donald Rumsfeld as secretary of defense in 2006. Rumsfeld had always been strongly opposed to military involvement in drug control and thus his departure is thought to have contributed to a "sea change" in the Department of Defense's attitude, which then became more engaged in counternarcotics.[76] However, the significance of staff changes should be downplayed when explaining the broad outlines of policy. It is not as if Rumsfeld had prevented single-handedly an army of drug warriors in the US government from carrying out counternarcotics operations in Afghanistan. As seen above, there were clear strategic reasons for the lack of military involvement in counternarcotics in the years immediately after 2001.

Congressional pressures have also been identified as a reason. This political pressure, the argument goes, eventually led the Pentagon and CIA to accept publicly that the insurgency was funded by drugs and to approve the 2005 counternarcotics strategy.[77] Indeed, in 2004–05, a host of critical pieces in the media urged more action in light of the large 2004 opium harvest. For example, Henry Hyde, Illinois Republican, stated that there was "a clear need at this stage for military action against the opium storage dumps and heroin laboratories" and that if the military did not get involved, the United States would need to send "troops from places like Turkey to take on this challenge." The Democrats also pitched in, as when John Kerry criticized Bush for failing to eliminate narcotics in Afghanistan.[78] Such explanations might be correct in terms of immediate causes, in that congressional pressures and debates contributed to putting the issue on policymakers' agenda and generating media coverage. However, they beg the question of why the narcotics issue became a more prominent debate within government circles in the first place?

Some have pointed to the explosion of poppy cultivation in Afghanistan and the political pressures it has generated in the United States to do something about the problem. For example, Ahmed Rashid noted how the greater emphasis on drugs in US policy from 2005 onwards was prompted in part by the fact that it had become too obvious that Afghan poppy cultivation was getting out of control. The United States could less easily afford to be seen as doing nothing, for public relations purposes. The 2004 massive opium harvest embarrassed Washington and London enough for them to begin addressing narcotics more seriously: farmland under poppy cultivation had just increased by 64 percent and for the first time poppies were cultivated in all 34 of Afghanistan's provinces. Similarly, opium production rose to 6,100 tons in 2006 and to 8,200 tons in 2007, the highest amount ever recorded, and Afghanistan now accounted for 93 percent of global heroin production. The skyrocketing of drug production in 2006 and 2007, publicized in UNODC reports, could not be ignored indefinitely.[79]

There is probably some truth to this interpretation. Even if drug control is not a US objective, the discourse that has been created around the issue has acquired a force of its own. Therefore, when poppy cultivation spread in Afghanistan to a point that it became difficult to ignore, it is plausible that Washington was forced to make some gesture seemingly addressing the problem, otherwise, its image as a government allegedly concerned with drug harms could have been tarnished.

Finally, another possible reason is that from 2004–05, it became useful politically to talk about a war on drugs to make the resurgent Taliban look evil by associating them with narcotics. Indeed, the intensification of counternarcotics rhetoric and operations "took place against the backdrop of an upsurge in armed opposition" to the US-backed Afghan government.[80] That is to say, whereas in the years immediately after 2001, the drug trade was largely controlled by US allies (warlords), from the time the Taliban reemerged as a significant force partly financed by drugs, narcotics became an issue that could be used to cast a negative light on them. Indeed, it is interesting that since 2004, the intensification of drug war rhetoric has grown in parallel with the rise of the insurgency.

In sum, while from 2001 to 2005, drugs were simply not part of the US agenda in Afghanistan, since 2005, there has been more talk about drug control, and more counternarcotics operations have taken place. However, this does not mean that the United States is moving closer to conducting a real war on drugs. It is not the intensification of militaristic counterdrug missions per se that makes a drug war real, but the implementation of strategies known to reduce drug problems. On that count, Washington has failed, as will be seen in the next chapter. Further, the United States has continued to support allies involved in trafficking, and Obama stated explicitly that his drug war is instrumental in fighting the insurgency and not about eliminating drugs per se. Indeed, in 2009, his administration presented its new approach to narcotics and elaborated a target list of 50 "major drug traffickers *who help finance the insurgency*" to be killed or captured by the military.[81] Therefore, if traffickers help the Taliban, they will be attacked—but if they support government forces, they apparently will be left alone. This suggests that the drug war is used to target enemies.

7
Solutions

There has been much discussion about what should be done to rid Afghanistan of its poppies and reduce global levels of addiction. The Bush administration called for crop eradication, while Obama favors arresting traffickers and rural development. The Senlis Council (now renamed ICOS, International Council on Security and Development) has argued that using Afghan opium to make painkilling medicines under license would go a long way toward solving the problem. A number of development specialists support alternative livelihoods for farmers. This chapter maintains that such solutions are inadequate because they are confined to Afghanistan. The most obvious way for the United States and Europe (and Russia) to reduce global addiction caused by Afghan drugs and reduce the size of the industry is first to stop supporting drug trafficking in Afghanistan and elsewhere. Second, they should work to reduce demand in consumer areas like Europe and Russia. Thus, conventional solutions for Afghanistan should either be discarded (eradication) or considered development projects rather than drug control schemes (alternative livelihoods and licensing). The first section below reviews the record of the main consumer countries and Afghanistan's neighbors in addressing narcotics problems and concludes that there is still much room for improvement.

The chapter then discusses the rising levels of addiction in Afghanistan in recent years due to the increase in drug production and examines what could be done to improve the situation. It concludes by exploring the likely benefits of legalizing and regulating drugs. It is argued that steps should be taken toward such a regime but that much of its success will depend on the extent to which the legalized industry can be regulated according to public health objectives, as opposed to commercial ones in place for the alcohol and tobacco industries.

DRUG POLICY

Europe and Russia are the world's two largest heroin markets, accounting together for nearly half of global consumption. The

United States is not an important consumer of Afghan opiates, importing its heroin mostly from Colombia and Mexico and accounting for 5 percent of global consumption.[1] How should drug problems in consumer countries be addressed? In addition to ending support for the drug trade in the many ways described in previous chapters, from protecting traffickers to neglecting to regulate banking practices seriously, governments should follow the well-established consensus reached by drug policy research. The latter ranks drug control policies from most to least effective as follows: 1) treatment of addicts, 2) prevention, 3) enforcement, and 4) overseas operations in producer countries. This assessment has been recently corroborated (again) by twelve leading scholars in a synthesis work, in addition to many other studies that have reached the same conclusions.[2] For example, a noted 1994 RAND report calculated that treatment of addicts domestically was the most effective method for reducing cocaine consumption in the United States, compared to targeting source countries overseas, interdiction, and domestic enforcement, which were respectively 23 times, 11 times, and 7 times less cost effective.[3] What works and what doesn't is therefore well known.

Treatment refers to various health-based methods to reduce drug use and its harms. Opioid substitution therapy (OST) has been particularly successful and consists in giving addicts regular doses of opiate substitutes like methadone to help them stop using illicit heroin. One major review of the scientific evidence found that "heroin users enrolled in OST programmes are more than twice as likely to cease heroin use as untreated users," that OST increases the chances of finding employment and "reduces criminal behavior by as much as 60%," while lowering the transmission of infectious diseases. Risk of death for patients who use methadone, particularly from overdoses, "is less than 25% of that for untreated heroin users." Needle exchange programs which provide clean needles to addicts are also effective in reducing HIV infections and have been widely adopted in Europe as part of a "harm reduction" agenda.[4] In sum, as Thomas Babor and his colleagues conclude: "If a society is committed to 'doing something' about its drug problem, a substantial expansion of [treatment] services, particularly for people dependent on opiates, is likely to produce the broadest range of benefits … yet … most societies invest in these services at a low level, resulting in limited access and inadequate quality."[5] Prevention, on its part, can be achieved through a variety of community programs and media campaigns. Overall, school and family programs "yield modest, but potentially important, benefits." A RAND report evaluated school-based prevention programs as a "good investment" for society.[6]

Enforcement includes a range of interventions such as arrests of traffickers and dealers and interdiction of drug shipments by custom officers. There is little, if any, systematic scientific evidence to evaluate such methods. In fact, most scholars view them in a negative light, particularly the very tough sort found in the United States, because although it "consumes the largest share of drug-related government spending in many countries ... so little can be said about how effective such enforcement is in accomplishing its goals." Finally, overseas operations may refer to eradication, alternative development, crop substitution, chemical precursors control, and police operations in producer countries. Such programs receive much exposure in the media, but the fact is that for decades, efforts "by wealthy countries to curtail cultivation of drug-producing plants in poor countries have not reduced aggregate drug supply or use in downstream markets, and probably never will ... it will fail even if current efforts are multiplied many times over."[7]

As mentioned previously, the West has consistently emphasized the strategies that have been shown not to work (enforcement and overseas operations) while neglecting those that do work (treatment and prevention). Babor and his colleagues state that "it is difficult to understand why policymakers would not want their policies to be based on good quality evidence." A plausible answer is that the war on drugs' role is to facilitate overseas intervention rather than addressing drug problems seriously. It would be surprising if rational government officials had indeed repeatedly failed, for decades, to select the methods that are well known to be effective and continually followed those known to be futile.[8]

The drug war has also neglected the most lethal drugs, tobacco and alcohol, which surely would have been targeted if the objective had been to reduce drug harms. One reason why they have been ignored is that they are consumed by many people in the top echelons of society, suggesting again that the war on drugs targets enemies and the underprivileged more so than allies and the powerful. According to the World Health Organization (WHO), tobacco kills about 5.4 million people every year—1 in 10 adult deaths worldwide—and alcohol accounts for another 1.8 million. In the twentieth century, tobacco killed 100 million people, and the number could reach one billion during the twenty-first century. On the other hand, all illegal drugs together kill about 200,000 every year, half of which is due to opiates. But tobacco and alcohol industry leaders are treated very differently than the Taliban. First, their products have not been made illegal; in fact, tobacco is the only legal consumer product which kills when it is used entirely as intended. Their industries spend tens of billions of dollars on marketing, but no one would think of giving the Taliban the privilege of conducting advertising campaigns in Europe or the United States for opium products.[9]

The Latin American Commission on Drugs and Democracy, conceived by ex-presidents Cardoso of Brazil, Gaviria of Colombia and Zedillo of Mexico, recently released a report that called the US war on drugs a "failure" and said that the "long-term solution for the drug problem is to reduce drastically the demand for drugs in the main consumer countries" and called for "emphasizing prevention and treatment."[10] But the United States and Russia have rejected the consensus on drug policy, with disastrous—and predictable—results. Europe has not done so poorly, but much improvement is still possible.

Washington's *National Drug Control Strategy* emphasizes enforcement, allocating 64 percent of the drug control budget to interdiction and to arresting, prosecuting and incarcerating drug offenders, including arresting about 750,000 each year for possession of small amounts of marijuana. Only 36 percent is reserved for treatment and other demand reduction activities.[11] But this has not always been the case. When President Nixon launched his "war on drugs" in 1971, drug law enforcement only received 30 percent of the budget, whereas demand reduction received the bulk of it—the opposite of the current situation. The shift came under President Reagan, who increased drastically federal spending on drug control, from about $1.5 billion in 1981 to $6.6 billion in 1989. The bulk of the increase was for enforcement and interdiction, and by 1989 less than 30 percent of the budget was allocated to demand reduction.[12] The United States now has the world's highest imprisonment rate, at more than 750 inmates per 100,000 residents, translating into over two million people behind bars, of which about 360,000 are held for drug offenses.[13] The consequences of such harsh policies have been disastrous, destroying lives, families and communities and leading to increased HIV infection rates. But drug use in the United States still ranks among the highest internationally. A global study found that "the US had among the highest levels of use of all drugs" and that in general, "countries with stringent user-level illegal drug policies did not have lower levels of use than countries with liberal ones."[14]

Europe has improved its record over the last two decades, as important advances have been made to bring harm reduction into the mainstream of policy and rates of usage for each category of drugs are relatively low compared to countries using a more criminalized approach. In the 1990s, many European countries introduced OST and needle and syringe exchange programs (NSP), making the continent the global leader in the implementation of harm reduction strategies. For example, all EU countries have one or more NSP and provide OST, and the latter is used by an estimated 670,000 addicts, about half the continent's problem drug users.[15]

Nevertheless, Europe still spends about three times more on enforcement than on harm reduction.[16] Moreover, there are still "huge national variations in coverage" in both OST and NSP. In particular, overall provision of "substitution treatment in the Baltic States and the central and south-east European regions" remains low. While some countries like Spain and the United Kingdom have many OST sites, at least ten European countries have fewer than 20. Thus, the proportion of addicts reached by those services varies from 5 percent in Cyprus and Slovakia to around 50 percent in the Czech Republic, Germany and Italy (40 percent is considered "good coverage"). Even when services are provided, long waiting lists can mean inadequate care, so that "in practice, treatment is sometimes least available to those who need it most." There is also a large variation in the number of NSP sites by country, "from several thousand (France), several hundred (United Kingdom, Portugal, Spain) to fewer than five (Cyprus, Greece, Romania and Sweden)." Further, as a European Commission review concluded: "Treatment and harm reduction programmes are often not tailored to address the specific needs and problems of different groups of problem or dependent drug users, e.g. women, under-aged young people, migrants, specific ethnic groups and vulnerable groups." The European prison system is not well serviced either: "Availability and accessibility of many key harm reduction measures in prisons lag far behind the availability and accessibility of these interventions in the community outside prisons."[17]

In 2002, the British government targeted a reduction of 70 percent of Afghan opium production over five years and complete elimination in ten years. It would be hard to have failed more completely: production increased from 3,400 tons in 2002 to 5,800 tons in 2011. But Britain would have done well to put its own house in order first. Since the mid 1980s, its drug policy has shifted from a focus on health to one on crime, a more coercive approach mirroring developments in the United States. Experts Peter Reuter and Alex Stevens report that despite "rhetorical commitments to the rebalancing of drug policy spending towards treatment ... the bulk of public expenditure continues to be devoted to criminal justice measures," just like in other European countries, even the Netherlands which still allocates 75 percent of its drug budget to law enforcement. From 1994 to 2005 in the United Kingdom, "the number of prison cell years handed out in annual sentences has tripled" and "the use of imprisonment has increased even more rapidly for drug offenders than other offenders," contributing significantly to the current "prison overcrowding crisis." Updated figures from 1996 to 2008 show the same trends, with the number of people in prison for drug offenses rising by 91 percent, faster than incarceration for other offenses (53 percent), while drug offenders made up 16 percent of the total prison population as of 2008. Yet, "the UK is at the top of the European ladder for drug use and dependence," and heroin now seems to be more available on the streets: its price fell from £70 to £45 per gram from 2000 to 2008 while purity rose from 32.7 to 46.5 percent between 2003 and 2005.[18]

Some European countries have successfully decriminalized drug use, as Portugal in 2001. Glenn Greenwald concluded that "judged by virtually every metric, the Portuguese decriminalization framework has been a resounding success," and "in virtually every category of any significance, Portugal, since decriminalization, has outperformed the vast majority of other states that continue to adhere to a criminalization regime." Addicts became more inclined to seek treatment as the fear of arrest and prosecution vanished. Drug usage in many categories has decreased and remains low or very low compared to other EU countries. Significantly, "the number of newly reported cases of HIV and AIDS among drug addicts has declined substantially every year since 2001" and "the total number of drug-related deaths has actually *decreased* from the predecriminalization year of 1999 (when it totaled close to 400) to 2006 (when the total was 290)." In 2000, there were 281 cases of deaths from opiates (including heroin), but that number decreased steadily to 133 by 2006.[19] And there are other successful cases. In the 1990s, France and Switzerland introduced large opioid substitution services nationally. Over a decade, the number of French addicts receiving such services zoomed from close to zero to about 100,000, and changes in Switzerland were also positive. France saw a 75 percent decline in heroin arrests between 1996 and 2003, along with decreases in drug-related mortality and AIDS cases, while Switzerland benefited from substantial reductions in crime.[20]

Russia often complains that US and NATO forces should crack down on narcotics more forcefully in Afghanistan, but Moscow is not in a position to give others lessons about drug control. During the Soviet era, its problem was relatively small as closed borders preempted trafficking and users consumed primarily homegrown substances. The drastic increase in use and related harms came with the collapse of the Soviet Union, which opened the floodgates to Afghan heroin, a situation exacerbated since 2001. Moscow estimates that heroin kills about 30,000 Russians every year, but has chosen a strategy that "serves the end of social control and enforcement" while doing little to treat addiction. Criminalization is emphasized and the largest share of public resources is directed to the arrest, prosecution and incarceration of users. This worsens the country's HIV epidemic, the fastest growing in the world—with nearly one million infections, some 80 percent of which are related to needle sharing—while syringe availability is still very limited and methadone and buprenorphine remain prohibited by law. Thus, as a recent New York University report states: "Nothing that happens in Afghanistan, for good or ill, would affect the Russian drug problem nearly as much as the adoption of methadone."[21]

Russia has the world's second highest incarceration rate after the United States, at 613 per 100,000 population, with as many as 20 percent of prisoners detained on drug charges.[22] Like Washington, Moscow uses its drug war to control certain segments of its own population and assert its influence abroad, as anti-immigration policies "can be advanced under the banner of drug control if ethnic minority immigrants are presented as responsible for Russia's crime problems." It is also apparent to a number of analysts that Moscow is "using the war-cry of combating drugs to reassert its influence in the former Soviet states."[23] While Obama recently announced plans to access seven military bases in Colombia under the pretext of fighting wars on terror and narcotics, Victor Ivanov, director of the Russian Federal Drug Control Service, stated that he would like to set up a second military base in Kyrgyzstan to combat drug trafficking. He explained how he was inspired by American tactics in Latin America:

The United States' experience is certainly quite effective. The powerful flow of cocaine from Colombia into the United States prompted Washington to set up seven military bases in the Latin

American nation in question. The US then used aircraft to destroy some 230,000 hectares of coca plantations ... Russia suggests building its military base in Kyrgyzstan since it is the republic's Osh region that is a centre of sorts whence drugs are channelled throughout Central Asia.[24]

Ivanov added that "such bases are likely to be set up along the drug traffic routes in other regional countries, too," as in Kazakhstan and Tajikistan. Otherwise, Russia would be in danger, he alleged, because "drug barons are uniting with Islamist militants to seize power in vulnerable Central Asian states" while NATO's failure to deal with Afghan drugs "threatens to create a security nightmare for Russia." The rationale was clearly explained by Tatiana Parkhalina, director of the Center for European Security in Moscow: "The former Soviet states of central Asia are our own backyard. Moscow doesn't want to stand by while the Taliban and terrorist networks convert the financial resources from drug trafficking into arms and political influence ... There is a practical alliance taking shape between drug traffickers and terrorists, and it is a very big threat."[25]

Russia has pushed for its strategies to be implemented by Central Asian republics as well. The consequences have been largely negative, including rising levels of narcotics use and one of the fastest-growing HIV epidemics in the world.[26] Corruption and the reported involvement of government officials has not helped either, while the United States and Western governments appear to be looking the other way to secure those authoritarian regimes' cooperation, in particular over operations in Afghanistan. For example, about 20 percent of Afghan drugs transit via Tajikistan toward Russia and Europe, but there has been little pressure put on Tajik President Emomali Rahmon to clamp down on narcotics. Western diplomats acknowledge the situation: "We send reports every month to our capitals, very negative, but they don't (care)," said one based in Dushanbe, the capital, and whose country has troops in Afghanistan. "Because it's a so-called stable country leading to Afghanistan, we accept it." William Lawrence, a chief adviser for a UN Afghan border-management program based in Dushanbe, said that the "Americans want to have a logistics base here, so do you think they're going to pressure the government about corruption? The answer is no." A State Department official conceded that there "is always going to be a tradeoff based on different foreign-policy objectives, different security objectives, the tolerance for different types of corruption, different levels of corruption [and] I don't think the situation in Tajikistan, frankly, is that much different than the rest of Central Asia in terms of these types of tradeoffs."[27]

Iran is a large consumer of Afghan opium. Following the 1979 revolution, it adopted tough anti-drug measures based on harsh enforcement—the death penalty was prescribed for serious drug offenses, and public health services offering treatment were closed. The country was then an opium producer but the mullahs' ban on cultivation succeeded in basically eliminating poppy crops, from 33,000 hectares in 1979 to virtually zero by the late 1990s. However, this merely shifted cultivation across the border into Afghanistan while Iran eventually became the most important transit country for the latter's opiates, steeply increasing consumption and harms, in particular HIV. In more recent years, Iran has kept enforcement very much alive: in 2002, for example, it accounted for no less than 25 percent of global opiates seizures. In the 1990s, more than 3,000 of its officials were killed and 10,000 disabled in fire fights with traffickers.[28] However, for the last decade and a half, Tehran has realized that the problem was not going away. For instance, thousands of drug users were incarcerated without receiving any health services, resulting in needle sharing and HIV infection in prisons. Thus, drug policies have been somewhat liberalized, returning to a strategy similar to that before 1979. While harsh laws have been preserved, moves toward harm reduction have been made, with great benefits. For example, between 2002 and 2008, the number of prisoners addicted to opiates receiving methadone maintenance treatment increased from 100 to more than 25,000, and needle and syringe programs have been established.[29]

Pakistan is a main transit country for Afghan opiates and the narcotics flow through its territory has increased since 2001. As a result, there are currently half a million chronic heroin users in the country and a rising number of HIV infections. Islamabad has reacted with harsh anti-drug laws, which grant the death penalty for possession of over 100g of heroin or 200g of opium. A number of barriers remain for those seeking treatment, in addition to criminalization and stigmatization. Drug users are often arrested and imprisoned and have to pay the police to prevent arrest, while they face severe discrimination in government-run health care facilities. Drug demand reduction programs are lacking, while prevention measures such as provision of clean needles remain inaccessible to most users.[30]

AFGHANISTAN

The above section has argued that demand reduction should be prioritized in consumer markets and reviewed the experience of countries suffering from Afghan drugs in this respect. But what should be done in Afghanistan in parallel? This section asserts that eradication should not be pursued (at least not as a primary method) as it does not lead to reductions in drug use, nor does it foster development. Alternative livelihood projects and licensing should not be seen primarily as narcotics control programs, but could be useful as development schemes whose impact will depend on the international community's willingness to fund them appropriately.

Also, drug consumption in Afghanistan itself will be examined. Although there are no easy solutions, the significant problems it has caused, in particular since 2001, would best be addressed through infusions of development aid to reduce social hardship and provide a social safety net, including services to addicts. The last section explores the potential benefits of drug legalization and regulation, globally and in Afghanistan.

Eradication

Eradication, in its ground-based or aerial variety, has been popular among drug warriors and carried out extensively in countries like Colombia and Afghanistan. But the strategy has been rightly discredited by many analysts for reasons mentioned in previous chapters, such as the fact that it threatens rural livelihoods.[31] Thomas Babor and his colleagues reviewed the decades-long evidence and concluded that despite "considerable efforts, there is almost no evidence that eradication has affected the supply of heroin or cocaine to Europe, the USA, or any other country." They added that there is "even less reason to believe that alternative development is an effective way to control drug use," even if it might gather broader political support in the West because it is perceived as helping poor farmers.[32]

It is true that supply control in producer countries can disturb production in the short term, but historically, the latter has emerged elsewhere to meet global demand. For example, in the early 1970s, within the context of Nixon's drug war, almost all of Turkey's opium poppy cultivation was eradicated and the heroin laboratories in Marseille closed. Because Turkey was the source of 80 percent of the heroin on American streets, the supply shock was felt relatively strongly, and by the mid-1970s, the retail price of heroin had tripled and purity dropped by half, indicating a shortage. But because demand remained constant, prices rose and stimulated production elsewhere, particularly in Southeast Asia. Alfred McCoy concluded that from this "market logic, every short-term victory, every successful eradication or crop substitution, would become a market stimulus that brought another defeat to America's drug wars." As a result, supply control resulted in "a paradoxical strengthening of the global narcotics traffic." Turkish eradication and the breakup of the French Connection stimulated heroin production in Mexico as well, which furnished the American market.[33] Afghanistan's production has been itself stimulated by bans in neighboring countries. As seen in chapter 3, poppy and opium bans in Iran in the aftermath of the 1979 revolution and in Pakistan around the same time resulted in those activities shifting across the border into Afghanistan.

In sum, as one well-informed analyst concluded, "sixty years of Asian opium bans have demonstrated that drug supply reduction is very rarely effective and, in fact, is most often counterproductive."[34] While crop elimination could work in theory if applied to every area of the world, in practice this is virtually impossible.

Alternative livelihoods and development

Overseas operations have been a failure for years. But could this be because they have emphasized coercive methods, while development projects could have been more successful? This is effectively the Obama administration's position. A number of analysts have also made this point and called for a range of agricultural and economic development programs to wean farmers from poppy cultivation. Farmers grow poppies because they face food insecurity and poverty, which is alleviated by selling opium for cash. Poppies are a good crop in situations of insecurity compared to, say, vegetables because traffickers come directly to farmers to buy the opium, whereas vegetables would need to be brought to a market, with all the associated transport costs. Opium is also a compact product that can be stored while demand is low whereas vegetables are bulky and perishable. Advocates of rural development maintain that the way to reduce poppy cultivation is to provide farmers with alternative livelihoods, whether it is growing other profitable crops or moving into other kinds of employment.[35]

But even proponents concede that more than 30 years after the United Nations launched its first crop substitution project, "so far alternative development has failed to achieve drug supply reduction,

whether worldwide or in any given country," let alone reduce
consumption in downstream markets. One important reason for
this failure is the balloon effect. However, some maintain that the
problem is not the strategy itself, but the fact that it has been poorly
funded and implemented, and thus it should not be abandoned. For
example, Pierre-Arnaud Chouvy argues that for three decades, it
"has not failed because it was the wrong approach to drug supply
reduction but rather because it has barely been tried" and because
"projects have been mostly poorly designed and implemented."[36]
While it is true that better funded and executed programs would
be desirable, and may indeed reduce poppy cultivation in certain
areas, the problem of the balloon effect would still remain. Even
if every Afghan farmer abandoned poppy cultivation thanks to
high levels of development aid, it would move to another country
where peasants are poor and where the government does not have
the ability or will to prevent it. In short, successful development
projects would have to be carried out over the whole world, which
would be desirable, but virtually impossible.

Alternative livelihoods advocates also tend to focus overly on
"micro" factors like rural households' decision-making processes
and why they decide to plant poppies, but neglect outside powers'
share of responsibility for the expansion of the drug trade. This leads
to the above argument that poverty and insecurity drive peasants
to grow poppies. This is true, but what are the more fundamental
causes behind opium cultivation? Global demand in consumer
countries is one, as seen above. In Afghanistan, farmers are poor
and insecure, but why? The lack of rural development is one reason,
but the US/NATO military occupation is another one, just like the
fact that Afghanistan has been embroiled in war for the last three
decades, with outside powers responsible in large part for wrecking
the country. The Soviet invasion destroyed subsistence agriculture
in the countryside and the United States has supported Afghan drug
lords for years, both of which have led to more poppy growing.
Therefore, neglecting to underline the negative consequences of
outside powers' intervention with regards to the drug trade gives
a partial picture of the problem. To focus on farmers' agricultural
decisions while overlooking the role of the United States at the many
levels documented in this book seems misleading, just as would be
a study focusing on cigarette users' psychology to explain smoking
rates while neglecting the role of the tobacco industry in marketing
its product.

Poppies for peace and licensing

The Senlis Council has proposed using Afghanistan's opium to make medicines under license, in particular morphine, to be exported to countries that need them. This would provide farmers with a legal income and cut money flows to traffickers and protectors of the trade, be they Taliban, warlords, police or government officials, while reducing corruption—in short, a "poppies for peace" scheme. The idea has received support in the media, but a number of experts have voiced their opposition.[37] From this book's perspective, although licensing could in theory rid Afghanistan of its illegal crops, cultivation would merely emerge somewhere else with global demand constant, the perennial limitation of crop reduction operations. However, this is not to say that licensing should not be encouraged as a development project, just like alternative livelihoods. In fact, licensing may be seen as one component of a national alternative livelihoods program.

Some have criticized licensing as unworkable, even as a development scheme. This may be true, but although many hurdles stand in the way, the West and the international community could significantly lower them. For instance, one objection is that there is not enough effective global demand for painkilling medicines. Many countries have restrictive national health care systems and laws that would prevent them from importing significant amounts of Afghan medicines and distributing them to the sick—even if there are large unmet needs for painkillers across the world. Nevertheless, restrictive laws can be and have been made more flexible in a number of countries, such as Uganda, Vietnam, Mongolia and Romania, which have expanded access to pain treatment services.[38] Also, one factor sustaining those restrictive laws is the global US-led war on drugs, which impedes the distribution of legal drugs like morphine. Worldwide, both legal and illegal substances fall under the domain of the International Narcotics Control Board (INCB), which regulates the amount of opiate-based painkillers like morphine that each country can import. But the INCB has directed most of its attention and resources to restricting the supply of illegal drugs. David Joranson, the founder of the University of Wisconsin's Pain & Policy Studies Group, says that in the process of trying to stem the global trade in illegal heroin, "morphine is controlled to the point of not being available." For example, even in Vietnam, where laws are relatively progressive, "doctors fear that they will be suspected of diverting morphine to the black market if they prescribe 'too many' pills," according to Dr. Nguyen Phi Yen of the National Cancer Hospital. Most pharmacists simply choose not to stock morphine to prevent arousing suspicions that they could be involved in contraband. Therefore, relaxing the global war on drugs could lead to more demand for morphine.[39]

Another objection to the Senlis proposal is that Afghan medicines would not be competitive on the world market and licensing would worsen farmers' lives by institutionalizing poverty. This is so, the argument goes, because there are currently 19 countries in the world that grow poppies for pharmaceutical use and meet global demand, and Afghanistan would not be competitive enough, unless it cut costs by paying its farmers so little that they would remain stuck in poverty.[40]

It is true that it would be difficult for Afghanistan to compete on its own on the global painkiller market. Morphine production costs and profitability depend on cultivation and manufacturing methods, environmental factors, and the type of poppy varieties used. In Afghanistan, farmers harvest by hand the opium gum which would be used to make morphine, a labor-intensive and costly process. Australia and other countries use a mechanized and less labor-intensive method (the poppy straw method, which does not require collecting opium gum but instead uses the actual plant directly). Further, Australia has developed varieties of poppies rich in thebaine (as opposed to morphine), for which there is a large demand. Those factors make Australia's production competitive.

But there is an obvious way to improve Afghanistan's weaknesses, which again would depend in large part on the will of the international community: subsidies. Some might object that this would amount to artificially propping up Afghanistan's economy, but there would be nothing unique in this arrangement: farmers in the West are heavily subsidized, just like a number of "infant industries" have been in industrial countries, so why not in Afghanistan? Moreover, international funding could be used to provide Afghanistan with competitive varieties of poppies and develop more efficient cultivation and morphine manufacturing processes. This would not be unique either: in Australia, the government played an important role in subsidizing the industry in its early years so that private enterprise can now reap the profits, a common way of fostering technological development. As A.J. Fist of Tasmanian Alkaloids, one of the companies growing poppies for the medicinal market in Australia, writes: "In the early stages of the industry, DPIWE [the government's Department of

Primary Industries Water and Environment] took a leadership role in much of the agronomic research for poppies. Poppy nutrition, irrigation requirements, responses to lime, optimum densities, and crop protection methods were determined by work conducted at government research stations. This research laid an important foundation for the industry." Production techniques could also be made safer to reduce the almost inevitable diversion to illicit markets.[41] Another way to subsidize Afghan production would be to reach bilateral trade agreements that could act as price support schemes between Afghanistan and customer countries. This has been implemented already for India's and Turkey's production through the "80/20 rule" under which the United States purchases at least 80 percent of its narcotic raw materials for pharmaceutical use from those two countries.[42]

In short, the viability of licensing in Afghanistan as a development scheme would depend to a good extent on the will of the international community to provide the needed resources. Similarly, the objection that Afghanistan's weak and corrupt government and institutions would make the manufacturing of medicines unmanageable certainly needs to be considered, but it would help if the coalition withdrew its support for corrupt individuals. Nevertheless, just like any alternative livelihoods schemes, licensing would most likely not reduce global drug consumption, as production would shift elsewhere.

Finally, none of the above should imply that licensing is indeed the best industry for Afghanistan to develop. Perhaps other industries, agricultural or not, would make more sense given the country's potential and resources. But this issue would require a larger analysis than is possible here.

Drug use in Afghanistan

The discussion so far has focused on the drug problems of the West and Russia and the most effective solutions for them. But what about solutions for Afghan addicts? A recent UNODC report estimated that following a dramatic increase in numbers over the last few years, there are now one million drug users in Afghanistan, or 8 percent of the population—twice the global average. Since 2005, the number of regular opium users has grown from 150,000 to 230,000 (a 53 percent increase) and for heroin, from 50,000 to 120,000 (a 140 percent increase). HIV/AIDS infection is also an issue because 87 percent of drug injectors say they share needles and syringes with others, and also because some addicts engage in unprotected sex in order to pay for their drugs.[43]

There has been relatively little research on the methods that could be employed to alleviate Afghanistan's own drug problems, but a few potential ones can be proposed. First, reducing demand in the West as discussed above could help lower Afghanistan's addiction levels by shrinking the size of its industry. Second, treatment and prevention would reduce addiction and drug harms, just as it does in developed countries. But such resources are very deficient in Afghanistan, facilities being small in number and of inadequate quality. Only about 10 percent of addicts have ever received treatment although 90 percent say they need it, meaning that about 700,000 nationwide are left without it, which prompted the former UNODC chief, Antonio Maria Costa, to call for much greater funds for such programs. The problem is that the Bush and Obama administrations are going in the opposite direction: between 2005 and 2009, less than $18 million was allocated to "demand reduction" activities in Afghanistan, an amount less than 1 percent of the $2 billion spent on eradication and interdiction. Put differently, over those same years, Washington has spent $2.5 billion on counter-narcotics programs, almost 80 percent of which was dedicated to crop elimination, while 0.7 percent went to demand reduction and 1.4 percent to public information.[44] Those numbers clearly show US priorities, which are diametrically opposed to what is known to work.[45]

Third, what about alternative livelihoods and eradication? As seen above, even if such methods did eliminate the entire harvest in Afghanistan, Western countries' consumption would not be affected because production would emerge somewhere else. On the other hand, Afghan consumption would decrease because an immediate source of narcotics would be removed from the country. But the problem with this approach is obvious. Even if all heroin production could be eliminated from Afghanistan and thus reduce problems there, cultivation would move to another country, which would in turn see its consumption and harms exacerbated. Therefore, problems would merely be shifted somewhere else.

Finally, it is important to keep in mind that addiction and its consequences are made worse by inequality and social hardship. Therefore, development aid and war reparations paid by Russia and the United States would go a long way toward addressing drug problems in Afghanistan by alleviating misery and reducing the need of many to supplement their income by selling and trafficking in narcotics, and by permitting adequate treatment programs to be put in place. Indeed, UNODC noted that many "Afghans seem to be taking drugs as a kind of self-medication against the hardships of life." Also, the typical Afghan user is "a 28-year-old father of three ... probably unemployed, cannot read or write and has little if any education ... he is poor [and] supplements his income, presumably to meet the costs of his drug use or to help his family, by either selling his assets, borrowing money, stealing, begging, or committing other crimes."[46]

LEGALIZATION?

An ambitious proposal would be to legalize and regulate drugs globally. The proposition remains somewhat moot because in practice, it will be many years before all drugs are legalized, if ever, as there is no desire to do so on the part of political elites. Nevertheless, there have been growing calls to move towards that goal—in fact, few researchers would defend the prohibition regime as it currently stands. Many analysts recognize that it "has caused substantial unintended harms; many were predictable."[47]

Debates about legalization are misleading when they imply that the only two available options are prohibition or full legalization in which all substances would become freely available like regular commercial goods. In fact, there are many intermediate alternatives which should be considered. A case will be made below in favor of legalization and regulation, although the specifics of such a regime would need to be adjusted over time in light of experience. The Global Commission on Drug Policy recently released a report calling for steps to be taken towards legalization and among its signatories are many establishment figures, showing that such proposals can no longer be caricatured as extreme.[48] The report notes that the prohibition regime has failed to reduce consumption, while generating a host of negative consequences, from the growth of a large, violent criminal market to a number of harms on users. Conservative economists like Milton Friedman and *The Economist* magazine have also endorsed similar strategies, in addition to the libertarian CATO Institute.[49]

At first glance, perhaps the most compelling argument against legalization is that alcohol and tobacco are two legal drugs that kill together about seven million people every year whereas illegal drugs together kill 200,000. Thus making illegal drugs legal would lead to sky-high addiction levels and deaths.[50]

Most analysts agree that legalizing drugs would probably increase use. However, it is unlikely that heroin and cocaine would become as popular as alcohol and tobacco. Among other things, alcohol's popularity is related to the fact that it goes well with a meal, quenches thirst, and is an inherent part of many countries' culture. Tobacco's psychoactive effects are so mild that they do not distract from conducting daily activities. Heroin and cocaine are less compatible with many daily tasks given their intense psychoactive effects.[51]

But the most important reason why legalization does not have to lead to the problems caused by tobacco and alcohol is that the latter's negative consequences could be mitigated significantly if a few policies known to be effective were implemented. First, raising taxes on tobacco is the best way to reduce use, especially with young people. A WHO report surveying the literature on the subject estimates that increasing prices by 70 percent could prevent over one million tobacco-related deaths worldwide every year. Tax revenues could be used to fund public health campaigns, but as of now, Western governments collect $110 billion in tobacco taxes each year, but only spend 0.3 percent of it on tobacco control. Second, bans on advertising, promotion and sponsorship do work: national studies found that consumption declined by 9 percent after such bans were in place. Those who deny that advertising in sports or cultural events has any influence on smoking should take note of the following tobacco company Philip Morris internal document, which stated that while "sports is by far the best avenue to attract, sample and influence our core target smokers, it's not the only way. International movies and videos also have tremendous appeal to our young adult consumers in Asia." Third, smoke-free areas are effective in reducing tobacco consumption and contrary to industry propaganda, don't affect businesses negatively. The industry knows this, as revealed by another Philip Morris internal document that stated that total "prohibition of smoking in the workplace strongly affects industry volume ... Milder workplace restrictions, such as smoking only in designated areas, have much less impact on quitting rates and very little effect on consumption."[52]

Therefore, the solutions are known, but not implemented. The WHO evaluated global anti-tobacco efforts and concluded that "progress is possible and is being made" but "there is still far more work that must be done." For example, only 21 countries (covering only 6 percent of the world population) have been judged to have fully implemented policy guidelines for tobacco taxation while corresponding data for advertising bans is 26 countries (9 percent), for smoke-free environments, 17 countries (5 percent), and for health warnings on cigarette packs, 15 countries (8 percent). In short, as former US Surgeon General David Satcher said: "Our lack of greater progress in tobacco control is more the result of failure to implement proven strategies than it is the lack of knowledge about what to do."[53]

The situation is similar for alcohol. Another WHO report states that contrary to popular belief, the deaths and harms associated with it can be reduced by rising taxes, implementing legal age limits to purchasing and consumption and setting lower limits for blood alcohol concentration while driving. But the problem, again, is that a "large proportion of countries, representing a high percentage of the global population, has weak alcohol policies and prevention programmes that do not protect the health and safety of the populace."[54]

One reason why it has been difficult to regulate alcohol and tobacco is the size and power of their industries, which have worked hard to block or weaken legislation: their tactics include "political lobbying and campaign contributions, financing of research, attempting to affect the course of regulatory and policy machinery and engaging in social responsibility initiatives as part of public relations campaigns." Moreover, "virtually all trade liberalisation agreements promote trade in tobacco products without consideration of public health concerns," leading to more consumption because of lower prices and increased advertising, which is also true for alcohol. This is why tobacco companies like Philip Morris have stated in internal discussions that they strongly support NAFTA and the Uruguay Round process to establish the World Trade Organization because the "removal of trade barriers will provide us with expanded market opportunities."[55] Governments have also helped tobacco companies break import restrictions in developing countries to increase market share. For example, when the US trade deficit reached $123 billion in 1984, the Reagan administration pressured Asian countries to open their borders, invoking the GATT's rules of non-discrimination: it worked. The GAO concluded that "in South Korea the smoking rate among young men increased from 18% to 30% in the year after the US companies moved in," as "cigarette advertising and promotional activities have increased appreciably ... as a result of the competitive marketing of U.S. cigarettes."[56]

Legalization in Afghanistan?

How does this apply to Afghanistan? Various proposals have been made to legalize, fully or partially, the country's narcotics industry.

For example, licensing would amount to partial legalization: medicinal production would be legal but production and sales on the black market would not. The problems associated with this approach have been seen above. Another idea would be for the international community to buy up all of Afghanistan's opium harvest every year and either destroy it or store it somewhere for eventual medical or other use, essentially making production legal and providing unlimited demand for it.[57] This could dry up supply initially, but quickly, producers elsewhere would pick up the demand. It would also become a price support system in Afghanistan, with farmers producing more and more opium to receive payments. It may be a good development scheme as funds would be channeled towards rural development, but such aid might as well be given directly without spreading poppy cultivation throughout the country.

Ethan Nadelmann, the founder of the Drug Policy Alliance, has proposed that Afghanistan should be treated as a global "red light district" and supply the world illicit market, as it currently does.[58] This would make the drug industry legal within Afghanistan (or at least tolerated and regulated), but illegal in the rest of the world. The Afghan government could even benefit from this situation by taxing the industry. This arrangement would recognize that as long as global demand exists, there will be supply, and it might as well be kept under control and concentrated at 90 percent in one place, as opposed to having it scattered around the globe. The idea would in fact amount to a situation similar to that under the Taliban regime, which taxed and regulated the drug industry and legalized it *de facto*.

The challenge would be to determine how exactly and to what extent this red light district would be regulated. A few suggestions can be made. Fully legalizing opium and heroin would not be the right solution, in particular for Afghans. Having heroin available in markets freely available for anyone to buy would simply increase the risks of addiction and destroy more lives. This is why almost no analyst recommends it for Western countries, and there is no reason why it should be any different for Afghanistan. But decriminalizing production and use would be a good start, meaning that counternarcotics operations targeting farmers and users would stop. The benefit would be that farmers would not see their livelihoods destroyed and addicts could receive help and get on with their lives more easily. Trafficking would also be tolerated and taxed like regular businesses. However, drawing on the discussion of legalization above, every effort should be made to restrict the marketing and promotion of the narcotics industry and its products, which should also be taxed heavily so that they do not become easily affordable. To what extent would this be possible? In today's Afghanistan, just as in the West, it is not an easy task to curb the aspirations of drug lords and tobacco industry executives. In both places, a lot would ultimately depend on changing the structure of power in society to make it more democratic, which would lead to more checks and regulations on the power of private and governmental entities. The key is to prevent the drug industry from being controlled by unaccountable institutions that have no interest in public health, whether they are corporations, governments, the mafia, or warlords. The more democratically-controlled is the industry, the more likely it is to take public health into account.

8
Conclusion: American Power, Drugs, and Drug Wars

It has been argued that American foreign policy is motivated by the political economic interests of US elites, which include expanding markets and investment opportunities overseas, as well as gaining access to raw materials and cheap labor to cut production costs. Fundamentally, a global political and economic order conducive to the realization of those objectives must be preserved. American hegemony also involves geopolitical motivations, such as attempts to establish a military presence in strategic locations and building alliances with states located in prized areas. The need to maintain credibility is crucial as well. It is a rather symbolic process by which Washington seeks to punish those that challenge its rule or adopt an independent path of development, sending a message to would-be challengers that dissent will not be tolerated. As such, even acts of defiance that do not threaten the United States on their own will often be rebuked.

In a general sense, economic interests drive policy and underpin geopolitical and credibility concerns. Indeed, during and after World War II, American officials made plans for the organization and recovery of the world economy along (state) capitalist lines, under the umbrella of US power. Overseas military operations in the postwar period have often been geared toward defending that system. For instance, intervention in the Middle East has been aimed at gaining control of its energy riches and the associated leverage it provides over the world economy. Likewise, the perceived need to react forcefully against dissenters would not arise if the United States was not a leading economic and military power in the first place.

Although strategic positioning and credibility concerns are ultimately related to defending American economic power and hegemony, they nevertheless sometimes become predominant in immediate terms. This has been the case of US relations with Afghanistan since the late 1970s, as Washington has never had significant economic stakes in the country itself. Therefore, American policies have been shaped mostly by strategic and credibility issues, although economic considerations have been in the background, more or less remotely depending on the particular time and event.[1]

Indeed, Afghanistan's central location on the Asian continent has long made it a coveted prize for great powers. In the nineteenth century, tsarist Russia expanded its reach in Central Asia while the British were moving west across India into Afghanistan. The country found itself squeezed by two colliding empires competing for influence and seeking to contain each other in the region during the so-called "Great Game." Lord Curzon, the viceroy of India, knew that the stakes were high for the British Empire, and saw Afghanistan as a piece "on a chessboard upon which is played out a game for the domination of the world."[2]

In the 1980s, following the Soviet invasion of the country, Washington sought to "bleed the Russians" in order to give them their Vietnam by supporting violent mujahideen fighters, in another show of military competition among great powers vying for international prestige. Russia got badly bruised, just like earlier imperial forces that had attempted to subjugate Afghanistan throughout history, explaining why some have referred to it as "the graveyard of empires."[3]

More recently, the United States and Russia have jousted over the country in what has been called a "New Great Game" for Central Asian energy resources.[4] Asian powers have taken steps toward continental integration while Washington has sought to counteract such moves by attempting to establish itself on the Eurasian landmass by building military bases in Afghanistan and leasing other facilities in the region. The United States has recently concluded a "Strategic Partnership Agreement" with Afghanistan through which it seeks "to cement an enduring partnership" and "long-term commitment" to the country. It "commits Afghanistan to provide U.S. personnel access to and use of Afghan facilities through 2014 and beyond" and "provides for the possibility of U.S. forces in Afghanistan after 2014" to train Afghan forces. Washington has also designated Afghanistan a "Major Non-NATO Ally" in order to bolster defense links further.[5] In addition to providing the United States with a foothold in Eurasia, a presence in the country means strategic proximity to the Persian Gulf's energy reserves and Iran. The Pentagon will be able to keep a watchful eye over Tehran, and perhaps eventually prepare a direct military intervention. Also, numerous competing pipelines, planned and completed, sponsored by the United States, Europe, Russia and China, illustrate the current geopolitical and geoeconomic struggle.

As seen in the previous chapters, for a few years in the 1990s, US government policy was aligned closely to Unocal's project to lay pipelines across Afghanistan to tap regional energy resources. The TAP pipeline could still materialize one day, but peace and stability will have to come first.[6]

Credibility concerns have also been key, most prominently in the aftermath of 9/11 when the United States responded by targeting al-Qaeda in Afghanistan. Similar motives were at play in the late 1990s when Washington labeled the Taliban regime a "rogue" one and isolated it internationally, in addition to launching missile strikes following the bombings of the American embassies in Africa. The point was to show the world and the Taliban, who refused to expel bin Laden, that defiance brings harsh consequences. Projecting an image of strength is also important in current developments in Afghanistan. After more than a decade spent in the country, and still battling an insurgency that seems determined to fight on, Washington has sought to portray itself as still fully in control of the situation as it announced plans for an eventual withdrawal. President Obama declared that the United States is "starting this drawdown from a position of strength" because "we have taken out more than half of Al Qaida's leadership" and the terrorists are now "under enormous strain," in addition to the "victory" achieved by killing Osama bin Laden.[7] When withdrawal happens, it will certainly be depicted as honorable.

It is the above factors that the book has sought to emphasize to explain what has shaped American policy toward Afghanistan. On the other hand, it has tried to show that some of the official rationales, such as those about drugs (and also human rights and women's rights), have not motivated policy. Drug wars and alleged outrage over rights violations have, on the contrary, facilitated intervention. For example, it is very revealing that during the last three decades of American involvement in Afghanistan, Washington has supported drug traffickers for two decades (1980–91 and 2001–present) and has largely ignored the growth of the drug industry during one decade (1991–2001). The result has been a significant increase in opium and heroin production since 1980. There is only one exception to this trend: 2000–01, when the Taliban implemented a ban that reduced narcotics production to virtually zero in most of Afghanistan—but the United States reacted by intensifying the sanctions on the regime. Finally, Washington has consistently favored the anti-drug methods known to be futile, concentrating on "solutions" within Afghanistan like eradication and alternative development, while neglecting the strategies that are well known to be effective, like treatment and prevention in consumer countries. In light of this record, it is clear that drug control is not an objective of the American government.

Following the money trail corroborates this point and reveals US and NATO priorities. From 2001 to 2011, the United States spent $443 billion in Afghanistan, and 94 percent of that sum was spent by the military, to pay for troops, operations, military equipment and other expenses. Counternarcotics, on the other hand, received just over 1 percent of total spending.[8] Also, aid makes up less than 10 percent of all international expenditures in Afghanistan, so that while "it costs approximately $1 million a year to support the deployment of one US soldier in Afghanistan, an average of just $93 in development aid has been spent per Afghan per year," leading agencies reported.[9]

Over the last three decades in Afghanistan, drug control has always been superseded by more important American priorities, and it has thus been argued that it is simply not an objective. Some might object, however, that drug control is an objective, but simply one less important than others like "bleeding the Russians" in the 1980s, isolating the Taliban in the 1990s, and smashing al-Qaeda after 9/11, and thus that it is exaggerated to claim that drug wars are mostly propaganda exercises facilitating overseas intervention.

It is true that some US government goals are more important than others, and it should not necessarily be concluded that anything that is not at the top of the list is irrelevant in shaping policy. However, in the case of drug control, the fact is that it has consistently been overridden by a number of other objectives for decades. In the case of Afghanistan, there has actually never been a time at which it could reasonably be argued that Washington was engaged in a real drug war. Thus, drug control principles have never seemed to influence government policy, and it is in this sense that it can be said that there is no such thing as a war on drugs.

Nevertheless, one could think of possible situations in which the United States could conduct some serious anti-drug operations. For example, it is conceivable that if at some point in time, Washington had no significant interests in Afghanistan, it could decide to implement some relatively effective counternarcotics projects in the country, perhaps for public relations purposes, since this would not distract from the pursuit of more important goals and would contribute to burnishing Washington's image. However, the first half of the 1990s approximated such a situation, and the United States simply chose to look the other way. Another situation could be that in the event that a friendly government is finally established in Afghanistan, the country stabilized, and a certain level of economic development reached, the narcotics industry could come to be perceived as too pervasive and disrupting the conduct of normal economic activities, fuelling corruption and violence. There might then be attempts at reducing its size to acceptable proportions. However, such situations remain, for the time being, hypothetical.

A second objection could be that the United States has conducted numerous counternarcotics operations in Afghanistan and elsewhere, and that it has arrested a number of traffickers. Therefore, although such missions might be carried out selectively, there are nevertheless drug wars taking place in specific settings and at specific times.

It is true that counternarcotics activities are taking place, but that doesn't mean that they constitute a real war on drugs. Even if the funds and the number of missions were increased substantially, this would still not translate into a real drug war. The latter would mean targeting all drugs (including tobacco and alcohol), not only a subset of them called "illegal." But even if only illegal substances are considered, a real drug war would have to target all players equally, not only enemies. Moreover, Washington would have to cease supporting the global narcotics traffic in the many ways described in the previous chapters, from its protection of drug lords to light regulation of the banking system and precursor industry. Finally, the right weapons would have to be employed, not the current losing tactics.

The future of Afghanistan's narcotics industry is unclear. It is difficult to imagine that drug production could still rise significantly, as it is already very high and global demand can only absorb so much heroin every year. On the other hand, if current political, economic and military conditions in the country remain more or less the same, it is also difficult to see why production would drop significantly. The withdrawal of international troops, if it leads to more stability, the disempowerment of drug lords and more development, could reduce the size of the trade. Or, it could leave the industry unchanged, if development is not forthcoming, fighting continues, and Afghanistan is forgotten by the international community. Thus, it remains to be seen how long poppies will grow in the graveyard of empires.

Notes

CHAPTER 1

1. For example, "Guns and Poppies," *New York Times*, 5 August 2008; see also Thomas Schweich, "Is Afghanistan a Narco-State?" *New York Times Magazine*, 27 July 2008.
2. "Blair's Speech—Full Text," *Press Association*, 2 October 2001; Transnational Institute, "Merging Wars: Afghanistan, Drugs and Terrorism" (Amsterdam: TNI, December 2001). See also Chris Johnson and Jolyon Leslie, *Afghanistan: The Mirage of Peace* (updated edition) (London: Zed Books, 2008), p. 146.
3. George W. Bush, "Remarks on the 2002 National Drug Control Strategy," 12 February 2002, www.presidency.ucsb.edu/ws/?pid=72976.
4. George W. Bush, "Remarks With President Vladimir Putin of Russia and a Question-and-Answer Session With Crawford High School Students in Crawford," 15 November 2001, www.presidency.ucsb.edu/ws/?pid=73461.
5. The United Nations Office on Drugs and Crime (UNODC) was formerly known as the United Nations International Drug Control Program (UNDCP). For more clarity, in this book, both will be referred to as UNODC.
6. For a recent summary of the Afghan drug trade, see UNODC, *The Global Afghan Opium Trade: A Threat Assessment* (Vienna: UNODC, July 2011). Numbers in this section are estimates taken from UNODC reports and other sources; the general trends outlined are more important than precise numbers, which are often impossible to obtain.
7. For details, see Pierre-Arnaud Chouvy, *Opium: Uncovering the Politics of the Poppy* (London: I.B. Tauris, 2009), chap. 7.
8. UNODC, *World Drug Report 2005* (New York: United Nations), pp. 16–17.
9. For a survey of the global heroin trade, see Letizia Paoli, Victoria Greenfield, and Peter Reuter, *The World Heroin Market: Can Supply Be Cut?* (Oxford: Oxford University Press, 2009). For a history, see Martin Booth, *Opium: A History* (New York: St. Martin's Press, 1996). On hashish in Afghanistan, see Robert Clarke, *Hashish!* (2nd edition) (Los Angeles: Red Eye Press, 2010); Julien Mercille, "Afghan Hash at an All-Time High," *Asia Times online*, 20 April 2010; UNODC, *Afghanistan Cannabis Survey 2009* (Vienna: UNODC).
10. Christopher Blanchard, *Afghanistan: Narcotics and U.S. Policy*, 7 October 2009 (Washington, DC: Congressional Research Service), p. 4; UNODC, *Afghanistan Opium Survey 2011* (Vienna: UNODC), p. 3.
11. UNODC, *Afghanistan Opium Survey 2008* (Vienna: UNODC), p. 5 and Section 2.17, pp. 125–9. On the importance of narcotics to the Afghan economy, see Christopher Ward and William Byrd, *Afghanistan's Opium Drug Economy* (Washington, DC: World Bank, December 2004).
12. UNODC, *The Global Afghan Opium Trade: A Threat Assessment*, pp. 143–4.
13. UNODC, *World Drug Report 2010* (New York: United Nations), pp. 39–42; UNODC, *World Drug Report 2011* (New York: United Nations), p. 15.

14. UNODC, *World Drug Report 2010*, p. 42. There is variation from year to year, but the trends remain similar. For example, in 2009, UNODC listed Russia as the largest opiates market and Europe second, accounting for $18 billion and $15 billion respectively of a $68 billion global market: UNODC, *The Global Afghan Opium Trade: A Threat Assessment*, p. 21.

CHAPTER 2

1. There now exist a number of studies and accounts of the Afghan drug trade. In addition to those mentioned below, there have been a few personal investigative accounts, such as Fariba Nawa, *Opium Nation: Child Brides, Drug Lords, and One Woman's Journey Through Afghanistan* (New York: Harper Perennial, 2011); Joel Hafvenstein, *Opium Season: A Year on the Afghan Frontier* (Guilford, CT: Guilford Press, 2007); Gregor Salmon, *Poppy: Life, Death and Addiction Inside Afghanistan's Opium Trade* (North Sydney: Ebury Press, 2009), as well as academic studies such as Deepali Gaur Singh, *Drugs Production and Trafficking in Afghanistan* (New Delhi: Pentagon Press, 2007); Amir Zada Asad and Robert Harris, *The Politics and Economics of Drug production on the Pakistan-Afghanistan Border* (Aldershot: Ashgate, 2003); Amalendu Misra, *Afghanistan: The Labyrinth of Violence* (Cambridge: Polity Press, 2004).
2. For examples of the conventional view in Afghanistan and elsewhere from US government officials or institutions, see Christopher Blanchard, *Afghanistan: Narcotics and U.S. Policy*, 7 October 2009 (Washington, DC: Congressional Research Service); US Department of State, *International Narcotics Control Strategy Report 2011*; Rand Beers, "Narco-Terror: The Worldwide Connection between Drugs and Terrorism," Hearing before the US Senate Judiciary Committee, Subcommittee on Technology, Terrorism, and Government Information, 13 March 2002 (Washington, DC: Government Printing Office); Michael Braun, Statement for the Record before the U.S. Senate Caucus on International Narcotics Control Regarding "U.S. Counternarcotics Strategy in Afghanistan," 21 October 2009, http://drugcaucus.senate.gov/Braun-Statement-10-21-09.pdf; Robert Charles, "U.S. Policy and Colombia," Testimony before the House Committee on Government Reform, 17 June 2004. Views from scholars and journalists will be discussed below.
3. Bush quoted in Karen Tandy (DEA), Statement before the Committee on International Relations, US House of Representatives, "United States Policy Towards Narco-Terrorism in Afghanistan," 12 February 2004, www.justice.gov/dea/pubs/cngrtest/ct021204.htm; Dianne Feinstein quoted in "Senate Caucus on International Narcotics Control Holds Hearing on Counternarcotics Efforts in Afghanistan," 20 July 2011, www.feinstein.senate.gov/public/index.cfm/press-releases?ID=4ac906e6-f2a4-4bf7-9f32-8d15dcca89d5; "narco-cartels" mentioned in "Commentary by the Executive Director" in UNODC, *Afghanistan Opium Survey 2009* (Summary Findings) (Vienna: UNODC, September 2009).
4. The hawala system is an informal financial transfer system used in Afghanistan in parallel with the formal banking sector. It handles financial transfers, currency exchange, and often, drug money. Under the Taliban regime (1996–2001), the hawala system fully replaced the formal banking sector. See Edwina Thompson, "The Nexus of Drug Trafficking and Hawala in Afghanistan,"

in Doris Buddenberg and William Byrd (eds.), *Afghanistan's Drug Industry: Structure, Functioning, Dynamics, and Implications for Counter-Narcotics Policy* (Vienna: UNODC; Washington, DC: World Bank, 2006), pp. 155–88.

5. Anthony Placido (DEA), "Transnational Drug Enterprises (Part II): Threats to Global Stability and U.S. Policy Responses," Statement before the House Oversight and Government Reform Subcommittee on National Security and Foreign Affairs, 3 March 2010, no page, www.justice.gov/dea/pubs/cngrtest/ct030310.pdf.

6. The issue is similar to that of terrorism, a label also reserved for enemies, even if Washington has a long record of supporting terrorism, as will be seen in the case of Afghanistan. For discussion, see Alexander George (ed.), *Western State Terrorism* (Cambridge: Polity Press, 1991).

7. US Senate, Caucus on International Narcotics Control, *U.S. Counternarcotics Strategy in Afghanistan*, July 2010, pp. 10–11; US State Department, *U.S. Counternarcotics Strategy for Afghanistan* (compiled by Thomas Schweich), August 2007, p. 13; Office of Inspectors General, *Interagency Assessment of the Counternarcotics Program in Afghanistan*, July 2007 (Department of State report no. ISP-I-07-34; Department of Defense report no. IE-2007-005), p. 10.

8. US Senate, *U.S. Counternarcotics Strategy in Afghanistan*, July 2010, p. 46.

9. McNeill quoted in US Department of State and UK Foreign and Commonwealth Office, "Fighting the Opium Trade in Afghanistan: Myths, Facts, and Sound Policy," 11 March 2008, p. 5, http://kabul.usembassy.gov/media/afghan_opium_myths_and_facts-final.pdf; Petraeus quoted in US Senate, Caucus on International Narcotics Control, *U.S. Counternarcotics Strategy in Afghanistan*, July 2010, p. 23.

10. US Department of State, *International Narcotics Control Strategy Report 2011*, Volume 1, pp. 101–2.

11. US State Department, *U.S. Counternarcotics Strategy for Afghanistan*, August 2007, p. 16; US Senate, *U.S. Counternarcotics Strategy in Afghanistan*, July 2010, pp. 22–3; US Department of State, *International Narcotics Control Strategy Report 2010*, p. 99.

12. Quoted in US Senate, Committee on Foreign Relations, *Afghanistan's Narco War: Breaking the Link between Drug Traffickers and Insurgents*, 10 August 2009 (Washington, DC: US Government Printing Office), p. 9. *The Sopranos* is an American television series about crime and the mafia.

13. US Senate, *Afghanistan's Narco War*, pp. 27–8.

14. US State Department, *U.S. Counternarcotics Strategy for Afghanistan*, August 2007, pp. 13–14; Office of Inspectors General, *Interagency Assessment of the Counternarcotics Program in Afghanistan*, July 2007, p. 10.

15. US Senate, *Afghanistan's Narco War*, p. 11; Office of Inspector General, *Status of the Bureau of International Narcotics and Law Enforcement Affairs Counternarcotics Programs in Afghanistan: Performance Audit*, Report Number MERO-A-10-02, December 2009, p. 21.

16. Office of Inspector General, *Status of the Bureau of International Narcotics and Law Enforcement Affairs Counternarcotics Programs in Afghanistan: Performance Audit*, December 2009, p. 24; Office of Inspectors General, *Interagency Assessment of the Counternarcotics Program in Afghanistan*, July 2007, pp. 14–15.

17. Office of Inspectors General, *Interagency Assessment of the Counternarcotics Program in Afghanistan*, July 2007, pp. 14, 30, 42; US Senate, *Afghanistan's*

Narco War, pp. 6–7, quoting Ronald Neumann, a former U.S. ambassador to Afghanistan, on the belief that "bad things come from planes."

18. For Bush's strategy, see US State Department, *U.S. Counternarcotics Strategy for Afghanistan*, August 2007; for Obama's strategy, see Blanchard, *Afghanistan: Narcotics and U.S. Policy*, 7 October 2009.

19. UK Foreign and Commonwealth Office (FCO), "Counternarcotics," http:// ukinafghanistan.fco.gov.uk/en/about-us/working-with-afghanistan/counter-narcotics# (specific page was removed as of April 2012, but available from the author); Catherine Ashton, speech to the European Parliament, Speech/10/756, 15 December 2010, http://europa.eu/rapid/pressReleasesAction.do?reference=S PEECH/10/756&type=HTML; "The UK's Foreign Policy towards Afghanistan and Pakistan," Written Evidence from the Foreign and Commonwealth Office, www.publications.parliament.uk/pa/cm201011/cmselect/cmfaff/writev/afpak/ afpak01.htm.

20. UK FCO, "Counternarcotics."

21. Gretchen Peters, *Seeds of Terror: How Heroin is Bankrolling the Taliban and al Qaeda* (New York: St. Martin's Press, 2009), pp. xvi–xvii.

22. Peters, *Seeds of Terror*, pp. 22, 4; Gretchen Peters, "The Taliban and the Opium Trade," in Antonio Giustozzi (ed.), *Decoding the New Taliban* (London: Hurst and Co., 2009), p. 7.

23. Peters, *Seeds of Terror*, pp. 9 (quoting Marvin Weinbaum, a former State Department intelligence analyst), 22, 10; Peters, "The Taliban and the Opium Trade," p. 17.

24. Peters, *Seeds of Terror*, pp. 216–7.

25. Vanda Felbab-Brown, *Shooting Up: Counterinsurgency and the War on Drugs* (Washington, DC: Brookings Institution Press, 2010), pp. 9, 179. See also Ahmed Rashid, *Descent into Chaos: How the War Against Islamic Extremism is Being Lost in Pakistan, Afghanistan and Central Asia* (London: Penguin, 2008), chap. 15, which presents a careful account, but whose chapter on narcotics is entitled "Drugs and Thugs: Opium Fuels the Insurgency," which makes explicit the association between the Taliban and opium. Another account is Frank Shanty, *The Nexus: International Terrorism and Drug Trafficking from Afghanistan* (Santa Barbara, CA: Praeger, 2011).

26. Thomas Schweich, "Is Afghanistan a Narco-State?" *New York Times Magazine*, 27 July 2008.

27. Rachel Ehrenfeld, *Funding Evil: How Terrorism is Financed—And How To Stop It* (expanded edition) (Chicago and Los Angeles: Bonus Books, 2005), pp. 31, 207; Drug Policy Alliance, *Repeating Mistakes of the Past: Another Mycoherbicide Research Bill*, March 2006, www.drugpolicy.org.

28. Felbab-Brown, *Shooting Up*, p. 163.

29. Thomas Friedman, "The Class Too Dumb to Quit," *New York Times*, 21 July 2009.

30. Michèle Alliot-Marie, "Afghanistan's Drug Boom; The Opium Problem Could Undo Everything that's Being Done to Help the Afghan People," *Washington Post*, 6 October 2004.

31. Joel Hafvenstein, "Afghanistan's Drug Habit," *New York Times*, 20 September 2006.

32. For example, Richard Holbrooke, "Still Wrong in Afghanistan," *Washington Post*, 23 January 2008.

33. "Guns and Poppies," *New York Times*, 5 August 2008.

34. Robert Draper, "Opium Wars" (photographs by David Guttenfelder), *National Geographic Magazine*, 219 (2) (2011), pp. 58–83.

35. Ted Galen Carpenter, "How the Drug War in Afghanistan Undermines America's War on Terror," Foreign Policy Briefing No. 84, 10 November 2004 (Washington, DC: CATO Institute), p. 6. See also *CATO Handbook for Policymakers* (7th edition), chap. 58, "The International War on Drugs" (Washington, DC: CATO Institute, 2009).

36. For example, Arnold Chien, Margaret Connors and Kenneth Fox, "The Drug War in Perspective," in Jim Yong Kim et al. (eds.), *Dying for Growth* (Monroe, ME: Common Courage, 2000), pp. 293–327; Noam Chomsky, *Deterring Democracy* (New York: Hill and Wang, 1992), pp. 107–38; *Rogue States: The Rule of Force in World Affairs* (Cambridge, MA: South End Press, 2000), pp. 62–81; Craig Reinerman and Harry G. Levine (eds.), *Crack in America: Demon Drugs and Social Justice* (Berkeley and Los Angeles: University of California Press, 1997); Doug Stokes, *America's Other War: Terrorizing Colombia* (London: Zed Books, 2005).

37. For a survey see for example Michael J. Hogan and Thomas G. Paterson (eds.), *Explaining the History of American Foreign Relations* (2nd edition) (Cambridge: Cambridge University Press, 2004).

38. US National Security Council, NSC-68, "United States Objectives and Programs for National Security," 14 April 1950, in US Department of State, *Foreign Relations of the United States*, 1950, 1: pp. 235–92 (Washington, DC: Government Printing Office, 1977); for commentary see Fred Block, "Economic Instability and Military Strength: The Paradoxes of the 1950 Rearmament Decision," *Politics & Society* 10(1) (1980): pp. 35–58.

39. This interpretation draws from the writings of a number of authors. For example, see Thomas J. McCormick, *America's Half-Century: United States Foreign Policy in the Cold War and After* (2nd edition) (Baltimore: Johns Hopkins University Press, 1995); Joyce Kolko and Gabriel Kolko, *The Limits of Power: The World and United States Foreign Policy 1945–1954* (New York: Harper & Row, 1972); Chomsky, *Deterring Democracy*; *World Orders Old and New* (New York: Columbia University Press, 1996); Howard Zinn, *A People's History of the United States* (New York: HarperCollins, 2003).

40. Melvyn Leffler, "The United States and the Strategic Dimensions of the Marshall Plan," *Diplomatic History* 12(3) (1988): p. 281.

41. Leffler, *Marshall Plan*, p. 302.

42. George Kennan, "Review of Current Trends in U.S. Foreign Policy," PPS/23, in US Department of State, *Foreign Relations of the United States*, 1948, volume 1, part 2 (Washington, DC: Government Printing Office, 1976), pp. 524–5.

43. Quoted in Michael Schaller, "Securing the Great Crescent: Occupied Japan and the Origins of Containment in Southeast Asia," *The Journal of American History* 69(2) (1982): p. 403.

44. Forrestal quoted in Ed Shaffer, *The United States and the Control of World Oil* (London: Croom Helm, 1983), p. 143; Kennan quoted in US State Department, "Transcript of Round Table Discussion on American Policy Toward China," 6, 7, 8 October 1949 (Washington: Department of State, Division of Central Services, 1949).

45. US National Security Council, NSC 5432/1, "United States Objectives and Courses of Action with Respect to Latin America," 3 September 1954.

46. On the need to maintain credibility, see Robert McMahon, "Credibility and World Power: Exploring the Psychological Dimension in Postwar American Diplomacy," *Diplomatic History* 15(4) (1991): pp. 455–71; Dean Acheson, *Present at the Creation: My Years in the State Department* (New York: Norton, 1987 [1969]), p. 219.
47. "The Iranian Accord," *New York Times*, 6 August 1954.
48. Alfred McCoy, "The Stimulus of Prohibition: A Critical History of the Global Narcotics Trade," in Michael K. Steinberg, Joseph J. Hobbs, and Kent Mathewson (eds.), *Dangerous Harvest: Drug Plants and the Transformation of Indigenous Landscapes* (Oxford: Oxford University Press, 2004), pp. 47–8. McCoy develops the same argument in a number of publications: *The Politics of Heroin: CIA Complicity in the Global Drug Trade* (revised edition) (Chicago: Lawrence Hill Books, 2003); "From Free Trade to Prohibition: A Critical History of the Modern Asian Opium Trade," *Fordham Urban Law Journal* 28 (2000): pp. 307–49; "Heroin as a Global Commodity: A History of Southeast Asia's Opium Trade," in Alfred McCoy and Alan Block (eds.), *War on Drugs: Studies in the Failure of U.S. Narcotics Policy* (Boulder: Westview Press, 1992), pp. 237–79.
49. Alfred McCoy, *The Politics of Heroin: CIA Complicity in the Global Drug Trade* (Brooklyn, NY: Lawrence Hill Books, 1991), p. 484. See also his discussion on pp. 484–92. The first edition appeared in 1972: Alfred McCoy (with Cathleen Read and Leonard Adams II), *The Politics of Heroin in Southeast Asia* (New York: Harper & Row, 1972). None of this should be seen as implying that McCoy is a naïve observer of the drug trade or of US politics, as he has probably done more than anybody to clarify our understanding of the relationship between the US government and global trafficking.
50. McCoy, *Politics of Heroin* (2003), pp. 456, 387, 455, 458.
51. McCoy, *Politics of Heroin* (2003), p. 459. For an argument similar to this book's on Nixon's drug war, see Jeremy Kuzmarov, *The Myth of the Addicted Army: Vietnam and the Modern War on Drugs* (Amherst: University of Massachusetts Press, 2009).
52. Peter Dale Scott, *Drugs, Oil, and War: The United States in Afghanistan, Colombia, and Indochina* (Lanham, MD: Rowman and Littlefield, 2003), p. 1.
53. Peter Dale Scott, *American War Machine: Deep Politics, the CIA Global Drug Connection, and the Road to Afghanistan* (Lanham, MD: Rowman and Littlefield, 2010), pp. 4, 193; see also Peter Dale Scott, "The CIA's secret powers," *Critical Asian Studies* 35 (2) (2003): pp. 233–58; *The Road to 9/11: Wealth, Empire, and the Future of America* (Berkeley and Los Angeles: University of California Press, 2007).
54. Scott, *Drugs, Oil, and War*, p. 43.

CHAPTER 3

1. Alfred McCoy, *The Politics of Heroin: CIA Complicity in the Global Drug Trade* (revised edition) (Chicago: Lawrence Hill, 2003), pp. 16–17.
2. Interview in the film "Our Own Private bin Laden" directed by Samira Goetschel, 2005, Chastè Films.
3. All quoted in Jeremy Kuzmarov, *The Myth of the Addicted Army: Vietnam and the Modern War on Drugs* (Amherst: University of Massachusetts Press, 2009), pp. 85–6.

4. This section relies mostly on McCoy, *Politics of Heroin*, chaps. 1–2 and Alexander Cockburn and Jeffrey St. Clair, *Whiteout: The CIA, Drugs and the Press* (London: Verso, 1998), chap. 5.

5. On US plans to revive the world economy under its hegemony, see for example Thomas J. McCormick, *America's Half-Century: United States Foreign Policy in the Cold War and After* (2nd edition) (Baltimore: Johns Hopkins University Press, 1995); McCoy, *Politics of Heroin*, p. 38.

6. McCoy, *Politics of Heroin*, p. 17.

7. On Marshall Plan aid from the US being made conditional on the exclusion of communists from government in France and Italy, see Melvyn Leffler, "The United States and the Strategic Dimensions of the Marshall Plan," *Diplomatic History* 12(3) (1988): pp. 277–306.

8. Zhou Yongming, *Anti-Drug Crusades in Twentieth-Century China: Nationalism, History, and State Building* (Lanham: Rowman & Littlefield, 1999).

9. For more details on this section, see Cockburn and St. Clair, *Whiteout*, chap. 9; McCoy, *Politics of Heroin*, chap. 4.

10. From the *Pentagon Papers*, quoted in McCoy, *Politics of Heroin*, p. 165.

11. McCoy, *Politics of Heroin*, p. 162.

12. Quoted in McCoy, *Politics of Heroin*, p. 140.

13. McCoy, *Politics of Heroin*, pp. xvii, 288, 300.

14. See McCormick, *America's Half-Century*; Patrick Hearden, *The Tragedy of Vietnam* (2nd ed.) (New York: Pearson Longman, 2005); Andrew Rotter, "The Triangular Route to Vietnam," *International History Review* vi(3) (1984): pp. 404–23.

15. US Senate, Committee on Foreign Relations, Subcommittee on Terrorism, Narcotics and International Operations, *Drugs, Law Enforcement and Foreign Policy*, December 1988 (Washington, DC: Government Printing Office, 1989), pp. 36, 42.

16. McCoy, *Politics of Heroin*, p. 492.

17. Doug Stokes, *America's Other War: Terrorizing Colombia* (London: Zed Books, 2005), pp. 101–103.

18. Luis Astorga, "Mexico: Drugs and Politics," in Menno Vellinga (ed.), *The Political Economy of the Drug Industry: Latin America and the International System* (Gainesville, FL: University Press of Florida, 2004), p. 88; Laurie Freeman and Jorge Luis Sierra, "Mexico: The Militarization Trap," in Coletta Youngers and Eileen Rosin (eds.), *Drugs and Democracy in Latin America* (Boulder, CO: Lynne Rienner, 2005), p. 267; Julien Mercille, "Violent Narco-Cartels or US Hegemony? The Political Economy of the 'War on Drugs' in Mexico," *Third World Quarterly* 32 (9) (2011): pp. 1637–1653.

19. McCoy, *Politics of Heroin*, p. 466.

20. Pierre-Arnaud Chouvy, *Opium: Uncovering the Politics of the Poppy* (London: I.B. Tauris, 2009), p. 30.

21. Bijan Nissaramanesh, Mike Trace and Marcus Roberts, "The Rise of Harm Reduction in the Islamic Republic of Iran," Beckley Foundation Briefing #8, July 2005, pp. 1–2, www.beckleyfoundation.org/pdf/paper_08.pdf; Chouvy, *Opium*, p. 149; for a slightly different view, see McCoy, *Politics of Heroin*, p. 471.

22. Chouvy, *Opium*, p. 150.

23. In addition to sources cited below, a good, critical history of Afghanistan is Paul Fitzgerald and Elizabeth Gould, *Invisible History: Afghanistan's Untold Story* (San Francisco, CA: City Lights, 2009).

24. Diego Cordovez and Selig Harrison, *Out of Afghanistan: The Inside Story of the Soviet Withdrawal* (Oxford: Oxford University Press, 1995), pp. 31–2; Robert Gates, *From the Shadows: The Ultimate Insider's Story of Five Presidents and How They Won the Cold War* (New York: Simon & Schuster, 1996), pp. 143–9; Steve Galster, "Afghanistan: The Making of U.S. Policy, 1973–1990," National Security Archive, 2001, www.gwu.edu/~nsarchiv/NSAEBB/NSAEBB57/essay. html. See also Ralph Magnus and Eden Naby, *Afghanistan: Mullah, Marx, and Mujahid* (Boulder, CO: Westview, 2002) and M. Hassan Kakar, *Afghanistan: The Soviet Invasion and the Afghan Response, 1979–1982* (Berkeley, CA: University of California Press, 1997).

25. Brzezinski interview in *Le Nouvel Observateur*, 15 January 1998 (in French); Counterpunch.org translation in English, 15 January 1998.

26. Michael Getler, "Sadat's Remarks on Afghan Arms Vex U.S.," *Washington Post*, 24 September 1981 (Sadat quote); Galster, "Making of U.S. Policy"; Gabriel Kolko, *The Age of War* (Boulder: Lynne Rienner, 2006), p. 54.

27. Olav Njolstad, "Shifting Priorities: The Persian Gulf in US Strategic Planning in the Carter Years," *Cold War History* 4(3) (April 2004): pp. 21–55; "Iran: The Crescent of Crisis," *TIME*, 15 January 1979; "An Interview with Brzezinski," *TIME*, 14 January 1980. See also Raymond Garthoff, *Détente and Confrontation: American-Soviet Relations from Nixon to Reagan* (revised edition) (Washington, DC: Brookings Institution, 1994), pp. 727–32.

28. Jimmy Carter, "State of the Union Address 1980," 23 January 1980, www. jimmycarterlibrary.gov/documents/speeches/su80jec.phtml.

29. Carter, "State of the Union Address 1980."

30. US National Security Council, PD-18, "U.S. National Strategy," 24 August 1977, www.jimmycarterlibrary.gov/documents/pddirectives/pd18.pdf; Fred S. Hoffman, *Associated Press*, 27 January 1978. See also Zbigniew Brzezinski, *Power and Principle: Memoirs of the National Security Advisor 1977–1981* (London: Weidenfeld and Nicolson, 1983), chap. 12.

31. Eisenhower and J.F. Dulles quoted in Noam Chomsky, *World Orders Old and New* (New York: Columbia University Press, 1996), pp. 201–2.

32. Melvyn Leffler, "From the Truman Doctrine to the Carter Doctrine: Lessons and Dilemmas of the Cold War," *Diplomatic History* 7(4) (1983): pp. 258–9.

33. Quoted in Gates, *From the Shadows*, p. 147.

34. Cordovez and Harrison, *Out of Afghanistan*, p. 55.

35. Galster, "Making of U.S. Policy."

36. For detailed accounts, see Gilles Dorronsoro, *Revolution Unending; Afghanistan: 1979 to the Present* (London: Hurst, 2005) and Olivier Roy, *Islam and Resistance in Afghanistan* (second edition) (Cambridge: Cambridge University Press, 1990).

37. Cordovez and Harrison, *Out of Afghanistan*, p. 63.

38. Edward Girardet, "Afghanistan Rebels Plan United Front Against Soviet Forces," *Christian Science Monitor*, 14 May 1980; "Afghan Rebels: More Time Squabbling Than Fighting," Christian Science Monitor, 24 June 1980; Cordovez and Harrison, *Out of Afghanistan*, pp. 62–3.

39. 1980 RAWA platform document cited in Sonali Kolhatkar and James Ingalls, *Bleeding Afghanistan: Washington, Warlords, and the Propaganda of Silence*

(New York: Seven Stories Press, 2006), p. 8. In general, see Anne Brodsky, *With All Our Strength: The Revolutionary Association of the Women of Afghanistan* (New York: Routledge, 2003).

40. Tim Weiner, *Blank Check: The Pentagon's Black Budget* (New York: Warner, 1990), p. 149; Kolhatkar and Ingalls, *Bleeding Afghanistan*, p. 9.

41. Jonathan Goodhand, "Frontiers and Wars: The Opium Economy in Afghanistan," *Journal of Agrarian Change* 5(2) (April 2005): pp. 191–216; McCoy, *Politics of Heroin*, pp. 479–80; Mariam Abou Zahab, "Pakistan: D'un Narco-État à une "Success Story" dans la Guerre Contre la Drogue?" CEMOTI 32 (2001): p. 144.

42. McCoy, *Politics of Heroin*, pp. 481, 483.

43. Barnett Rubin, *The Fragmentation of Afghanistan: State Formation and Collapse in the International System* (second edition) (New Haven: Yale University Press, 2002), p. 199; Ahmed Rashid, *Taliban: Militant Islam, Oil and Fundamentalism in Central Asia* (New Haven: Yale University Press, 2001), p. 120.

44. Lifschultz, L. (1992) "Pakistan: The Empire of Heroin," in A. McCoy and A. Block (eds.), *War on Drugs: Studies in the Failure of U.S. Narcotics Policy* (Boulder: Westview Press), pp. 340–341; Rashid, *Taliban*, pp. 120–1.

45. McCoy, *Politics of Heroin*, p. 486.

46. McCoy, *Politics of Heroin*, p. 481; Rashid, *Taliban*, p. 121.

47. McCoy, *Politics of Heroin*, 478–9.

48. James Rupert and Steve Coll, "U.S. Declines to Probe Afghan Drug Trade; Rebels, Pakistani Officers Implicated," *Washington Post*, 13 May 1990.

49. McCoy, *Politics of Heroin*, pp. 484–5; Arthur Bonner, "Afghan Rebel's Victory Garden: Opium," *New York Times*, 18 June 1986.

50. Peter Truell and Larry Gurwin, *False Profits: The Inside Story of BCCI, the World's Most Corrupt Financial Empire* (Boston: Houghton Mifflin Company, 1992), p. xvii.

51. M. Emdad-ul Haq, *Drugs in South Asia: From the Opium Trade to the Present Day* (London: Macmillan, 2000), p. 204; Truell and Gurwin, *False Profits*, pp. 133, 160.

52. Truell and Gurwin, *False profits*, pp. 217 (Sakhia), 222–4 (Noriega); Jonathan Beaty and S.C. Gwynne, *The Outlaw Bank: A Wild Ride into The Secret Heart of BCCI* (New York: Random House, 1993), p. xx.

53. US Senate, *The BCCI Affair: A Report to the Committee on Foreign Relations*, by Senator John Kerry and Senator Hank Brown, December 1992, 102d Congress 2d Session, Senate Print 102–40.

54. Charles Shepard and Anne Swardson, "Warnings of Wrongdoing at BCCI Went Unheeded Since 1984," *Washington Post*, 6 September 1991; Sharon Walsh, "U.S. Warned about BCCI in 1978, Panel Told," *Washington Post*, 20 February 1992; George Lardner Jr., "CIA Probed, Used BCCI, Official Says, *Washington Post*, 3 August 1991; Elaine Sciolino, "Intelligence Agency Used B.C.C.I., Official Says," *New York Times*, 3 August 1991.

55. J.W. Anderson, "Two Banks, Blended Scandal," *Washington Post*, 16 November 1992.

56. Alexander Cockburn, "Bankers to the New World Scum Class BCCI and its Ilk Flourish Because They Serve the Needs of Spies, Tyrants and Crooks," *Los Angeles Times*, 1 August 1991; "Shady, Yes, but Not the Least Bit Unusual: Are We Pretending that, Unlike BCCI, Western Banks Don't Launder Dirty Money?" *Los Angeles Times*, 21 July 1991.

CHAPTER 4

1. Christopher Blanchard, *Afghanistan: Narcotics and U.S. Policy*, 7 October 2009 (Washington, DC: Congressional Research Service).
2. Amnesty International, "Afghanistan: International Responsibility for Human Rights Disaster," 1995, pp. 6–7, www.amnesty.org/en/library/info/ASA11/009/1995/en.
3. Amnesty International, "International Responsibility," p. 9.
4. Sonali Kolhatkar and James Ingalls, *Bleeding Afghanistan: Washington, Warlords, and the Propaganda of Silence* (New York: Seven Stories Press, 2006), 12; Alfred McCoy, *The Politics of Heroin: CIA Complicity in the Global Drug Trade* (revised edition) (Chicago: Lawrence Hill Book, 2003), p. 505. See also Paul Fitzgerald and Elizabeth Gould, *Invisible History: Afghanistan's Untold Story* (San Francisco, CA: City Lights, 2009), chap. 11.
5. Barnett Rubin, *The Search for Peace in Afghanistan: From Buffer State to Failed State* (New Haven: Yale University Press, 1995), p. 111.
6. Barnett Rubin, *The Fragmentation of Afghanistan: State Formation and Collapse in the International System* (second edition) (New Haven: Yale University Press, 2002), p. x.
7. John F. Burns, "Afghan Capital Grim as War Follows War," *New York Times*, 5 February 1996.
8. John F. Burns, "With Kabul Largely in Ruins, Afghans Get Respite From War," *New York Times*, 20 February 1995.
9. Kolhatkar and Ingalls, *Bleeding Afghanistan*, p. 17.
10. Thomas Friedman, "U.S. Urges Afghan Factions to Avoid Violent Anarchy," *New York Times*, 17 April 1992.
11. Rubin, *Fragmentation of Afghanistan*, p. x.
12. Rubin, *Search for Peace*, pp. 128–9.
13. Amnesty International, "International Responsibility," p. 3.
14. Amnesty International, "International Responsibility," pp. 12–13.
15. Blanchard, "Afghanistan: Narcotics and U.S. Policy," 7 October 2009.
16. McCoy, *Politics of Heroin*, p. 505.
17. Barnett Rubin, "The Political Economy of War and Peace in Afghanistan," *World Development* 28(10) (2000): pp. 1789–1803.
18. McCoy, *Politics of Heroin*, p. 507.
19. For an account of the Taliban regime in Afghanistan, see Michael Griffin, *Reaping the Whirlwind: The Taliban Movement in Afghanistan* (London: Pluto, 2001); Fitzgerald and Gould, *Invisible History*, chap. 12.
20. U.S. Embassy (Islamabad) Cable, "Afghanistan: [Excised] Briefs the Ambassador on his Activities. Pleads for Greater Activism by U.N.," 27 August 1997; Sajit Gandhi, "The Taliban File Part III," National Security Archive (NSA), 19 March 2004, www.gwu.edu/~nsarchiv/NSAEBB/NSAEBB97/index4.htm.
21. Sajit Gandhi, The September 11th Sourcebooks, Volume VII: The Taliban File, NSA Electronic Briefing Book No. 97, 11 September 2003, www.gwu.edu/~nsarchiv/NSAEBB/NSAEBB97/index.htm.
22. Rubin, *Fragmentation of Afghanistan*, p. xii.
23. Barnett Rubin, "Testimony on the Situation in Afghanistan Before the United States Senate Committee on Foreign Relations," 8 October 1998, www.cfr.org/afghanistan/testimony-situation-afghanistan-before-united-states-senate-committee-foreign-relations/p3088.

24. US Department of State Report, "Pakistan-Afghanistan Relations," circa January 1996, Confidential, available at The Taliban File Part III, NSA, 19 March 2004, www.gwu.edu/~nsarchiv/NSAEBB/NSAEBB97/index4.htm.

25. The best source of relevant declassified documents on this period is the NSA website: http://nsarchive.chadwyck.com/marketing/index.jsp.

26. Milton Bearden, "Afghanistan, Graveyard of Empires," *Foreign Affairs* 80(6) (Nov-Dec 2001): p. 26; Rubin, "Testimony."

27. US Department of State, Cable, "Dealing with the Taliban in Kabul," 28 September 1996, NSA, www.gwu.edu/~nsarchiv/NSAEBB/NSAEBB97/index.htm.

28. U.S. Embassy (Islamabad) Cable, "Official Informal for SA Assistant Secretary Robin Raphel and SA/PAB," 10 March 1997, NSA, www.gwu.edu/~nsarchiv/NSAEBB/NSAEBB295/

29. Doug Stokes and Sam Raphael, *Global Energy Security and American Hegemony* (Baltimore: The Johns Hopkins University Press, 2010).

30. Michael Klare, *Rising Powers, Shrinking Planet: The New Geopolitics of Energy* (Oxford: Oneworld, 2008), pp. 118–19.

31. Quoted in Stokes and Raphael, *Global Energy Security*, p. 118.

32. "U.S. Interests in the Central Asian Republics," Hearings Before the Subcommittee on Asia and the Pacific of the Committee on International Relations, House of Representatives, 12 February 1998, http://commdocs. house.gov/committees/intlrel/hfa48119.000/hfa48119_0.HTM.

33. "U.S. Interests in the Central Asian Republics," Hearings, 12 February 1998.

34. Michael Klare, *Resource Wars: The New Landscape of Global Conflict* (New York: Metropolitan Books, 2002), p. 103.

35. Steve Coll, *Ghost Wars: The Secret History of the CIA, Afghanistan, and Bin Laden, from the Soviet Invasion to September 10, 2001* (New York: Penguin, 2004), pp. 305, 307–10.

36. U.S. Department of State, Cable, "Dealing with the Taliban in Kabul," 28 September 1996, NSA, www.gwu.edu/~nsarchiv/NSAEBB/NSAEBB97/index.htm.

37. Marvin Weinbaum, quoted in *The 9/11 Commission Report* (authorized edition) (New York: W.W. Norton & Company, 2004), p. 111.

38. Coll, *Ghost Wars*, p. 330.

39. "Turkmenistan-Afghanistan-Pakistan Pipelines: Nature of USG Support and Relation to Policy on Afghanistan," September 1996, STATE 197375, made available to the author by the NSA; see also Elaine Sciolino, "State Dept. Becomes Cooler to the New Rulers of Kabul," *New York Times*, 23 October 1996.

40. US Embassy (Islamabad), Cable, "Ambassador Meets Taliban: We Are the People," 12 November 1996, NSA, www.gwu.edu/~nsarchiv/NSAEBB/NSAEBB97/index.htm.

41. Rubin, *Fragmentation of Afghanistan*, p. xxxiii.

42. Zalmay Khalilzad, "Afghanistan: Time to Reengage," *Washington Post*, 7 October 1996; Zalmay Khalilzad and Daniel Byman, "Afghanistan: The Consolidation of a Rogue State," *The Washington Quarterly* 23(1) (Winter 2000): pp. 65–78.

43. Rubin, "Testimony."

44. Bearden, "Graveyard of Empires," p. 28.

45. US Embassy (Islamabad), Cable, "Pakistan: Ambassador Raises bin Laden with Foreign Secretary Shamshad Ahmed," 6 October 1998, NSA, www.gwu. edu/~nsarchiv/NSAEBB/NSAEBB134/index2.htm.

46. Coll, *Ghost Wars*, p. 417.

47. Rubin, *Fragmentation of Afghanistan*, pp. xxv, xxviii.

48. US Department of State report, "U.S. Engagement with the Taliban on Usama bin Laden," circa July 2001, NSA, www.gwu.edu/~nsarchiv/NSAEBB/ NSAEBB97/index3.htm; "Usama bin Laden's Statement About Jihad Against the U.S.," STATE 034310, 26 February 1998, Wikileaks, www.cablegatesearch.net/ cable.php?id=98STATE34310&q=afghanistan; "Approach to EU on Taleban Support for Usama bin Laden," STATE 055357, 27 March 1998, Wikileaks, www.cablegatesearch.net/cable.php?id=98STATE55357&q=afghanistan.

49. Coll, *Ghost Wars*, pp. 422–3; *9/11 Commission Report*, p. 116; Kolhatkar and Ingalls, *Bleeding Afghanistan*, p. 30. The target in Sudan was the al-Shifa Pharmaceutical Factory in Khartoum, which was destroyed by the missiles, with one person killed and eleven injured. US officials argued that bombing the plant would prevent bin Laden from putting his hands on the nerve gas precursors allegedly produced at the factory. But as the German ambassador to Sudan at the time stated, the factory produced basic medicines "covering 20 to 60 percent of Sudan's market and 100 percent of the market for intravenous liquids," and its destruction resulted in the deaths of "several tens of thousands" of people. After the strikes, Sudan asked the UN Security Council to conduct an investigation to find out whether there were indeed chemical weapons at the factory site, but the US blocked the investigation. Moreover, Washington refused to provide evidence to support its allegations that the plant or its owners were involved in chemical weapons production or terrorism, Human Rights Watch reported. Later investigations found no evidence of the presence of the chemicals at the plant sites, or of direct links between the plant owner and Osama bin Laden. See Werner Daum, "Universalism and the West," *Harvard International Review* (Summer 2001), p. 19; Human Rights Watch, *Sudan, Oil, and Human Rights*, 2003, p. 481; Michael Barletta, "Chemical Weapons in the Sudan: Allegations and Evidence," *The Nonproliferation Review* (Fall 1998): pp. 115–36; James Risen and David Johnston, "Experts Find No Arms Chemicals at Bombed Sudan Plant," *New York Times*, 9 February 1999.

50. "Press Briefing by Secretary of State Madeleine Albright and National Security Advisor Sandy Berger," 20 August 1998, www.presidency.ucsb.edu/; "Clinton's Words: 'There Will Be No Sanctuary for Terrorists'," *New York Times*, 21 August 1998; Thomas Friedman, "Motives For the Bombing," *New York Times*, 8 August 1998; "Air Raids Necessary," *Los Angeles Times*, 21 August 1998.

51. Bill Clinton, "Statement on the National Emergency With Respect to the Taliban," 6 July 1999, www.presidency.ucsb.edu/ws/?pid=57840 and "Statement on United Nations Sanctions Against the Taliban," 15 November 1999, www.presidency.ucsb.edu/ws/?pid=56938#axzz1q3k4SwiB.

52. Nancy Soderberg, at Security Council meeting on 15 October 1999, www. undemocracy.com/securitycouncil/meeting_4051#pg002-bk10.

53. Human Rights Watch, "Letter to U.N. Security Council," 14 December 2000, www.hrw.org/en/news/2000/12/13/letter-un-security-council.

54. Office of the UN Coordinator for Afghanistan, *Vulnerability And Humanitarian Implications of UN Security Council Sanctions in Afghanistan*, December 2000

(Islamabad: United Nations), p. 36; "Oxfam Warns that Tighter UN Sanctions on Afghanistan Will Deepen Humanitarian Crisis," 13 December 2000, http://reliefweb.int/node/73059.

55. Richard Mackenzie, "The United States and the Taliban," in William Maley (ed.), *Fundamentalism Reborn? Afghanistan and the Taliban* (London: Hurst & Company, 2001 [1998]), p. 100.

56. UNODC, *The Opium Economy in Afghanistan: An International Problem* (Vienna: UNODC, 2003), p. 92.

57. UNODC, *The Opium Economy in Afghanistan: An International Problem*, pp. 91–2.

58. Rashid, *Taliban*, p. 117.

59. UNDCP, *Strategic Study* #6 (2000), cited in McCoy, *Politics of Heroin*, p. 508.

60. Rubin, "Political Economy of War and Peace," p. 1796; UNODC, *Addiction, Crime and Insurgency: The Transnational Threat of Afghan Opium* (Vienna: UNODC, 2009), p. 17; Rashid, *Taliban*, p. 118; McCoy, *Politics of Heroin*, p. 509; UNODC, *The Opium Economy in Afghanistan: An International Problem*, chap. 2. For an investigative account of the drug trade during the Taliban years, see Stéphane Allix, *La Petite Cuillère de Shéhérazade: Sur la Route de l'Héroine* (Paris: Ramsay, 1998). See also John Cooley, *Unholy Wars: Afghanistan, America and International Terrorism* (Third Edition) (London: Pluto, 2002), chap. 7.

61. Rashid, *Taliban*, p. 122; Mariam Abou Zahab, "Pakistan: D'un Narco-État à une "Success Story" dans la Guerre Contre la Drogue?" CEMOTI 32 (2001): p. 158.

62. On the balloon effect, see Pierre-Arnaud Chouvy, *Opium: Uncovering the Politics of the Poppy* (London: I.B. Tauris, 2009), p. 150. For details on drug corruption in Pakistan in the 1990s, see Abou Zahab, "Success Story," pp. 148–53, which cites the UNDCP report on p. 151; M. Emdad-ul Haq, *Drugs in South Asia: From the Opium Trade to the Present Day* (London: Macmillan, 2000), chap. 5. The $8–10 billion figure is from McCoy, *Politics of Heroin*, p. 483.

63. Major Donors Mission, "The Impact of the Taliban Prohibition on Opium Poppy Cultivation in Afghanistan. A Mission Report Presented to the Major Donors Countries of UNDCP," 25 May 2001. For discussion of the ban's motives, see Alain Labrousse, *Opium de Guerre, Opium de Paix* (Paris: Mille et Une Nuits, 2005), pp. 149–54; David Macdonald, *Drugs in Afghanistan: Opium, Outlaws and Scorpion Tales* (London: Pluto, 2007), pp. 79–85.

64. Major Donors Mission, "The impact of the Taliban Prohibition."

65. UNDCP, *Afghanistan Annual Opium Poppy Survey 2001* (Islamabad: UNDCP), p. ii; Transnational Institute, "Merging Wars: Afghanistan, Drugs and Terrorism" (Amsterdam: TNI, December 2001), p. 17.

66. UNODC, *The Opium Economy in Afghanistan: An International Problem*, p. 93; Martin Jelsma, "Learning Lessons from the Taliban Opium Ban," *International Journal of Drug Policy* 16 (2005): p. 98.

67. UNSCR 1333, 19 December 2000, www.unhcr.org/refworld/docid/3b00f51e14.html; TNI, "Merging Wars," p. 5; Nancy Soderberg, at Security Council meeting on 15 October 1999, www.undemocracy.com/securitycouncil/meeting_4051#pg002-bk10.

68. The drop in opium production was reached in part thanks to a drought, which diminished the credibility of the Taliban's intentions regarding drug control.

69. TNI, "Merging Wars," pp. 11–12; UNODC, *The Opium Economy in Afghanistan: An International Problem*, pp. 92–3; Rashid, *Taliban*, pp. 123–4.

70. Barbara Crossette, "U.S. Sends 2 to Assess Drug Program for Afghans," *New York Times*, 25 April 2001.

71. Talat Aslam, "Shift in U.S. Policy as Envoys Visit Afghanistan," *Dawn* (Pakistan), 18 April 2001, cited in Kolhatkar and Ingalls, *Bleeding Afghanistan*, p. 37.

72. Thalif Deen, "Drugs: U.N. Pays Rare Compliment to Taliban Over Opium Ban," *Inter Press Service*, 9 August 2001.

73. *Reuters*, "Bush Decides to Keep Afghan Sanctions," *New York Times*, 3 July 2001; George W. Bush, "Letter to Congressional Leaders on Continuation of the National Emergency With Respect to the Taliban," 30 June 2001, www.presidency.ucsb.edu/ws/?pid=64110.

74. "Powell Reveals $43 Million in New Aid to Afghans," US Department of State report, 17 May 2001, http://reliefweb.int/node/407386.

75. Mackenzie, "The United States and the Taliban," p. 101.

76. William Maley, *The Foreign Policy of the Taliban* (New York: Council on Foreign Relations Press, 2000), p. 11.

77. Ahmed Rashid, *Taliban: Militant Islam, Oil and Fundamentalism in Central Asia* (New Haven: Yale Nota Bene/Yale University Press, 2001), pp. 180–2.

78. Rahul Mahajan, "We Think the Price is Worth it," *Extra!* (November/December 2001), www.fair.org/index.php?page=1084.

79. Maley, *The Foreign Policy of the Taliban*, p. 13; Kolhatkar and Ingalls, *Bleeding Afghanistan*, pp. 18–19.

80. Maley, *The Foreign Policy of the Taliban*, p. 14; Dan Morgan and David B. Ottaway, "Women's Fury Toward Taliban Stalls Pipeline; Afghan Plan Snagged In U.S. Political Issues," *Washington Post*, 11 January 1998.

81. Sharon Waxman, "A Cause Unveiled; Hollywood Women Have Made the Plight of Afghan Women Their Own—Sight Unseen," *Washington Post*, 30 March 1999; Kathleen Kenna, "Hollywood's Cause; Celebrities Challenge the Taleban Stars Say Their Campaign's Goal is to Restore Women's Rights," *Toronto Star*, 22 November 1998. See also Janelle Brown, "A Coalition of Hope," *Ms. Magazine* (Spring 2002), which relates how the Feminist Majority campaign for Afghan women built momentum from 1997 to shortly after 9/11. Their successes always seem to coincide with more fundamental US foreign policy shifts towards Afghanistan and the Taliban.

82. Maley, *The Foreign Policy of the Taliban*, p. 14.

83. Mavis Leno in an interview with the Real News Network, "The Rights of Women in Afghanistan," 1 April 2009, http://therealnews.com/t2/index.php?option=com_content&task=view&id=31&Itemid=74&jumival=3463; interview by the author with Norma Gattsek (Feminist Majority official), 6 December 2011.

CHAPTER 5

1. For a good account of the American campaign against al-Qaeda in Afghanistan and elsewhere, see Jason Burke, *Al-Qaeda: The True Story of Radical Islam* (third edition) (London: Penguin, 2007).

2. George W. Bush, "Address Before a Joint Session of the Congress on the United States Response to the Terrorist Attacks of September 11," 20 September 2001, www.presidency.ucsb.edu/ws/?pid=64731.

3. George W. Bush, "The President's Radio Address," 15 September 2001, www.presidency.ucsb.edu/ws/?pid=25001.

4. Bob Woodward, *Bush at War* (London: Pocket Books/Simon & Schuster, 2003), p. 103.

5. Charles Krauthammer, "The Real New World Order: The American and the Islamic Challenge," *The Weekly Standard* 7(9), 12 November 2001.

6. Woodward, *Bush at War*, pp. 38–9.

7. Woodward, *Bush at War*, p.103.

8. Woodward, *Bush at War*, p. 63.

9. Woodward, *Bush at War*, p. 98.

10. DOD Dictionary of Military Terms, "Terrorism," www.dtic.mil/doctrine/dod_dictionary/data/t/7591.html.

11. Michael R. Gordon, "A Nation Challenged: The Strategy; Allies Preparing for a Long Fight as Taliban Dig in," *New York Times*, 28 October 2001.

12. US Embassy (Islamabad), "Musharraf [EXCISED]," 13 September 2001; "'No-Go' Tribal Areas Became Basis for Afghan Insurgency Documents Show," Digital National Security Archive (DNSA), electronic briefing book No. 325, 13 September 2010, www.gwu.edu/~nsarchiv/NSAEBB/NSAEBB325/index.htm.

13. US Embassy (Islamabad), "Mahmud Plans 2nd Mission to Afghanistan," 24 September 2001, DNSA, www.gwu.edu/~nsarchiv/NSAEBB/NSAEBB325/index.htm.

14. US Department of State, "Deputy Secretary Armitage-Mamoud Phone Call—September 18, 2001," 18 September 2001, DNSA, www.gwu.edu/~nsarchiv/NSAEBB/NSAEBB325/index.htm.

15. Said Mohammad Azam, "US Attacks Taliban Frontline, Rejects Bin Laden Trial Offer," *AFP*, 14 October 2001; *ABC News*, World News Tonight Sunday, "The President; Bush Rejects Taliban's Offer to Hand over Osama bin Laden to Neutral Country for Trial," 14 October 2001 (transcript available on Nexis database); Laura King, "Taliban Delivers Message to bin Laden; Aid Workers' Trial Resume; Rebel Patrol Pushes Close to Kabul," *Associated Press Worldstream*, 27 September 2001.

16. Zbigniew Brzezinski, *The Grand Chessboard: American Primacy and Its Geostrategic Imperatives* (New York: Basic Books, 1997).

17. *National Energy Policy*, Report of the National Energy Policy Development Group, May 2001, pp. 8–7, 8–12, www.ne.doe.gov/pdfFiles/nationalEnergyPolicy.pdf.

18. US Senate, Committee on Foreign Relations, *Central Asia and the Transition in Afghanistan*, 19 December 2011 (Washington, DC: US Government Printing Office), pp. 1–2.

19. Dilip Hiro, "Shanghai Surprise: The Summit of the Shanghai Cooperation Organisation Reveals How Power is Shifting in the World," *Guardian*, 16 June 2006.

20. Siddharth Varadarajan, "Pipelines, Power Grids and the New Silk Road in Asia," *The Hindu*, 11 July 2005; Siddharth Srivastava, "The Foundations for an Asian Oil and Gas Grid," *Asia Times online*, 1 December 2005.

21. Michael Klare, "Danger Waters: The Three Hot Spots of Potential Conflict in the Geo-Energy Era," 10 January 2012, TomDispatch.com.

22. Doug Stokes and Sam Raphael, *Global Energy Security and American Hegemony* (Baltimore: Johns Hopkins University Press, 2010), p. 121.

23. Nick Turse, "The 700 Military Bases of Afghanistan: Black Sites in the Empire of Bases," TomDispatch.com, 9 February 2010.

24. US Department of Defense, 30 September 2011, http://siadapp.dmdc.osd.mil/personnel/MILITARY/history/hst1109.pdf.

25. Zdzislaw Lachowski, *Foreign Military Bases in Central Asia*, SIPRI (Stockholm International Peace Research Institute) Policy Paper No. 18, June 2007, pp. 47–8; US Senate, *Central Asia and the Transition in Afghanistan*, p. 6.

26. Wayne Madsen, "Afghanistan, the Taliban and the Bush Oil Team," 23 January 2002, http://globalresearch.ca/articles/MAD201A.html.

27. Ilene R. Prusher, Scott Baldauf, and Edward Girardet, "Afghan Power Brokers," *Christian Science Monitor*, 10 June 2002.

28. Interview with David Barsamian at Alternative Radio, quoted in Sonali Kolhatkar and James Ingalls, *Bleeding Afghanistan: Washington, Warlords, and the Propaganda of Silence* (New York: Seven Stories Press, 2006), p. 227.

29. Jon Lee Anderson, "American Viceroy: Zalmay Khalilzad's Mission," *The New Yorker*, 19 December 2005.

30. Michel Chossudovsky, "The Spoils of War: Afghanistan's Multibillion Heroin Trade," *Global Research*, 5 April 2004, www.globalresearch.ca/articles/CHO404A.html.

31. Michel Chossudovsky, "Who Benefits from the Afghan Opium Trade?" *Global Research*, 21 September 2006, www.globalresearch.ca/index.php?context=va&aid=3294.

32. Peter Dale Scott, *American War Machine: Deep Politics, the CIA Global Drug Connection, and the Road to Afghanistan* (Lanham, MD: Rowman and Littlefield, 2010), pp. 237, 232–3; Peter Dale Scott, *Drugs, Oil, and War: The United States in Afghanistan, Colombia, and Indochina* (Lanham, MD: Rowman and Littlefield, 2003), pp. 28, xv.

33. Scott, *Drugs, Oil, and War*, p. 43.

34. UNODC, *Estimating Illicit Financial Flows Resulting from Drug Trafficking and Other Transnational Organized Crimes*, October 2011 (Vienna: UNODC), p. 32 (Table 23). Note that those estimates vary greatly. The $220 billion figure is calculated by estimating that about two-thirds of annual total drug profits ($322 billion, i.e., the total street value of drugs) are available for laundering through the financial system annually. The other third is spent by traffickers and dealers on their own consumption, living expenses and luxury lifestyle without being laundered. To be precise, the $220 billion is not all laundered through the financial system but can also be laundered through direct investments into the real estate sector or other legal activities. It is unclear what proportion of the $220 billion goes into such investments. But in any case, in developed countries, such investments (say, buying a house) will usually not be made by using cash directly but through banks (although cash is more used in developing countries). In short, the $220 billion figure can be used as a maximum estimate of drug money laundered through the financial system annually. Thank you to Thomas Pietschmann, UNODC research officer, for clarifications on this subject.

35. Deposit data taken from Federal Deposit Insurance Corporation statistics. Deposits for 2001 taken from the following table: www.fdic.gov/bank/statistical/stats/2001dec/industry.html and deposits for 2011 taken from the following table: www.fdic.gov/bank/statistical/stats/2011dec/industry.html.

36. Alfred McCoy, *The Politics of Heroin: CIA Complicity in the Global Drug Trade* (revised edition) (Chicago: Lawrence Hill Books, 2003), p. 519; David Macdonald, *Drugs in Afghanistan: Opium, Outlaws and Scorpion Tales* (London: Pluto, 2007), p. 84; Pierre-Arnaud Chouvy, *Opium: Uncovering the Politics of the Poppy* (London: I.B. Tauris, 2009), p. 151.

37. UNODC, *The Opium Economy in Afghanistan: An International Problem* (Vienna: UNODC, 2003), p. 93.

38. Steve Coll, *Ghost Wars: The Secret History of the CIA, Afghanistan, and Bin Laden, from the Soviet Invasion to September 10, 2001* (New York: Penguin, 2004).

39. Norimitsu Onishi, "Afghan Warlords and Bandits Are Back in Business," *New York Times*, 28 December 2001.

40. Human Rights Watch, *Blood-Stained Hands: Past Atrocities in Kabul and Afghanistan's Legacy of Impunity* (2005); Human Rights Watch, "Letter to President Barack Obama on Afghanistan," 26 March 2009, www.hrw.org/en/news/2009/03/26/human-rights-watch-letter-president-barack-obama-afghanistan.

41. Ahmed Rashid, *Descent into Chaos: How the War Against Islamic Extremism is Being Lost in Pakistan, Afghanistan and Central Asia* (London: Allen Lane, 2008), pp. 128–9; Woodward, *Bush at War*, p. 317.

42. Human Rights Watch, *World Report 2003*, Afghanistan.

43. Human Rights Watch, *Afghanistan: Return of the Warlords*, June 2002, pp. 1–2; John Sifton, "Afghanistan's Warlords Still Call the Shots," 24 December 2003, www.hrw.org/news/2003/12/23/afghanistans-warlords-still-call-shots; Human Rights Watch, *The Rule of the Gun: Human Rights Abuses and Political Repression in the Run-up to Afghanistan's Presidential Election*, September 2004, pp. 1, 43. See also Human Rights Watch, *"Killing You is a Very Easy Thing for Us": Human Rights Abuses in Southeast Afghanistan*, July 2003.

44. Andrew Wilder, *A House Divided? Analysing the 2005 Afghan Elections*, December 2005 (Kabul: AREU), p. 14; Human Rights Watch, "Letter to President Barack Obama on Afghanistan," 26 March 2009.

45. Matthew Rosenberg, "U.S. Courts Former Warlords in its Bid for Afghan Stability," *Wall Street Journal*, 20 March 2009; Saeed Shah, "Karzai's Pick for Parliament Speaker Accused of Atrocities," *McClatchy Newspapers*, 26 January 2011. On warlordism in Afghanistan, see Antonio Giustozzi, *Empires of Mud: Wars and Warlords in Afghanistan* (London: Hurst, 2009).

46. *Radio Free Europe*, "Human Rights Watch Chief 'Appalled' by Afghan VP Choice," 7 May 2009, www.rferl.org/content/Human_Rights_Watch_Chief_Appalled_by_Afghan_VP_Choice/1623813.html; Abubakar Siddique, "Afghan President's Choice Of Running Mate Draws Criticism," *Radio Free Europe*, 5 May 2009, www.rferl.org/content/Afghan_Presidents_Choice_Of_Running_Mate_Draws_Criticism/1622135.html ; for details, see Human Rights Watch, *Blood-Stained Hands*, 2005, and Afghan Rights Monitor, *The Winning Warlords*, (Kabul: ARM, June 2009).

47. Malalai Joya, *Raising my Voice: The Extraordinary Story of the Afghan Woman Who Dares to Speak Out* (London: Rider, 2009); Anne E. Brodsky, *With All Our Strength: The Revolutionary Association of the Women of Afghanistan* (New York: Routledge, 2003); www.rawa.org.
48. Human Rights Watch, "Letter to President Barack Obama on Afghanistan," 26 March 2009.

CHAPTER 6

1. It had decreased to 5,800 tons by 2011. UNODC, *Afghanistan Opium Survey 2010* (Vienna: UNODC), p. 58; UNODC, *Afghanistan Opium Survey 2011* (Vienna: UNODC), p. 3. An earlier version of this chapter appeared in Julien Mercille, "The U.S. 'War on Drugs' in Afghanistan: Reality or Pretext?" *Critical Asian Studies* 43(2) (2011): pp.285–309, available at www.tandfonline.com.
2. UNODC, *Addiction, Crime and Insurgency: The Transnational Threat of Afghan Opium* (Vienna: UNODC), pp. 113–14.
3. It is unclear whether the increase from $75–100 million to $125 million in Taliban revenues from drugs is in inflation-adjusted dollars, but if not (as appears likely), this would make the increase even less significant. UNODC, *Addiction*, pp. 2–3, 18, 113.
4. The total revenue generated by opiates within Afghanistan is about $3 billion per year; insurgents take $125 million, farmers $600 million. We can therefore estimate that insurgents and farmers take approximately 5 percent and 20 percent respectively of total opiates revenue in Afghanistan. For data, see for example UNODC, *Afghanistan Opium Survey 2009* (Vienna: UNODC), p. 5. For details on how UNODC calculates the allocation of drug revenues in Afghanistan, see *Afghanistan Opium Survey 2008* (Vienna: UNODC), Section 2.17, pp. 125–9.
5. UNODC, *Addiction*, p. 102.
6. Jonathan Caulkins, Jonathan Kulick, and Mark Kleiman, "Think Again: The Afghan Drug Trade," *Foreign Policy*, 1 April 2011, www.foreignpolicy.com/articles/2011/04/01/think_again_the_afghan_drug_trade?page=full. See also, making the same point: Julien Mercille, "UN Report Misleading on Afghanistan," *Foreign Policy in Focus*, November 2009, www.fpif.org/articles/un_report_misleading_on_afghanistans_drug_problem.
7. Gretchen Peters, "The Taliban and the Opium Trade," in Antonio Giustozzi (ed.), *Decoding the New Taliban* (London: Hurst and Co., 2009), p. 19; Interview by the author with UNODC official, 2 November 2009.
8. For an excellent account of the structure of the Afghan drug industry, see Mark Shaw, "Drug Trafficking and the Development of Organized Crime in Post-Taliban Afghanistan," in Doris Buddenberg and William Byrd (eds.), *Afghanistan's Drug Industry: Structure, Functioning, Dynamics, and Implications for Counter-Narcotics Policy* (Vienna: UNODC and Washington, DC: World Bank, 2006), pp. 189–214.
9. Ron Moreau and Sami Yousafzai, "A Harvest Of Treachery; Afghanistan's Drug Trade Is Threatening the Stability of a Nation America Went to War to Stabilize. What Can Be Done?" *Newsweek*, 9 January 2006.
10. "Afghanistan: Running on Drugs, Corruption and Aid," IRIN, 10 May 2010, www.irinnews.org/Report.aspx?ReportID=89078.

11. Ahmed Rashid, *Descent into Chaos: How the War Against Islamic Extremism is Being Lost in Pakistan, Afghanistan and Central Asia* (London: Allen Lane, 2008), p. 328.
12. Quoted in Shaw, "Drug Trafficking," p. 205; Thomas Schweich, "Is Afghanistan a Narco-State?" *New York Times Magazine*, 27 July 2008.
13. UNODC, *Addiction*, p. 3.
14. US Department of State, *International Narcotics Control Strategy Report 2011*, Volume I, pp. 7, 433, www.state.gov/j/inl/rls/nrcrpt/2011/vol1/index.htm.
15. US Senate, Committee on Foreign Relations, *Afghanistan's Narco War: Breaking the Link between Drug Traffickers and Insurgents*, 10 August 2009 (Washington, DC: US Government Printing Office), p. 17.
16. Elizabeth Rubin, "Karzai in His Labyrinth," *New York Times Magazine*, 4 August 2009; Vanda Felbab-Brown, *Shooting Up: Counterinsurgency and the War on Drugs* (Washington, DC: Brookings Institution Press, 2010), p. 150.
17. Dexter Filkins, "Rule of the Gun: Convoy Guards in Afghanistan Face Inquiry," *New York Times*, 6 June 2010.
18. Gretchen Peters, *Seeds of Terror: How Heroin Is Bankrolling the Taliban and al Qaeda* (New York: St. Martin's Press, 2009), pp. 133–34; David Mansfield, "Where Have All the Flowers Gone? Assessing the Sustainability of Current Reductions in Opium Production in Afghanistan," 1 May 2010 (Kabul: AREU), p. 22.
19. Ahmed Rashid, *Descent into Chaos*, pp. 327–8; Vishal Chandra, "Warlords, Drugs and the "War on Terror" in Afghanistan: The Paradoxes," *Strategic Analysis* 30(1) (2006): pp. 64–92; Barnett Rubin, *Road to Ruin: Afghanistan's Booming Opium Industry* (New York: New York University, Center on International Cooperation, 2004).
20. Moreau and Yousafzai, "Harvest of Treachery," *Newsweek*, 9 January 2006. See also Andrew Wilder, *A House Divided? Analysing the 2005 Afghan Elections* (Kabul: AREU, 2005).
21. US Senate, *Afghanistan's Narco War*; GAO, *Afghanistan Drug Control: Strategy Evolving and Progress Reported, but Interim Performance Targets and Evaluation of Justice Reform Efforts Needed*, March 2010, www.gao.gov/new.items/d10291.pdf, Table 1.
22. Schweich, "Is Afghanistan a Narco-State?"
23. James Risen, "An Afghan's Path from Ally of U.S. to Drug Suspect," *New York Times*, 2 February 2007.
24. Peters, *Seeds of Terror*, pp. 202, 193; Larry Neumeister, "Federal officials in New York Say Afghan Tribal Chief Had Strong Links to Taliban in 2005," *Associated Press*, 3 May 2008; Benjamin Weiser, "Afghan Linked to Taliban Sentenced to Death in Drug Trafficking Case," *New York Times*, 1 May 2009.
25. James Risen, "Propping up a Drug Lord, then Arresting Him," *New York Times*, 12 December 2010.
26. James Risen, "Poppy Fields Are Now a Front Line in Afghanistan's War," *New York Times*, 16 May 2007; Elizabeth Rubin, "Karzai in His Labyrinth."
27. Matthew Pennington, "Afghan Anti-Corruption Chief Is a Convicted Heroin Trafficker," *Associated Press*, 9 March 2007.
28. Dexter Filkins, Mark Mazzetti and James Risen, "Brother of Afghan Leader Said to Be Paid by CIA," *New York Times*, 27 October 2009; James Risen, "Reports Link Karzai's Brother to Afghanistan Heroin Trade," *New York Times*, 4 October 2008; Scott Schane and Andrew Lehren, "Leaked Cables

Offer a Raw Look Inside U.S. Diplomacy," *New York Times*, 29 November 2010; Mark Mazzetti, "Reported Ties from C.I.A. to a Karzai Spur Rebukes," *New York Times*, 29 October 2009.

29. James Risen and Mark Landler, "Drug Accusations Against Afghan Official Pose Dilemma for U.S.," *New York Times*, 27 August 2009.

30. Jake Sherman and Victoria DiDomenico, *The Public Cost of Private Security* (New York: Center on International Cooperation, New York University, September 2009), pp. 1, 7.

31. Matthieu Aikins, "The Master of Spin Boldak: Undercover with Afghanistan's Drug-Trafficking Border Police," *Harper's*, December 2009; Matthieu Aikins, "Our Man in Kandahar," *The Atlantic*, November 2011.

32. For example, see the map in UNODC, *World Drug Report 2011* (New York: United Nations, 2011), p. 58.

33. UNODC, *Addiction*, p. 22.

34. Barnett Rubin, "Counter-Narcotics in Afghanistan: First Installment," 24 August 2007, icga.blogspot.com/2007/08/counter-narcotics-in-afghanistan-first.html.

35. Shaw, "Drug Trafficking," p. 206.

36. UNODC, *The Global Afghan Opium Trade: A Threat Assessment*, July 2011 (Vienna: UNODC), pp. 143–4; UNODC, *Addiction*, pp. 76, 110.

37. UNODC, *Addiction*, p. 15; UNODC, *Global Afghan Opium Trade*, p. 91.

38. Author's calculations from data reported in UNODC, *Addiction*.

39. For example, UNODC, *Addiction*, p. 17.

40. UNODC, *Global Afghan Opium Trade*, p. 5; see also US Department of State, *International Narcotics Control Strategy Report 2011*, p. 57, which reaches similar conclusions.

41. International Narcotics Control Board (INCB), *Precursors and Chemicals Frequently Used in the Illicit Manufacture of Narcotic Drugs and Psychotropic Substances, 2009* (New York: United Nations), p. 17; INCB, *Precursors and Chemicals Frequently Used in the Illicit Manufacture of Narcotic Drugs and Psychotropic Substances, 2010* (New York: United Nations), pp. xi, 16, 14.

42. UNODC, *Addiction*, pp. 70, 73; UNODC, *Afghanistan Opium Survey 2008*, p. 156.

43. *International Narcotics Control Strategy Report 2011*, p. 7; UNODC, *Addiction*, pp. 71–2.

44. Edwina Thompson, "The Nexus of Drug Trafficking and Hawala in Afghanistan," in Buddenberg and Byrd, *Afghanistan's Drug Industry*, p. 162; Peters, *Seeds of Terror*, p. 231.

45. See chapter 5. UNODC, *Addiction*, p. 7. Although his assertion may be exaggerated, former UNODC chief Antonio Maria Costa even claimed that drug money may have recently rescued some failing banks: "Interbank loans were funded by money that originated from drug trade and other illegal activities," he said, and there are "signs that some banks were rescued in that way." "At a time of major bank failures, *money doesn't smell*, bankers seem to believe," he wrote in the 2009 *World Drug Report*. See "UN Crime Chief Says Drug Money Flowed into Banks," *Reuters*, 25 January 2009; UNODC, *World Drug Report 2009* (New York: United Nations), p. 3 (emphasis in original).

46. See chapter 5. UNODC, *Estimating Illicit Financial Flows Resulting from Drug Trafficking and Other Transnational Organized Crimes*, October 2011 (Vienna: UNODC), p. 32 (Table 23) ($220 billion figure) and p. 7 (0.2 percent figure).

47. Jefferson Morley, "Contradictions of Cocaine Capitalism," *The Nation*, 2 October 1989, pp. 341–7.
48. "Remarks by President Obama and President Calderon of Mexico at Joint Press Conference," 3 March 2011, www.whitehouse.gov/the-press-office/2011/03/03/remarks-president-obama-and-president-calder-n-mexico-joint-press-confer.
49. Ed Vulliamy, "How a Big US Bank Laundered Billions From Mexico's Murderous Drug Gangs," *Observer* (London), 3 April 2011.
50. D. Tedford, "Bank Gets Record Penalty in Money-Laundering Case," *Houston Chronicle*, 22 November 1994.
51. GAO, *Private Banking: Raul Salinas, Citibank, and Alleged Money Laundering*, October 1998, p. 3, www.gao.gov/archive/1999/os99001.pdf; Tim Golden, "Swiss Recount Key Drug Role of Salinas Kin," *New York Times*, 19 September 1998. See also Alexander Cockburn and Jeffrey St. Clair, *Whiteout: The CIA, Drugs and the Press* (London: Verso, 1998), pp. 365–71.
52. Franks in Eric Schmitt, "U.S. to Add to Forces in Horn of Africa," *New York Times*, 30 October 2002; Rumsfeld quoted in Rashid, *Descent into Chaos*, p. 324; Sarles quoted in Tim McGirk, "Drugs? What drugs?" TIME, 18 August 2003; US colonel quoted in Rashid, *Descent into Chaos*, p. 325; Ron Moreau and Sami Yousafzai, "Flowers of Destruction," *Newsweek*, 14 July 2003.
53. Felbab-Brown, *Shooting Up*, pp. 138–40; John F. Burns, "Afghan Warlords Squeeze Profits from the War on Drugs, Critics Say," *New York Times*, 5 May 2002; "The Poppies Bloom Again," *The Economist* (London), 18 April 2002.
54. Rowan Scarborough, "Military Resists Afghan Drug War," *Washington Times*, 14 October 2004.
55. Schweich, "Is Afghanistan a Narco-State?"
56. McGirk, "Drugs? What drugs?"; James Risen, *State of War: The Secret History of the CIA and the Bush Administration* (London: The Free Press, 2006), p. 154; Josh Meyer, "Pentagon Doing Little In Afghan Drug Fight," *Los Angeles Times*, 5 December 2006; Barnett Rubin, "Afghanistan's Fatal Addiction," *International Herald Tribune*, 28 October 2004.
57. US Senate, *Afghanistan's Narco War*, p. 5.
58. Felbab-Brown, *Shooting Up*, p. 135; Pankaj Mishra, "The Real Afghanistan", *New York Review of Books* 52 (4), 10 March 2005.
59. Mishra, "The Real Afghanistan"; Moreau and Yousafzai, "Flowers of Destruction," *Newsweek*, 14 July 2003.
60. Antonio Giustozzi, *Koran, Kalashnikov and Laptop: The Neo-Taliban Insurgency in Afghanistan* (New York: Columbia University Press, 2008), p. 87; James Risen, "Poppy Fields Are Now a Front Line in Afghan War," *New York Times*, 16 May 2007.
61. Giustozzi, *Koran, Kalashnikov and Laptop*, p. 69.
62. US Senate, *Afghanistan's Narco War*, p. 6.
63. Tom Shanker, "Pentagon Sees Aggressive Antidrug Effort in Afghanistan," *New York Times*, 25 March 2005. See also Jim Hoagland, "A New Afghan Policy," *Washington Post*, 8 August 2004; Eric Schmitt, "Afghans' Gains Face Big Threat in Drug Traffic," *New York Times*, 11 December 2004.
64. Felbab-Brown, *Shooting Up*, pp. 143–4.
65. Transnational Institute, "Plan Afghanistan," Drug Policy Briefing No. 10, January 2005 (Amsterdam: TNI); "Afghanistan: Are the British Counternarcotics Efforts Going Wobbly?" Hearing Before the Subcommittee on Criminal Justice, Drug Policy and Human Resources of the Committee on Government Reform,

US House of Representatives, 1 April 2004 (Washington, DC: US Government Printing Office).

66. Schweich, "Is Afghanistan a Narco-State?"
67. Rajiv Chandrasekaran, "Skeptical Administration Keeping Karzai at Arm's Length," *Washington Post*, 6 May 2009.
68. Jim Hoagland, "Poppies vs. Power in Afghanistan," *Washington Post*, 23 December 2007; Schweich, "Is Afghanistan a Narco-State?"
69. Schweich, "Is Afghanistan a Narco-State?"
70. Felbab-Brown, *Shooting Up*, p. 163.
71. Barnett Rubin and Jake Sherman, *Counter-Narcotics to Stabilize Afghanistan: The False Promise of Crop Eradication* (New York: Center on International Cooperation, New York University, 2008), pp. 7–8.
72. Holbrooke quoted in "Envoy Damns US Afghan Drug Effort", *BBC News*, 21 March 2009, http://news.bbc.co.uk/2/hi/south_asia/7957237.stm; David Mansfield and Adam Pain, *Alternative Livelihoods: Substance or Slogan?* (Kabul: AREU, 2005).
73. GAO, *Afghanistan Drug Control* (March 2010).
74. GAO, *Afghanistan Drug Control* (March 2010), p. 11; Holbrooke quoted in US Senate, Caucus on International Narcotics Control, *U.S. Counternarcotics Strategy in Afghanistan*, July 2010, p. 20, http://drugcaucus.senate.gov.
75. Kenneth Katzman, *Afghanistan: Post-Taliban Governance, Security, and U.S. Policy*, 22 November 2011, (Washington, DC: Congressional Research Service), p. 19; GAO, *Afghanistan Drug Control* (March 2010), pp. 11, 20, 22.
76. James Risen, "Poppy Fields Are Now a Front Line in Afghanistan's War," *New York Times*, 16 May 2007.
77. Rashid, *Descent into Chaos*, pp. 325–8.
78. Rowan Scarborough, "Military Resists Afghan Drug War," *Washington Times*, 14 October 2004; Felbab-Brown, *Shooting Up*, p. 141.
79. Rashid, *Descent into Chaos*, pp. 325–9. See also Felbab-Brown, *Shooting Up*, p. 141.
80. Felbab-Brown, *Shooting Up*, p. 147.
81. US Senate, *Afghanistan's Narco War*, p. 1 (emphasis added). See also James Risen, "Drug Chieftains Tied to Taliban Are US Targets", *New York Times*, 10 August 2009.

CHAPTER 7

1. UNODC, *World Drug Report 2010* (New York: United Nations); see this book's Introduction for details.
2. Thomas Babor et al., *Drug Policy and the Public Good* (Oxford: Oxford University Press, 2010). Different authors adopt slightly different classification schemes and the four methods listed overlap: for example, many overseas operations can in part be considered as enforcement. There is a large literature associated with treatment and prevention strategies, and a smaller body of work on enforcement and overseas operations. See also Robert MacCoun and Peter Reuter, *Drug War Heresies: Learning from Other Vices, Times, and Places* (Cambridge: Cambridge University Press, 2001).
3. Peter Rydell and Susan Everingham, *Controlling Cocaine: Supply Versus Demand Programs* (Santa Monica, CA: RAND, 1994).

4. Babor et al. *Drug Policy*, pp. 124–6; D. Hedrich et al., "From Margin to Mainstream: The Evolution of Harm Reduction Responses to Problem Drug Use in Europe," *Drugs: Education, Prevention and Policy* 15(6) (December 2008): pp. 503–17.

5. Babor et al., *Drug Policy*, p. 255.

6. Babor et al., *Drug Policy*, pp. 120, 263; Jonathan Caulkins, Rosalie Liccardo Pacula, Susan Paddock and James Chiesa, *School-Based Drug Prevention: What Kind of Drug Use Does It Prevent?* (Santa Monica, CA: RAND, 2002), p. 32.

7. Babor et al., *Drug Policy*, p. 160. Mark Kleiman has argued that a policy of "coerced abstinence" could reduce drug use, by using certain, immediate and short sanctions (for example, 24 hours in jail) for dependent drug users who fail urine tests. Kleiman, *When Brute Force Fails: How To Have Less Crime and Less Punishment* (Princeton: Princeton University Press, 2009). There have been a few unconvincing attempts to demonstrate the effectiveness of enforcement. The Institute for Defense Analysis did a study arguing that source-country interventions like Bush Sr.'s war on drugs in Latin America, initiated in 1989, can reduce consumption in the United States. However, the study was so flawed that the National Research Council concluded that major "concerns about data and methods make it impossible to accept the IDA findings as a basis for the assessment of interdiction policies." See Barry Crane, Rex Rivolo and Gary Comfort, *An Empirical Examination of Counterdrug Interdiction Program Effectiveness* (Alexandria: Institute for Defense Analyses, 1997); Charles Manski, John Pepper and Yonette Thomas, *Assessment of Two Cost-Effectiveness Studies on Cocaine Control Policy* (Washington, DC: National Academy Press, 1999). It could also be suggested that enforcement and prohibition act as deterrents to drug use and hence reduce drug problems, although this is difficult to measure. See Robert MacCoun, "Drugs and the Law: A Psychological Analysis of Drug Prohibition," *Psychological Bulletin* 113(3) (1993): pp. 497–512.

8. Babor et al., *Drug Policy*, p. 258. See also Charles Manski, John Pepper and Carol Petrie (eds.), *Informing America's Policy on Illegal Drugs: What We Don't Know Keeps Hurting Us* (Washington, DC: National Academy Press, 2001).

9. WHO, *Report on the Global Tobacco Epidemic, 2008: The MPOWER Package* (Geneva: World Health Organization, 2008); WHO, *Report on the Global Tobacco Epidemic, 2009: Implementing Smoke-Free Environments* (Geneva: World Health Organization, 2009); WHO, *Global Status Report on Alcohol and Health* (Geneva: World Health Organization, 2011).

10. Latin American Commission on Drugs and Democracy, *Drugs & Democracy: Towards a Paradigm Shift* (2009), pp. 8, 10, www.drogasedemocracia.org/.

11. And the proportion going to demand reduction is inflated because the $2 billion spent annually to imprison people who violate federal drug laws is no longer counted in the drug control budget. Ethan Nadelmann, "An Imperfect Improvement: Obama's New Drug War Strategy," *Huffington Post*, 11 May 2010, www.huffingtonpost.com/ethan-nadelmann/ethan-nadelmann-critiques_b_571672.html.

12. Alex Stevens, *Drugs, Crime and Public Health: The Political Economy of Drug Policy* (New York: Routledge, 2011), p. 109; David Boyum and Peter Reuter, *An Analytic Assessment of U.S. Drug Policy* (Washington, DC: The American Enterprise Institute Press, 2005), p. 7.

13. Imprisonment numbers refer to both state and federal custody. Stevens, *Crime and Public Health*, p. 109.
14. Louisa Degenhardt et al., "Toward a Global View of Alcohol, Tobacco, Cannabis, and Cocaine Use: Findings from the WHO World Mental Health Surveys," *PLoS Medicine* 5(7) (July 2008): pp. 1061, 1053. See also Stevens, *Drugs, Crime and Public Health*, pp. 110–12.
15. Tim Rhodes and Dagmar Hedrich, "Harm Reduction and the Mainstream," in Tim Rhodes and Dagmar Hedrich (eds.), *Harm Reduction: Evidence, Impacts and Challenges*, European Monitoring Centre for Drugs and Drug Addiction (EMCDDA) Monographs (Luxembourg: Publications Office of the European Union, 2010), p. 24; EMCDDA, *2010 Annual Report on the State of the Drugs Problem in Europe* (Luxembourg: Publications Office of the European Union, 2010), pp. 71, 75–6.
16. EMCDDA, *2009 Annual Report on the State of the Drugs Problem in Europe* (Luxembourg: Publications Office of the European Union, 2009), p. 32.
17. Catherine Cook, Jamie Bridge, and Gerry Stimson, "The Diffusion of Harm Reduction in Europe and Beyond," in Rhodes and Hedrich, *Harm Reduction*, pp. 46–9; Hedrich et al., "From Margin to Mainstream," p. 507; EMCDDA, *2010 Annual Report*, p. 5; European Commission, *Report of the Final Evaluation of the EU Drugs Action Plan (2005–2008)* (2008), p. 83, http://ec.europa.eu/health/; Alex Stevens, Heino Stöver and Cinzia Brentari, "Criminal Justice Approaches to Harm Reduction in Europe," in Rhodes and Hedrich, *Harm Reduction*, p. 83.
18. Peter Reuter and Alex Stevens, "Assessing UK Drug Policy from a Crime Control Perspective," *Criminology and Criminal Justice* 8(4) (2008): pp. 467, 461, 470, 474; Stevens, *Crime and Public Health*, p. 101.
19. Glenn Greenwald, *Drug Decriminalization in Portugal* (Washington, DC: CATO Institute, 2009), pp. 1, 11, 16–17. See also Caitlin Hughes and Alex Stevens, "What Can We Learn from the Portuguese Decriminalization of Illicit Drugs?" *British Journal of Criminology* 50(6) (2010).
20. Babor et al., *Drug Policy*, p. 244.
21. Richard Elovich and Ernest Drucker, "On Drug Treatment and Social Control: Russian Narcology's Great Leap Backwards," *Harm Reduction Journal* 5(23) (2008); Jonathan Caulkins, Mark Kleiman and Jonathan Kulick, *Drug Production and Trafficking, Counterdrug Policies, and Security and Governance in Afghanistan*, June 2010 (New York: New York University Center on International Cooperation), p. 25.
22. Daniel Wolfe and Kasia Malinowska-Sempruch, *Illicit Drug Policies and the Global HIV Epidemic: Effects of UN and National Government Approaches* (New York: Open Society Institute, 2004), p. 46.
23. Alexandra Orlova, "The Russian 'War on Drugs': A Kinder, Gentler Approach?", *Problems of Post-Communism* 56(1) (January/February 2009), p. 30.
24. "Russia to Set Up Antidrug Military Base in Kyrgyzstan", *The Voice of Russia*, 25 June 2010, http://english.ruvr.ru/2010/06/25/10660878.html.
25. "Russia to Set Up Antidrug Military Base in Kyrgyzstan"; "Russia plans counter-drug deployment in Kyrgyzstan", *The Voice of Russia*, 24 June 2010, http://english.ruvr.ru/2010/06/24/10631393.html; Fred Weir, "Moscow Furious, Says US Not Pushing Drug War in Afghanistan," *Christian Science Monitor*, 19 May 2010.

26. Open Society Institute, *At What Cost? HIV and Human Rights Consequences of the Global "War on Drugs"* (New York: Open Society Institute, 2009); UNODC, *Illicit Drug Trends in Central Asia*, April 2008 (Tashkent: UNODC).

27. Tom Lasseter, "U.S.-Built Bridge Is Windfall—For Illegal Afghan Drug Trade," *McClatchy Newspapers*, 28 June 2009; see also David Lewis, "High Times on the Silk Road: The Central Asian Paradox," *World Policy Journal* 27(1) (Spring 2010): pp. 39–49.

28. Bijan Nissaramanesh, Mike Trace, and Marcus Roberts, "The Rise of Harm Reduction in the Islamic Republic of Iran," Beckley Foundation Briefing Paper No. 8, July 2005, pp. 2–3.

29. Marziyeh Farniaa, Bahman Ebrahimia, Ali Shamsa and Saman Zamanib, "Scaling Up Methadone Maintenance Treatment for Opioid-Dependent Prisoners in Iran," *International Journal of Drug Policy* 21(5) (2010): p. 422.

30. Gul Shamim, "Twin Epidemics—Drug Use and HIV/AIDS in Pakistan," in Open Society Institute, *At What Cost?*, pp. 165–80.

31. For a defense of eradication, see Thomas Schweich, "Is Afghanistan a Narco-State?" *New York Times Magazine*, 27 July 2008. For arguments against it, see Vanda Felbab-Brown, *Shooting Up: Counterinsurgency and the War on Drugs* (Washington, DC: Brookings Institution Press, 2010) and Pierre-Arnaud Chouvy, *Opium: Uncovering the Politics of the Poppy* (London: I.B. Tauris, 2009).

32. Babor et al., *Drug Policy*, p. 148.

33. Alfred McCoy, "From Free Trade to Prohibition: A Critical History of the Modern Asian Opium Trade," *Fordham Urban Law Journal* XXVIII (2000): pp. 331, 333.

34. Chouvy, *Opium*, p. 156.

35. David Mansfield and Adam Pain, *Alternative Livelihoods: Substance or Slogan?* (Kabul: AREU, 2005); David Mansfield, "Where Have All the Flowers Gone? Assessing the Sustainability of Current Reductions in Opium Production in Afghanistan," 1 May 2010 (Kabul: AREU); Barnett Rubin, *Road to Ruin: Afghanistan's Booming Opium Industry* (New York: Center on International Cooperation, New York University, 2004); Barnett Rubin and Jake Sherman, *Counter-Narcotics to Stabilize Afghanistan: The False Promise of Crop Eradication* (New York: Center on International Cooperation, New York University, 2008); Chouvy, *Opium*, pp. 131ff.

36. Chouvy, *Opium*, pp. 186, 183, 187.

37. The Senlis Council proposals are available at www.icosgroup.net/report/. For a recent debate on medicinal opium production in Afghanistan, see Victoria Greenfield, Letizia Paoli, and Peter Reuter, "Is Medicinal Opium Production Afghanistan's Answer?: Lessons from India and the World Market," *Journal of Drug Policy Analysis* 2(1) (2009); Romesh Bhattacharji and Jorrit Kamminga, "Poppy for Medicine: An Essential Part of a Balanced Economic Development Solution for Afghanistan's Illegal Opium Economy," *Journal of Drug Policy Analysis* 3(1) (2010); V. Greenfield et al., "Is Medicinal Opium Production Afghanistan's Answer?: A Reply to Comments," *Journal of Drug Policy Analysis* 3(1) (2010). For supportive commentary in the media, see editorial, "The Afghan Poppy Trade," *Globe and Mail*, 21 November 2006; Anne Applebaum, "Ending an Opium War: Poppies and Afghan Recovery Can Both Bloom," *Washington Post*, 16 January 2007. For opposition and/or reservations, see Chouvy, *Opium*, pp. 191–7 and "Licensing Afghanistan's Opium: Solution

or Fallacy?" *Caucasian Review of International Affairs* 2(2) (Spring 2006); Vanda Felbab-Brown, "Opium Licensing in Afghanistan: Its Desirability and Feasibility," August 2007, Policy Paper No. 1 (Washington, DC: Brookings Institution).

38. Human Rights Watch, *Please, Do Not Make Us Suffer Any More...: Access to Pain Treatment as a Human Right*, 2009.
39. Martha Ann Overland, "Global Pain-Law Reform: Morphine Still Scarce for Many," *TIME*, 7 June 2010.
40. David Mansfield, "An Analysis of Licit Opium Poppy Cultivation: Turkey and India," 2001, www.davidmansfield.org/; Chouvy, *Opium*, pp. 191–7.
41. A.J. Fist, "The Tasmanian Poppy Industry: A Case Study of the Application of Science and Technology," 2001, www.regional.org.au/au/asa/2001/plenary/1/fist.htm.
42. Mansfield, "Turkey and India."
43. UNODC, *Drug Use in Afghanistan: 2009 Survey* (Executive Summary) (Vienna: UNODC); for a detailed analysis of the history of drug use in Afghanistan, see Macdonald, *Outlaws and Scorpion Tales*.
44. UNODC, *Drug Use in Afghanistan: 2009 Survey*; GAO, *Afghanistan Drug Control: Strategy Evolving and Progress Reported, but Interim Performance Targets and Evaluation of Justice Reform Efforts Needed*, March 2010, pp. 4–5 (Table 1 and Figure 2), www.gao.gov/new.items/d10291.pdf.
45. Note that the above numbers do not include US funds for agricultural development in Afghanistan, including for alternative livelihoods. Over 2002–10, the US allocated about $1.4 billion to agricultural development. See GAO, *Afghanistan Development: Enhancements to Performance Management and Evaluation Efforts Could Improve USAID's Agricultural Programs*, July 2010, GAO-10-368 (Washington, DC: GAO).
46. UNODC, *Drug Use in Afghanistan: 2009 Survey*, pp. 3, 9; see also Macdonald, *Outlaws and Scorpion Tales*, chap. 3.
47. Stevens, *Drugs, Crime and Public Health*, p. 109.
48. Such as George Shultz, former US secretary of state, Paul Volcker, former chairman of the Federal Reserve, Kofi Annan, former secretary general of the United Nations, Fernando Henrique Cardoso, former president of Brazil, Ernesto Zedillo, former president of Mexico, and Javier Solana, former European Union high representative for foreign and security policy.
49. Global Commission on Drug Policy, *War on Drugs*, June 2011, www.globalcommissionondrugs.org/; for commentary see Martin Wolf, "We Should End Our Disastrous War on Drugs," *Financial Times*, 3 June 2011; for an earlier case, see Ethan Nadelmann, "Drug Prohibition in the United States: Costs, Consequences, and Alternatives," *Science*, New Series, 245(4921) (1 September 1989): pp. 939–47 and Letters, *Science* 246(4934) (1 December 1989): pp. 1102–05. "How to Stop the Drug Wars," *The Economist*, 7–13 March 2009; Milton Friedman and Thomas Szasz, *On Liberty and Drugs: Essays on the Free Market and Prohibition* (Washington, DC: The Drug Policy Foundation Press, 1992); Ted Galen Carpenter, "How the Drug War in Afghanistan Undermines America's War on Terror," Foreign Policy Briefing No. 84, 10 November 2004 (Washington, DC: CATO Institute); for a debate and alternative views, see Douglas Husak and Peter de Marneffe, *The Legalization of Drugs* (Cambridge: Cambridge University Press, 2005) and James Inciardi

(ed.), *The Drug Legalization Debate (second edition)* (Thousand Oaks, CA: Sage, 1999).

50. Antonio Maria Costa, "Legalise Drugs and a Worldwide Epidemic of Addiction Will Follow," *Observer* (London), 5 September 2010.

51. Nadelmann, "Drug Prohibition in the United States."

52. WHO, *Report on the Global Tobacco Epidemic, 2008*. The Philip Morris documents are internal company documents quoted on pp. 37 and 26 of the WHO report.

53. WHO, *Report on the Global Tobacco Epidemic, 2009*, p. 64 (2008 data); Satcher quoted in WHO, *Report on the Global Tobacco Epidemic, 2008*, p. 47.

54. WHO, *Global Status Report on Alcohol and Health*, p. 46.

55. WHO, *Tobacco Industry Interference with Tobacco Control* (Geneva: WHO, 2008), p. v; E.R. Shaffer, J.E. Brenner, and T.P. Houston, "International Trade Agreements: A Threat to Tobacco Control Policy," *Tobacco Control* 14 (2005): p. ii24; the Philip Morris quote is from the text of discussion document used at top management meeting, 29 March 1985, and is quoted on p. ii23. See also Donald Zeigler, "International Trade Agreements Challenge Tobacco and Alcohol Control Policies," *Drug and Alcohol Review* 25 (November 2006).

56. GAO, *Trade and Health Issues*, May 1990 (Washington, DC: GAO), p. 6.

57. James Nathan, "Ending the Taliban's Money Stream: U.S. Should Buy Afghanistan's Opium," *Washington Times*, 8 January 2009.

58. Ethan Nadelmann, "Let Afghanistan Grow the World's Opium Supply," 31 August 2007, www.alternet.org/world/61144/.

CHAPTER 8

1. True, recent news reports have emphasized the presence of potentially large mineral deposits in Afghanistan, including copper and lithium, which could allegedly give a direct economic rationale for Washington's occupation of the country. China and India have already shown interest in those resources. Nevertheless, it will take many years before the minerals can be extracted, and their profitability remains uncertain. In any case, they are not the reason why the United States intervened in Afghanistan. James Risen, "U.S. Identifies Vast Mineral Riches in Afghanistan," *New York Times*, 13 June 2010; Robert Cutler, "Kabul Starts Race for Afghan Resources," *Asia Times online*, 15 December 2011; Jim Lobe, "Pentagon Strikes it Rich," *Asia Times online*, 16 June 2010.

2. Quoted in Ahmed Rashid, *Taliban: Militant Islam, Oil and Fundamentalism in Central Asia* (New Haven: Yale University Press, 2001), p. 145.

3. Milton Bearden, "Afghanistan, Graveyard of Empires," *Foreign Affairs* 80(6) (2001): pp. 17–30; Seth Jones, *In the Graveyard of Empires: America's War in Afghanistan* (New York: W.W. Norton, 2009).

4. Rashid, *Taliban*; Lutz Kleveman, *The New Great Game: Blood and Oil in Central Asia* (London: Atlantic Books, 2004); Elizabeth Gould and Paul Fitzgerald, *Crossing Zero: The AfPak War at the Turning Point of American Empire* (San Francisco, CA: City Lights, 2011).

5. White House, "Fact Sheet: The U.S.-Afghanistan Strategic Partnership Agreement," 1 May 2012, www.whitehouse.gov/the-press-office/2012/05/01/fact-sheet-us-afghanistan-strategic-partnership-agreement; Matthew Rosenberg and Graham Bowley, "U.S. Grants Special Ally Status to Afghans, Easing Fears of Abandonment," *New York Times*, 7 July 2012.

6. Robert Cutler, "TAPI Deals Nudge Pipeline Nearer Reality," *Asia Times online*, 19 August 2011; M.K. Bhadrakumar, "US Breathes Life Into a New Cold War," *Asia Times online*, 7 June 2011.

7. Barack Obama, "Address to the Nation on the Drawdown of United States Military Personnel in Afghanistan," 22 June 2011, www.presidency.ucsb.edu/ws/?pid=90556.

8. Kenneth Katzmann, *Afghanistan: Post-Taliban Governance, Security, and U.S. Policy*, 4 April 2012 (Washington, DC: Congressional Research Service), Tables 13 and 14; Amy Belasco, *The Cost of Iraq, Afghanistan, and Other Global War on Terror Operations Since 9/11*, 29 March 2011 (Washington, DC: Congressional Research Service). The $443 billion figure is about incremental costs only, that is, costs incurred due to the conduct of the war in Afghanistan. For example, it includes special combat pay for troops, but not troops' regular salaries, which would be paid even in the absence of war. Total counternarcotics funding was $5.227 billion for 2002–10.

9. Lydia Poole, *Afghanistan: Tracking Major Resource Flows 2002–2010* (London: Global Humanitarian Assistance, January 2011). Concern Worldwide et al., "Quick Impact, Quick Collapse: The Dangers of Militarized Aid in Afghanistan," January 2010, www.oxfam.org/sites/www.oxfam.org/files/quick-impact-quick-collapse-jan-2010.pdf. See also Curt Tarnoff, *Afghanistan: U.S. Foreign Assistance*, 12 August 2010 (Washington, DC: Congressional Research Service).

Bibliography

ABC News (2001) "The President; Bush Rejects Taliban's Offer to Hand over Osama bin Laden to Neutral Country for Trial," World News Tonight Sunday, 14 October.

Acheson, D. (1987 [1969]) *Present at the Creation: My Years in the State Department* (New York: Norton).

Afghan Rights Monitor (2009) *The Winning Warlords*, (Kabul: ARM).

Aikins, M. (2009) "The Master of Spin Boldak: Undercover with Afghanistan's Drug-Trafficking Border Police," *Harper's*, December.

Aikins, M. (2011) "Our Man in Kandahar," *The Atlantic*, November.

Albright, M. and Berger, S. (1998) "Press Briefing by Secretary of State Madeleine Albright and National Security Advisor Sandy Berger," 20 August, www.presidency.ucsb.edu/.

Alliot-Marie, M. (2004) "Afghanistan's Drug Boom; The Opium Problem Could Undo Everything That's Being Done To Help the Afghan People," *Washington Post*, 6 October.

Allix, S. (1998) *La Petite Cuillère de Shéhérazade: Sur la Route de l'Héroïne* (Paris: Ramsay).

Amnesty International (1995a) "Afghanistan: International Responsibility for Human Rights Disaster," www.amnesty.org/en/library/info/ASA11/009/1995/en.

Amnesty International (1995b) "Afghanistan: Foreign-Sponsored Human Rights Disaster Ignored by the World," November, www-secure.amnesty.org/en/library/asset/ASA11/016/1995/en/89d6399f-eb28-11dd-92ac-295bdf97101f/asa110161995en.html.

Anderson, J.L. (2005) "American Viceroy: Zalmay Khalilzad's Mission," *The New Yorker*, 19 December.

Anderson, J.W. (1992) "Two Banks, Blended Scandal," *Washington Post*, 16 November.

Applebaum, A. (2007) "Ending an Opium War: Poppies and Afghan Recovery Can Both Bloom," *Washington Post*, 16 January.

Asad, A.Z. and Harris, R. (2003) *The Politics and Economics of Drug production on the Pakistan-Afghanistan Border* (Aldershot: Ashgate).

Ashton, C. (2010) Speech to the European Parliament, Speech/10/756, 15 December, http://europa.eu/rapid/pressReleasesAction.do?reference=SPEECH/10/756&type=HTML.

Astorga, L. (2004) "Mexico: Drugs and Politics," in M. Vellinga (ed.), *The Political Economy of the Drug Industry: Latin America and the International System* (Gainesville, FL: University Press of Florida), pp. 85–102.

Azam, S.M. (2001) "US Attacks Taliban Frontline, Rejects Bin Laden Trial Offer," *AFP*, 14 October.

Babor, T. et al. (2010) *Drug Policy and the Public Good* (Oxford: Oxford University Press).

Barletta, M. (1998) "Chemical Weapons in the Sudan: Allegations and Evidence," *The Nonproliferation Review* (Fall):115–36.

BBC News (2009) "Envoy Damns US Afghan Drug Effort", 21 March, http://news.
bbc.co.uk/2/hi/south_asia/7957237.stm.

Bearden, M. (2001) "Afghanistan, Graveyard of Empires," *Foreign Affairs*
80(6):17–30.

Beaty, J. and Gwynne, S.C. (1993) *The Outlaw Bank: A Wild Ride into The Secret
Heart of BCCI* (New York: Random House).

Beers, R. (2002) "Narco-Terror: The Worldwide Connection between Drugs and
Terrorism," Hearing before the US Senate Judiciary Committee, Subcommittee
on Technology, Terrorism, and Government Information, 13 March (Washington,
DC: Government Printing Office).

Belasco, A. (2011) *The Cost of Iraq, Afghanistan, and Other Global War on Terror
Operations Since 9/11*, 29 March (Washington, DC: Congressional Research
Service).

Bhadrakumar, M.K. (2011) "US Breathes Life Into a New Cold War," *Asia Times
online*, 7 June.

Bhattacharji, R. and Kamminga, J. (2010) "Poppy for Medicine: An Essential Part
of a Balanced Economic Development Solution for Afghanistan's Illegal Opium
Economy," *Journal of Drug Policy Analysis* 3(1):1–9.

Blanchard, C. (2009) *Afghanistan: Narcotics and U.S. Policy*, 7 October (Washington,
DC: Congressional Research Service).

Block, F. (1980) "Economic Instability and Military Strength: The Paradoxes of the
1950 Rearmament Decision," *Politics & Society* 10(1):35–58.

Bonner, A. (1986) "Afghan Rebel's Victory Garden: Opium," *New York Times*,
18 June.

Booth, M. (1996) *Opium: A History* (New York: St. Martin's Press).

Boyum, D. and Reuter, P. (2005) *An Analytic Assessment of U.S. Drug Policy*
(Washington, DC: The American Enterprise Institute Press).

Braithwaite, R. (2011) *Afgantsy: The Russians in Afghanistan 1979–1989* (London:
Profile Books).

Braun, M. (2009) Statement for the Record before the U.S. Senate Caucus on
International Narcotics Control Regarding "U.S. Counternarcotics Strategy
in Afghanistan," 21 October, http://drugcaucus.senate.gov/Braun-State-
ment-10-21-09.pdf.

Brodsky, A. (2003) *With All Our Strength: The Revolutionary Association of the
Women of Afghanistan* (New York: Routledge).

Brookings Institution (various dates) *Afghanistan Index*, www.brookings.edu/
foreign-policy/afghanistan-index.aspx.

Brown, J. (2002) "A Coalition of Hope," *Ms. Magazine* (Spring).

Brzezinski, Z. (1983) *Power and Principle: Memoirs of the National Security Advisor
1977–1981* (London: Weidenfeld and Nicolson).

Brzezinski, Z. (1997) *The Grand Chessboard: American Primacy and Its Geostrategic
Imperatives* (New York: Basic Books).

Burke, J. (2007) *Al-Qaeda: The True Story of Radical Islam* (third edition) (London:
Penguin).

Burns, J.F. (1995) "With Kabul Largely in Ruins, Afghans Get Respite From War,"
New York Times, 20 February.

Burns, J.F. (1996) "Afghan Capital Grim as War Follows War," *New York Times*,
5 February.

Burns, J.F. (2002) "Afghan Warlords Squeeze Profits from the War on Drugs, Critics
Say," *New York Times*, 5 May.

Bush, G.W. (2001a) "Letter to Congressional Leaders on Continuation of the National Emergency With Respect to the Taliban," 30 June, www.presidency.ucsb.edu/ws/?pid=64110.

Bush, G.W. (2001b) "The President's Radio Address," 15 September 2001, www.presidency.ucsb.edu/ws/?pid=25001.

Bush, G.W. (2001c) "Address Before a Joint Session of the Congress on the United States Response to the Terrorist Attacks of September 11," 20 September, www.presidency.ucsb.edu/ws/?pid=64731.

Bush, G.W. (2001d) "Remarks With President Vladimir Putin of Russia and a Question-and-Answer Session With Crawford High School Students in Crawford," 15 November, www.presidency.ucsb.edu/ws/?pid=73461.

Bush, G.W. (2002) "Remarks on the 2002 National Drug Control Strategy," 12 February, www.presidency.ucsb.edu/ws/?pid=72976.

Carpenter, T.G. (2004) "How the Drug War in Afghanistan Undermines America's War on Terror," Foreign Policy Briefing No. 84, 10 November (Washington, DC: CATO Institute).

Carter, J. (1980) "State of the Union Address 1980," 23 January, www.jimmycarterlibrary.gov/documents/speeches/su80jec.phtml.

CATO Institute (2009) CATO Handbook for Policymakers (7th edition) (Washington, DC: CATO Institute).

Caulkins, J., Kleiman, M. and Kulick, J. (2010) Drug Production and Trafficking, Counterdrug Policies, and Security and Governance in Afghanistan (New York: New York University Center on International Cooperation).

Caulkins, J. Kulick, J. and Kleiman, M. (2011) "Think Again: The Afghan Drug Trade," Foreign Policy, 1 April, www.foreignpolicy.com/articles/2011/04/01/think_again_the_afghan_drug_trade?page=full.

Caulkins, J. Pacula, R.L., Paddock, S. and Chiesa, J. (2002) School-Based Drug Prevention: What Kind of Drug Use Does It Prevent? (Santa Monica, CA: RAND).

Chandra, V. (2006) "Warlords, Drugs and the "War on Terror" in Afghanistan: The Paradoxes," Strategic Analysis 30(1):64–92.

Charles, R. (2004) "U.S. Policy and Colombia," Testimony before the House Committee on Government Reform, 17 June, merln.ndu.edu/archivepdf/colombia/State/33663.pdf.

Chien, A., Connors, M. and Fox, K. (2000) "The Drug War in Perspective," in J.Y. Kim et al. (eds.), Dying for Growth (Monroe, ME: Common Courage), pp. 293–327.

Chomsky, N. (1992) Deterring Democracy (New York: Hill and Wang).

Chomsky, N. (1996) World Orders Old and New (New York: Columbia University Press).

Chomsky, N. (2000) Rogue States: The Rule of Force in World Affairs (Cambridge, MA: South End Press).

Chossudovsky, M. (2004) "The Spoils of War: Afghanistan's Multibillion Heroin Trade," Global Research, 5 April, www.globalresearch.ca/articles/CHO404A.html.

Chossudovsky, M. (2006) "Who Benefits from the Afghan Opium Trade?," Global Research, 21 September, www.globalresearch.ca/index.php?context=va&aid=3294.

Chouvy, P.-A. (2006) "Licensing Afghanistan's Opium: Solution or Fallacy?," Caucasian Review of International Affairs 2(2):101–06.

Chouvy, P.-A. (2009) *Opium: Uncovering the Politics of the Poppy* (London: I.B. Tauris).

Clarke, R. (2010) *Hashish!* (2nd edition) (Los Angeles: Red Eye Press).

Clinton, B. (1999a) "Statement on the National Emergency With Respect to the Taliban," 6 July, www.presidency.ucsb.edu/ws/?pid=57840.

Clinton, B. (1999b) "Statement on United Nations Sanctions Against the Taliban," 15 November, www.presidency.ucsb.edu/ws/?pid=56938#axzz1q3k4SwiB.

Cockburn, A. (1991) "Bankers to the New World Scum Class BCCI and its Ilk Flourish Because They Serve the Needs of Spies, Tyrants and Crooks," *Los Angeles Times*, 1 August.

Cockburn, A. (1991) "Shady, Yes, but Not the Least Bit Unusual : Are We Pretending that, Unlike BCCI, Western Banks Don't Launder Dirty Money?," *Los Angeles Times*, 21 July.

Cockburn, A. and St. Clair, J. (1998) *Whiteout: The CIA, Drugs and the Press* (London: Verso).

Coll, S. (2004) *Ghost Wars: The Secret History of the CIA, Afghanistan, and Bin Laden, from the Soviet Invasion to September 10, 2001* (New York: Penguin).

Concern Worldwide et al. (2010) "Quick Impact, Quick Collapse: The Dangers of Militarized Aid in Afghanistan," January, www.oxfam.org/sites/www.oxfam.org/files/quick-impact-quick-collapse-jan-2010.pdf.

Cook, C., Bridge, J. and Stimson, G. (2010) "The Diffusion of Harm Reduction in Europe and Beyond," in T. Rhodes and D. Hedrich (eds.), *Harm Reduction: Evidence, Impacts and Challenges*, European Monitoring Centre for Drugs and Drug Addiction (EMCDDA) Monographs (Luxembourg: Publications Office of the European Union), pp. 37–58.

Cooley, J. (2002) *Unholy Wars: Afghanistan, America and International Terrorism* (third edition) (London: Pluto).

Costa, A.M. (2010) "Legalise Drugs and a Worldwide Epidemic of Addiction Will Follow," *The Observer* (London), 5 September.

Cordovez, D. and Harrison, S. (1995) *Out of Afghanistan: The Inside Story of the Soviet Withdrawal* (Oxford: Oxford University Press).

Crane, B., Rivolo, R. and Comfort, G. (1997) *An Empirical Examination of Counterdrug Interdiction Program Effectiveness* (Alexandria: Institute for Defense Analyses).

Crossette, B. (2001) "U.S. Sends 2 to Assess Drug Program for Afghans," *New York Times*, 25 April.

Cutler, R. (2011) "TAPI Deals Nudge Pipeline Nearer Reality," *Asia Times online*, 19 August.

Cutler, R. (2011) "Kabul Starts Race for Afghan Resources," *Asia Times online*, 15 December.

Daum, W. (2001) "Universalism and the West," *Harvard International Review* 23(2):19–23.

Deen, T. (2001) "Drugs: U.N. Pays Rare Compliment to Taliban Over Opium Ban," *Inter Press Service*, 9 August.

Degenhardt, L. et al. (2008) "Toward a Global View of Alcohol, Tobacco, Cannabis, and Cocaine Use: Findings from the WHO World Mental Health Surveys," *PLoS Medicine* 5(7):1053–67.

Dorronsoro, G. (2005) *Revolution Unending; Afghanistan: 1979 to the Present* (London: Hurst).

Draper, R. and Guttenfelder, D. (2011) "Opium Wars," *National Geographic Magazine*, 219(2):58–83.

Drug Policy Alliance (2006) *Repeating Mistakes of the Past: Another Mycoherbicide Research Bill*, March, www.drugpolicy.org.

The Economist (London) (2002) "The Poppies Bloom Again," 18 April.

The Economist (London) (2009) "How to Stop the Drug Wars," 7–13 March.

Ehrenfeld, R. (2005) *Funding Evil: How Terrorism is Financed—And How To Stop It* (expanded edition) (Chicago and Los Angeles: Bonus Books).

EMCDDA (2010) *2010 Annual Report on the State of the Drugs Problem in Europe* (Luxembourg: Publications Office of the European Union).

EMCDDA (2009) *2009 Annual Report on the State of the Drugs Problem in Europe* (Luxembourg: Publications Office of the European Union).

Elovich, R. and Drucker, E. (2008) "On Drug Treatment and Social Control: Russian Narcology's Great Leap Backwards," *Harm Reduction Journal* 5(23).

European Commission (2008) *Report of the Final Evaluation of the EU Drugs Action Plan (2005–2008)*, http://ec.europa.eu/health/.

Farniaa, M., Ebrahimia, B., Shamsa, A. and Zamanib, S. (2010) "Scaling Up Methadone Maintenance Treatment for Opioid-Dependent Prisoners in Iran," *International Journal of Drug Policy* 21(5):422–4.

Feifer, G. (2009) *The Great Gamble: The Soviet War in Afghanistan* (New York: Harper).

Felbab-Brown, V. (2007) "Opium Licensing in Afghanistan: Its Desirability and Feasibility," August, Policy Paper No. 1 (Washington, DC: Brookings Institution).

Felbab-Brown, V. (2010) *Shooting Up: Counterinsurgency and the War on Drugs* (Washington, DC: Brookings Institution Press).

Filkins, D. (2010) "Rule of the Gun: Convoy Guards in Afghanistan Face Inquiry," *New York Times*, 6 June.

Filkins, D., Mazzetti, M., and Risen, J. (2009) "Brother of Afghan Leader Said to Be Paid by CIA," *New York Times*, 27 October.

Fist, A.J. (2001) "The Tasmanian Poppy Industry: A Case Study of the Application of Science and Technology," www.regional.org.au/au/asa/2001/plenary/1/fist.htm.

Fitzgerald, P. and Gould, E. (2009) *Invisible History: Afghanistan's Untold Story* (San Francisco, CA: City Lights).

Freeman, L. and Sierra, J.L. (2005) "Mexico: The Militarization Trap," in C. Youngers and E. Rosin (eds.), *Drugs and Democracy in Latin America* (Boulder, CO: Lynne Rienner), pp. 263–302.

Friedman, M. and Szasz, T. (1992) *On Liberty and Drugs: Essays on the Free Market and Prohibition* (Washington, DC: The Drug Policy Foundation Press).

Friedman, T. (1992) "U.S. Urges Afghan Factions To Avoid Violent Anarchy," *New York Times*, 17 April.

Friedman, T. (1998) "Motives For the Bombing," *New York Times*, 8 August.

Friedman, T. (2009). "The Class Too Dumb to Quit," *New York Times*, 21 July.

Gandhi, S. (2003) The September 11th Sourcebooks, Volume VII: The Taliban File, National Security Archive Electronic Briefing Book No. 97, 11 September, www.gwu.edu/~nsarchiv/NSAEBB/NSAEBB97/index.htm.

Gandhi, S. (2004) "The Taliban File Part III," National Security Archive, 19 March, www.gwu.edu/~nsarchiv/NSAEBB/NSAEBB97/index4.htm.

GAO (1990) *Trade and Health Issues*, May (Washington, DC: GAO).

GAO (1998) *Private Banking: Raul Salinas, Citibank, and Alleged Money Laundering*, October, www.gao.gov/archive/1999/os99001.pdf.

GAO (2006) *Afghanistan Drug Control: Despite Improved Efforts, Deteriorating Security Threatens Success of U.S. Goals*, November, www.gao.gov/assets/260/253513.pdf.

GAO (2010a) *Afghanistan Drug Control: Strategy Evolving and Progress Reported, but Interim Performance Targets and Evaluation of Justice Reform Efforts Needed*, March, www.gao.gov/new.items/d10291.pdf.

GAO (2010b) *Afghanistan Development: Enhancements to Performance Management and Evaluation Efforts Could Improve USAID's Agricultural Programs*, July, GAO-10–368 (Washington, DC: GAO).

Garthoff, R. (1994) *Détente and Confrontation: American-Soviet Relations from Nixon to Reagan* (revised edition) (Washington, DC: Brookings Institution).

Gates, R. (1996) *From the Shadows: The Ultimate Insider's Story of Five Presidents and How They Won the Cold War* (New York: Simon & Schuster).

Galster, S. (2001) "Afghanistan: The Making of U.S. Policy, 1973–1990," National Security Archive, www.gwu.edu/~nsarchiv/NSAEBB/NSAEBB57/essay.html.

George, A. (ed.) (1991) *Western State Terrorism* (Cambridge: Polity Press).

Getler, M. (1981) "Sadat's Remarks on Afghan Arms Vex U.S.," *Washington Post*, 24 September.

Girardet, E. (1980a) "Afghanistan Rebels Plan United Front Against Soviet Forces," *Christian Science Monitor*, 14 May.

Girardet, E. (1980b) "Afghan Rebels: More Time Squabbling Than Fighting," *Christian Science Monitor*, 24 June.

Giustozzi, A. (2008) *Koran, Kalashnikov and Laptop: The Neo-Taliban Insurgency in Afghanistan* (New York: Columbia University Press).

Giustozzi, A. (2009) *Empires of Mud: Wars and Warlords in Afghanistan* (London: Hurst).

Globe and Mail (2006) "The Afghan Poppy Trade," editorial, 21 November.

Goetschel, S. (dir.) (2005) "Our Own Private bin Laden" Chastè Films.

Golden, T. (1998) "Swiss Recount Key Drug Role of Salinas Kin," *New York Times*, 19 September.

Goodhand, J. (2005) "Frontiers and Wars: The Opium Economy in Afghanistan," *Journal of Agrarian Change* 5(2):191–216.

Gordon, M.R. (2001) "A Nation Challenged: The Strategy; Allies Preparing for a Long Fight as Taliban Dig In," *New York Times*, 28 October.

Gould, E. and Fitzgerald, P. (2011) *Crossing Zero: The AfPak War at the Turning Point of American Empire* (San Francisco, CA: City Lights).

Greenfield, V., Paoli, L., and Reuter, P. (2009) "Is Medicinal Opium Production Afghanistan's Answer?: Lessons from India and the World Market," *Journal of Drug Policy Analysis* 2(1):1–15.

Greenfield, V., Paoli, L. and Reuter, P. (2010) "Is Medicinal Opium Production Afghanistan's Answer?: A Reply to Comments," *Journal of Drug Policy Analysis* 3(1):1–2.

Greenwald, G. (2009) *Drug Decriminalization in Portugal* (Washington, DC: CATO Institute).

Griffin, M. (2001) *Reaping the Whirlwind: The Taliban Movement in Afghanistan* (London: Pluto).

Hafvenstein, J. (2006) "Afghanistan's Drug Habit," *New York Times*, 20 September.

Hafvenstein, J. (2007) *Opium Season: A Year on the Afghan Frontier* (Guilford, CT: Guilford Press).

Haq, M.E. (2000) *Drugs in South Asia: From the Opium Trade to the Present Day* (London: Macmillan).

Hearden, P. (2005) *The Tragedy of Vietnam* (2nd ed.) (New York: Pearson Longman).

Hedrich, D. et al. (2008) "From Margin to Mainstream: The Evolution of Harm Reduction Responses to Problem Drug Use in Europe," *Drugs: Education, Prevention and Policy* 15(6): 503–17.

Hiro, D. (2006) "Shanghai Surprise: The Summit of the Shanghai Cooperation Organisation Reveals How Power Is Shifting in the World," *The Guardian*, 16 June.

Hoagland, J. (2004) "A New Afghan Policy," *Washington Post*, 8 August.

Hoagland, J. (2007) "Poppies vs. Power in Afghanistan," *Washington Post*, 23 December.

Hogan, M.J. and Paterson, T.G. (eds.) (2004) *Explaining the History of American Foreign Relations* (2nd edition) (Cambridge: Cambridge University Press).

Holbrooke, R. (2008) "Still Wrong in Afghanistan," *Washington Post*, 23 January.

Hughes, C. and Stevens, A. (2010) "What Can We Learn from the Portuguese Decriminalization of Illicit Drugs?," *British Journal of Criminology* 50(6):1–24.

Human Rights Watch (2000) "Letter to U.N. Security Council," 14 December, www.hrw.org/en/news/2000/12/13/letter-un-security-council.

Human Rights Watch (2002) *Afghanistan: Return of the Warlords*, June, http://reliefweb.int/sites/reliefweb.int/files/resources/7340173745BD5C6E49256BD0001BEEF0-hrw-afg-6jun.pdf.

Human Rights Watch (2003a) *World Report 2003* (New York: HRW).

Human Rights Watch (2003b) *"Killing You Is a Very Easy Thing for Us": Human Rights Abuses in Southeast Afghanistan*, July (New York: HRW).

Human Rights Watch (2003c) *Sudan, Oil, and Human Rights*, www.unhcr.org/refworld/docid/3fe4807d7.html.

Human Rights Watch (2004) *The Rule of the Gun: Human Rights Abuses and Political Repression in the Run-up to Afghanistan's Presidential Election*, September, www.hrw.org/legacy/backgrounder/asia/afghanistan0904/afghanistan0904.pdf.

Human Rights Watch (2005) *Blood-Stained Hands: Past Atrocities in Kabul and Afghanistan's Legacy of Impunity* (New York: HRW).

Human Rights Watch (2009a) *Please, Do Not Make Us Suffer Any More...: Access to Pain Treatment as a Human Right* (New York: HRW).

Human Rights Watch (2009b) "Letter to President Barack Obama on Afghanistan," 26 March, www.hrw.org/en/news/2009/03/26/human-rights-watch-letter-president-barack-obama-afghanistan.

Husak, D. and de Marneffe, P. (2005) *The Legalization of Drugs* (Cambridge: Cambridge University Press).

ICOS (2009) "Eight Years After 9/11 Taliban Now Have a Permanent Presence in 80% of Afghanistan," 10 September, www.icosgroup.net/2009/media/media-press-releases/eight_years_after_911/

Inciardi, J. (ed.) (1999) *The Drug Legalization Debate (second edition)* (Thousand Oaks, CA: Sage).

International Narcotics Control Board (2010) *Precursors and Chemicals Frequently Used in the Illicit Manufacture of Narcotic Drugs and Psychotropic Substances, 2009* (New York: United Nations).

International Narcotics Control Board (2011) *Precursors and Chemicals Frequently Used in the Illicit Manufacture of Narcotic Drugs and Psychotropic Substances, 2010* (New York: United Nations).

IRIN (2010) "Afghanistan: Running on Drugs, Corruption and Aid," IRIN, 10 May, www.irinnews.org/Report.aspx?ReportID=89078.

Jelsma, M. (2005) "Learning Lessons from the Taliban Opium Ban," *International Journal of Drug Policy* 16(2):98–103.

Johnson, C. and Leslie, J. (2008) *Afghanistan: The Mirage of Peace* (updated edition) (London: Zed Books).

Jones, S. (2009) *In the Graveyard of Empires: America's War in Afghanistan* (New York: W.W. Norton).

Joya, M. (2009) *Raising my Voice: The Extraordinary Story of the Afghan Woman Who Dares to Speak Out* (London: Rider).

Kakar, M.H. (1997) *Afghanistan: The Soviet Invasion and the Afghan Response, 1979–1982* (Berkeley, CA: University of California Press).

Katzman, K. (2011) *Afghanistan: Post-Taliban Governance, Security, and U.S. Policy*, 22 November, (Washington, DC: Congressional Research Service).

Katzman, K. (2012) *Afghanistan: Post-Taliban Governance, Security, and U.S. Policy*, 4 April, (Washington, DC: Congressional Research Service).

Kenna, K. (1998) "Hollywood's Cause; Celebrities Challenge the Taleban Stars Say Their Campaign's Goal is to Restore Women's Rights," *Toronto Star*, 22 November.

Kennan, G. (1948) "Review of Current Trends in U.S. Foreign Policy," PPS/23, in US Department of State, *Foreign Relations of the United States*, 1948, volume 1, part 2 (Washington, DC: Government Printing Office, 1976), pp. 524–5.

Khalilzad, Z. (1996) "Afghanistan: Time to Reengage," *Washington Post*, 7 October.

Khalilzad, Z. and Byman, D. (2000) "Afghanistan: The Consolidation of a Rogue State," *The Washington Quarterly* 23(1):65–78.

King, L. (2001) "Taliban Delivers Message to bin Laden; Aid Workers' Trial Resume; Rebel Patrol Pushes Close to Kabul," *Associated Press Worldstream*, 27 September.

Klare, M. (1980) "Resurgent Militarism," in H. Sklar (ed.), *Trilateralism: The Trilateral Commission and Elite Planning for World Management* (Boston: South End Press), pp. 269–91.

Klare, M. (2002) *Resource Wars: The New Landscape of Global Conflict* (New York: Metropolitan Books).

Klare, M. (2008) *Rising Powers, Shrinking Planet: The New Geopolitics of Energy* (Oxford: Oneworld).

Klare, M. (2012) "Danger Waters: The Three Hot Spots of Potential Conflict in the Geo-Energy Era," 10 January, TomDispatch.com.

Kleiman, M. (2009) *When Brute Force Fails: How To Have Less Crime and Less Punishment* (Princeton: Princeton University Press).

Kleveman, L. (2004) *The New Great Game: Blood and Oil in Central Asia* (London: Atlantic Books).

Kolhatkar, S. and Ingalls, J. (2006) *Bleeding Afghanistan: Washington, Warlords, and the Propaganda of Silence* (New York: Seven Stories Press).

Kolko, G. (2006) *The Age of War* (Boulder: Lynne Rienner).

Kolko, J. and Kolko, G. (1972) *The Limits of Power: The World and United States Foreign Policy 1945–1954* (New York: Harper & Row).

Krauthammer, C. (2001) "The Real New World Order: The American and the Islamic Challenge," *The Weekly Standard* 7(9), 12 November.

Kuzmarov, J. (2009) *The Myth of the Addicted Army: Vietnam and the Modern War on Drugs* (Amherst: University of Massachusetts Press).

Labrousse, A. (2005) *Opium de Guerre, Opium de Paix* (Paris: Mille et Une Nuits).

Lachowski, Z. (2007) *Foreign Military Bases in Central Asia*, SIPRI Policy Paper No. 18 (Solna: SIPRI).

Lardner, G. Jr (1991) "CIA Probed, Used BCCI, Official Says, *Washington Post*, 3 August.

Lasseter, T. (2009) "U.S.-Built Bridge Is Windfall—For Illegal Afghan Drug Trade," *McClatchy Newspapers*, 28 June.

Latin American Commission on Drugs and Democracy (2009) *Drugs & Democracy: Towards a Paradigm Shift*, www.drogasedemocracia.org/.

Leffler, M. (1983) "From the Truman Doctrine to the Carter Doctrine: Lessons and Dilemmas of the Cold War," *Diplomatic History* 7(4):245–66.

Leffler, M. (1988) "The United States and the Strategic Dimensions of the Marshall Plan," *Diplomatic History* 12(3):277–306.

Lewis, D. (2010) "High Times on the Silk Road: The Central Asian Paradox," *World Policy Journal* 27(1):39–49.

Lifschultz, L. (1992) "Pakistan: The Empire of Heroin," in A. McCoy and A. Block (eds.), *War on Drugs: Studies in the Failure of U.S. Narcotics Policy* (Boulder: Westview Press), pp. 319–58.

Lobe, J. (2010) "Pentagon Strikes it Rich," *Asia Times online*, 16 June.

Los Angeles Times (1998) "Air Raids Necessary," editorial, 21 August.

MacCoun, R. (1993) "Drugs and the Law: A Psychological Analysis of Drug Prohibition," *Psychological Bulletin* 113(3):497–512.

MacCoun, R. and Reuter, P. (2001) *Drug War Heresies: Learning from Other Vices, Times, and Places* (Cambridge: Cambridge University Press).

Macdonald, D. (2007) *Drugs in Afghanistan: Opium, Outlaws and Scorpion Tales* (London: Pluto).

Mackenzie, R. (2001 [1998]) "The United States and the Taliban," in W. Maley (ed.), *Fundamentalism Reborn? Afghanistan and the Taliban* (London: Hurst & Company), pp. 90–103.

Madsen, W. (2002) "Afghanistan, the Taliban and the Bush Oil Team," 23 January, http://globalresearch.ca/articles/MAD201A.html.

Magnus, R. and Naby, E. (2002) *Afghanistan: Mullah, Marx, and Mujahid* (Boulder, CO: Westview).

Mahajan, R. (2001) "We Think the Price Is Worth It," *Extra!* (November/December), www.fair.org/index.php?page=1084.

Major Donors Mission (2001) "The Impact of the Taliban Prohibition on Opium Poppy Cultivation in Afghanistan. A Mission Report Presented to the Major Donors Countries of UNDCP," 25 May.

Maley, W. (2000) *The Foreign Policy of the Taliban* (New York: Council on Foreign Relations Press).

Mansfield, D. (2001) "An Analysis of Licit Opium Poppy Cultivation: Turkey and India," www.davidmansfield.org/.

Mansfield, D. (2010) "Where Have All the Flowers Gone? Assessing the Sustainability of Current Reductions in Opium Production in Afghanistan," (Kabul: AREU).

Mansfield, D. and Pain, A. (2005) *Alternative Livelihoods: Substance or Slogan?* (Kabul: AREU).

Manski, C., Pepper, J. and Petrie, C. (eds.) (2001) *Informing America's Policy on Illegal Drugs: What We Don't Know Keeps Hurting Us* (Washington, DC: National Academy Press).

Manski, C., Pepper, J. and Thomas, Y. (1999) *Assessment of Two Cost-Effectiveness Studies on Cocaine Control Policy* (Washington, DC: National Academy Press).

Mazzetti, M. (2009) "Reported Ties from C.I.A. to a Karzai Spur Rebukes," *New York Times*, 29 October.

McCormick, T.J. (1995) *America's Half-Century: United States Foreign Policy in the Cold War and After* (2nd edition) (Baltimore: Johns Hopkins University Press).

McCoy, A. (with Read, C. and Adams, L. II) (1972) *The Politics of Heroin in Southeast Asia* (New York: Harper & Row).

McCoy, A. (1991) *The Politics of Heroin: CIA Complicity in the Global Drug Trade* (Brooklyn, NY: Lawrence Hill Books).

McCoy, A. (1992) "Heroin as a Global Commodity: A History of Southeast Asia's Opium Trade," in A. McCoy and A. Block (eds.), *War on Drugs: Studies in the Failure of U.S. Narcotics Policy* (Boulder: Westview Press), pp. 237–79.

McCoy, A. (2000) "From Free Trade to Prohibition: A Critical History of the Modern Asian Opium Trade," *Fordham Urban Law Journal* 28:307–49.

McCoy, A. (2003) *The Politics of Heroin: CIA Complicity in the Global Drug Trade* (revised edition) (Chicago: Lawrence Hill Books).

McCoy, A. (2004) "The Stimulus of Prohibition: A Critical History of the Global Narcotics Trade," in M. Steinberg, J. Hobbs and K. Mathewson (eds.), *Dangerous Harvest: Drug Plants and the Transformation of Indigenous Landscapes* (Oxford: Oxford University Press), pp. 24–111.

McGirk, T. (2003) "Drugs? What drugs?," *TIME*, 18 August.

McMahon, R. (1991) "Credibility and World Power: Exploring the Psychological Dimension in Postwar American Diplomacy," *Diplomatic History* 15(4):455–71.

Mercille, J. (2009) "UN Report Misleading on Afghanistan," *Foreign Policy in Focus*, November, www.fpif.org/articles/un_report_misleading_on_afghanistans_drug_problem.

Mercille, J. (2010) "Afghan Hash At an All-Time High," *Asia Times online*, 20 April.

Mercille, J. (2011) "The U.S. 'War on Drugs' in Afghanistan: Reality or Pretext?" *Critical Asian Studies* 43(2):285–309.

Mercille, J. (2011) "Violent Narco-Cartels or US Hegemony? The Political Economy of the 'War on Drugs' in Mexico," *Third World Quarterly* 32(9):1637–53.

Meyer, J. (2006) "Pentagon Doing Little In Afghan Drug Fight," *Los Angeles Times*, 5 December.

Mishra, P. (2005) "The Real Afghanistan", *New York Review of Books* 52 (4), 10 March.

Misra, A. (2004) *Afghanistan: The Labyrinth of Violence* (Cambridge: Polity Press).

Moreau, R. and Yousafzai, S. (2003) "Flowers of Destruction," *Newsweek*, 14 July.

Moreau, R. and Yousafzai, S. (2006) "A Harvest Of Treachery; Afghanistan's Drug Trade Is Threatening the Stability of a Nation America Went to War to Stabilize. What Can Be Done?," *Newsweek*, 9 January.

Morgan, D. and Ottaway, D.B. (1998) "Women's Fury Toward Taliban Stalls Pipeline; Afghan Plan Snagged In U.S. Political Issues," *Washington Post*, 11 January.

Morley, J. (1989) "Contradictions of Cocaine Capitalism," *The Nation*, 2 October.

Nadelmann, E. (1989) "Drug Prohibition in the United States: Costs, Consequences, and Alternatives," *Science*, New Series, 245(4921):939–47.

Nadelmann, E. (2007) "Let Afghanistan Grow the World's Opium Supply," 31 August, www.alternet.org/world/61144/.

Nadelmann, E. (2010) "An Imperfect Improvement: Obama's New Drug War Strategy," *Huffington Post*, 11 May, www.huffingtonpost.com/ethan-nadelmann/ethan-nadelmann-critiques_b_571672.html.

Nathan, J. (2009) "Ending the Taliban's Money Stream: U.S. Should Buy Afghanistan's Opium," *Washington Times*, 8 January.

National Commission on Terrorist Attacks upon the United States (2004) *The 9/11 Commission Report* (authorized edition) (New York: W.W. Norton & Company).

National Energy Policy Development Group (2001) *National Energy Policy*, May, www.ne.doe.gov/pdfFiles/nationalEnergyPolicy.pdf.

National Security Archive (NSA) (2010) "'No-Go' Tribal Areas Became Basis for Afghan Insurgency Documents Show," electronic briefing book No. 325, 13 September, www.gwu.edu/~nsarchiv/NSAEBB/NSAEBB325/index.htm.

Nawa, F. (2011) *Opium Nation: Child Brides, Drug Lords, and One Woman's Journey Through Afghanistan* (New York: Harper Perennial).

Neumeister, L. (2008) "Federal officials in New York Say Afghan Tribal Chief Had Strong Links to Taliban in 2005," *Associated Press*, 3 May.

New York Times (1954) "The Iranian Accord," editorial, 6 August.

New York Times (1998) "Clinton's Words: 'There Will Be No Sanctuary for Terrorists'," 21 August.

New York Times (2001) "Bush Decides to Keep Afghan Sanctions," 3 July.

New York Times (2008) "Guns and Poppies," editorial, 5 August.

Nissaramanesh, B., Trace, M. and Roberts, M. (2005) "The Rise of Harm Reduction in the Islamic Republic of Iran," Beckley Foundation Briefing #8, July, www.beckleyfoundation.org/pdf/paper_08.pdf.

Njolstad, O. (2004) "Shifting Priorities: The Persian Gulf in US Strategic Planning in the Carter Years," *Cold War History* 4(3):21–55.

Le Nouvel Observateur [Paris] (1998) "Les Révélations d'un Ancien Conseiller de Carter: 'Oui, la CIA Est Entrée en Afghanistan Avant les Russes'," 15 January.

Obama, B. (2011) "Address to the Nation on the Drawdown of United States Military Personnel in Afghanistan," 22 June, www.presidency.ucsb.edu/ws/?pid=90556.

Obama, B. and Calderón, F. (2011) "Remarks by President Obama and President Calderon of Mexico at Joint Press Conference," 3 March, www.whitehouse.gov/the-press-office/2011/03/03/remarks-president-obama-and-president-calder-n-mexico-joint-press-confer.

Office of Inspectors General (2007) *Interagency Assessment of the Counternarcotics Program in Afghanistan*, July, (Department of State report no. ISP-I-07–34; Department of Defense report no. IE-2007-005), www.dodig.mil/inspections/ie/Reports/Counternarcotics_Pgr_Afghan%20_Final%20Rpt.pdf.

Office of Inspector General (2009) *Status of the Bureau of International Narcotics and Law Enforcement Affairs Counternarcotics Programs in Afghanistan: Performance Audit*, Report Number MERO-A-10-02, December, http://oig.state.gov/documents/organization/134183.pdf.

Office of the UN Coordinator for Afghanistan (2000) *Vulnerability And Humanitarian Implications of UN Security Council Sanctions in Afghanistan*, (Islamabad: United Nations).

Onishi, N. (2001) "Afghan Warlords and Bandits Are Back in Business," *New York Times*, 28 December.

Open Society Institute (2009) *At What Cost? HIV and Human Rights Consequences of the Global "War on Drugs"* (New York: Open Society Institute).

Orlova, A. (2009) "The Russian 'War on Drugs': A Kinder, Gentler Approach?", *Problems of Post-Communism* 56(1):23–34.

Overland, M.A. (2010) "Global Pain-Law Reform: Morphine Still Scarce for Many," TIME, 7 June.

Paoli, L., Greenfield, V. and Reuter, P. (2009) *The World Heroin Market: Can Supply Be Cut?* (Oxford: Oxford University Press).

Pennington, M. (2007) "Afghan Anti-Corruption Chief Is a Convicted Heroin Trafficker," *Associated Press*, 9 March.

Peters, G. (2009a) *Seeds of Terror: How Heroin is Bankrolling the Taliban and al Qaeda* (New York: St. Martin's Press).

Peters, G. (2009b) "The Taliban and the Opium Trade," in A. Giustozzi (ed.), *Decoding the New Taliban* (London: Hurst and Co., 2009).

Placido, A. (2010) "Transnational Drug Enterprises (Part II): Threats to Global Stability and U.S. Policy Responses," Statement before the House Oversight and Government Reform Subcommittee on National Security and Foreign Affairs, 3 March, www.justice.gov/dea/pubs/cngrtest/ct030310.pdf.

Poole, L. (2011) *Afghanistan: Tracking Major Resource Flows 2002–2010* (London: Global Humanitarian Assistance).

Press Association (2001) "Blair's Speech—Full Text, ", 2 October.

Prusher, I., Baldauf, S., and Girardet, E. (2002) "Afghan Power Brokers," *Christian Science Monitor*, 10 June.

Radio Free Europe (2009) "Human Rights Watch Chief "Appalled" by Afghan VP Choice," 7 May, www.rferl.org/content/Human_Rights_Watch_Chief_Appalled_by_Afghan_VP_Choice/1623813.html.

Rashid, A. (2001) *Taliban: Militant Islam, Oil and Fundamentalism in Central Asia* (New Haven: Yale University Press).

Rashid, A. (2008) *Descent into Chaos: How the War Against Islamic Extremism is being Lost in Pakistan, Afghanistan and Central Asia* (London: Penguin).

Reinerman, C. and Levine, H.G. (eds.) (1997) *Crack in America: Demon Drugs and Social Justice* (Berkeley and Los Angeles: University of California Press).

Reuter, P. (2009) "Ten Years After the United Nations General Assembly Special Session (UNGASS): Assessing Drug Problems, Policies and Reform Proposals," *Addiction* 104(4):510–17.

Reuter, P. and Stevens, A. (2008) "Assessing UK Drug Policy from a Crime Control Perspective," *Criminology and Criminal Justice* 8(4):461–82.

Reuters (2009) "UN Crime Chief Says Drug Money Flowed into Banks," 25 January.

Rhodes, T. and Hedrich, D. (2010) "Harm Reduction and the Mainstream," in T. Rhodes and D. Hedrich (eds.), *Harm Reduction: Evidence, Impacts and Challenges*, European Monitoring Centre for Drugs and Drug Addiction (EMCDDA) Monographs (Luxembourg: Publications Office of the European Union), pp. 19–36.

Risen, J. (1999) "Sudan, Angry at U.S. Attack, Freed Bomb Suspects, Officials Say," *New York Times*, 30 July.

Risen, J. (2006) *State of War: The Secret History of the CIA and the Bush Administration* (London: The Free Press).

Risen, J. (2007a) "An Afghan's Path from Ally of U.S. to Drug Suspect," *New York Times*, 2 February.

Risen, J. (2007b) "Poppy Fields Are Now a Front Line in Afghanistan's War," *New York Times*, 16 May.

Risen, J. (2008) "Reports Link Karzai's Brother to Afghanistan Heroin Trade," *New York Times*, 4 October.

Risen, J. (2009) "Drug Chieftains Tied to Taliban Are US Targets", *New York Times*, 10 August.

Risen, J. (2010a) "U.S. Identifies Vast Mineral Riches in Afghanistan," *New York Times*, 13 June.

Risen, J. (2010b) "Propping Up a Drug Lord, then Arresting Him," *New York Times*, 12 December.

Risen, J. and Johnston, D. (1999) "Experts Find No Arms Chemicals at Bombed Sudan Plant," *New York Times*, 9 February.

Risen, J. and Landler, M. (2009) "Drug Accusations Against Afghan Official Pose Dilemma for U.S.," *New York Times*, 27 August.

Rosenberg, M. (2009) "U.S. Courts Former Warlords in Its Bid for Afghan Stability," *Wall Street Journal*, 20 March.

Rosenberg, M. and Bowley, G. (2012) "U.S. Grants Special Ally Status to Afghans, Easing Fears of Abandonment," *New York Times*, 7 July.

Rotter, A. (1984) "The Triangular Route to Vietnam," *International History Review* vi(3):404–23.

Roy, O. (1990) *Islam and Resistance in Afghanistan* (second edition) (Cambridge: Cambridge University Press).

Rubin, B. (1995) The *Search for Peace in Afghanistan: From Buffer State to Failed State* (New Haven: Yale University Press).

Rubin, B. (1998) "Testimony on the Situation in Afghanistan Before the United States Senate Committee on Foreign Relations," 8 October, www.cfr.org/afghanistan/testimony-situation-afghanistan-before-united-states-senate-committee-foreign-relations/p3088.

Rubin, B. (2000) "The Political Economy of War and Peace in Afghanistan," *World Development* 28(10):1789–1803.

Rubin, B. (2002) *The Fragmentation of Afghanistan: State Formation and Collapse in the International System* (second edition) (New Haven: Yale University Press).

Rubin, B. (2004a) *Road to Ruin: Afghanistan's Booming Opium Industry* (New York: New York University, Center on International Cooperation).

Rubin, B. (2004b) "Afghanistan's Fatal Addiction," *International Herald Tribune*, 28 October.

Rubin, B. (2007) "Counter-Narcotics in Afghanistan: First Installment," 24 August, icga.blogspot.com/2007/08/counter-narcotics-in-afghanistan-first.html.

Rubin, B. and Sherman, J. (2008) *Counter-Narcotics to Stabilize Afghanistan: The False Promise of Crop Eradication* (New York: Center on International Cooperation, New York University).

Rubin, E. (2009) "Karzai in His Labyrinth," *New York Times Magazine*, 4 August.

Rupert, J. and Coll, S. (1990) "U.S. Declines to Probe Afghan Drug Trade; Rebels, Pakistani Officers Implicated," *Washington Post*, 13 May.

Rydell, P. and Everingham, S. (1994) *Controlling Cocaine: Supply Versus Demand Programs* (Santa Monica, CA: RAND).

Salmon, G. (2009) *Poppy: Life, Death and Addiction Inside Afghanistan's Opium Trade* (North Sydney: Ebury Press).

Scarborough, R. (2004) "Military Resists Afghan Drug War," *Washington Times*, 14 October.

Schaller, M. (1982) "Securing the Great Crescent: Occupied Japan and the Origins of Containment in Southeast Asia," *The Journal of American History* 69(2):392–414.

Schane, S. and Lehren, A. (2010) "Leaked Cables Offer a Raw Look Inside U.S. Diplomacy," *New York Times*, 29 November.

Schmitt, E. (2002) "U.S. to Add to Forces in Horn of Africa," *New York Times*, 30 October.

Schmitt, E. (2004) "Afghans' Gains Face Big Threat in Drug Traffic," *New York Times*, 11 December.

Schweich, T. (2008) "Is Afghanistan a Narco-State?" *New York Times Magazine*, 27 July.

Sciolino, E. (1991) "Intelligence Agency Used B.C.C.I., Official Says," *New York Times*, 3 August.

Sciolino, E. (1996) "State Dept. Becomes Cooler To the New Rulers of Kabul," *New York Times*, 23 October.

Scott, P.D. (2003a) *Drugs, Oil, and War: The United States in Afghanistan, Colombia, and Indochina* (Lanham, MD: Rowman and Littlefield).

Scott, P.D. (2003b) "The CIA's secret powers," *Critical Asian Studies* 35(2):233–58.

Scott, P.D. (2007) *The Road to 9/11: Wealth, Empire, and the Future of America* (Berkeley and Los Angeles: University of California Press).

Scott, P.D. (2010) *American War Machine: Deep Politics, the CIA Global Drug Connection, and the Road to Afghanistan* (Lanham, MD: Rowman and Littlefield).

Shaffer, E. (1983) *The United States and the Control of World Oil* (London: Croom Helm).

Shaffer, E.R., Brenner, J.E., and Houston, T.P. (2005) "International Trade Agreements: A Threat to Tobacco Control Policy," *Tobacco Control* 14:ii19–ii25.

Shah, S. (2011) "Karzai's Pick for Parliament Speaker Accused of Atrocities," *McClatchy Newspapers*, 26 January.

Shamim, G. (2009) "Twin Epidemics—Drug Use and HIV/AIDS in Pakistan," in Open Society Institute (2009) *At What Cost? HIV and Human Rights Consequences of the Global "War on Drugs"* (New York: Open Society Institute), pp. 165–80.

Shanker, T. (2005) "Pentagon Sees Aggressive Antidrug Effort in Afghanistan," *New York Times*, 25 March.

Shanty, F. (2011) *The Nexus: International Terrorism and Drug Trafficking from Afghanistan* (Santa Barbara, CA: Praeger).

Shaw, M. (2006) "Drug Trafficking and the Development of Organized Crime in Post-Taliban Afghanistan," in D. Buddenberg and W. Byrd (eds.), *Afghanistan's Drug Industry: Structure, Functioning, Dynamics, and Implications for Counter-Narcotics Policy* (Vienna: UNODC and Washington, DC: World Bank), pp. 189–214.

Shepard, C. and Swardson, A. (1991) "Warnings of Wrongdoing at BCCI Went Unheeded Since 1984," *Washington Post*, 6 September.

Sherman, J. and DiDomenico, V. (2009) *The Public Cost of Private Security* (New York: Center on International Cooperation, New York University).

Sifton, J. (2003) "Afghanistan's Warlords Still Call the Shots," 24 December, www.hrw.org/news/2003/12/23/afghanistans-warlords-still-call.shots.

Singh, D.G. (2007) *Drugs Production and Trafficking in Afghanistan* (New Delhi: Pentagon Press).

Srivastava, S. (2005) "The Foundations for an Asian Oil and Gas Grid," *Asia Times online*, 1 December.

Stevens, A. (2011) *Drugs, Crime and Public Health: The Political Economy of Drug Policy* (New York: Routledge).

Stevens, A., Stöver, H., and Brentari, C. (2010) "Criminal Justice Approaches to Harm Reduction in Europe," in T. Rhodes and D. Hedrich (eds.), *Harm Reduction: Evidence, Impacts and Challenges*, European Monitoring Centre for Drugs and Drug Addiction (EMCDDA) Monographs (Luxembourg: Publications Office of the European Union), pp. 379–404.

Stokes, D. (2005) *America's Other War: Terrorizing Colombia* (London: Zed Books).

Stokes, D. and Raphael, S. (2010) *Global Energy Security and American Hegemony* (Baltimore: The Johns Hopkins University Press).

Tandy, K. (2004) Statement before the Committee on International Relations, US House of Representatives, "United States Policy Towards Narco-Terrorism in Afghanistan," 12 February, www.justice.gov/dea/pubs/cngrtest/ct021204.htm.

Tedford, D. (1994) "Bank Gets Record Penalty in Money-Laundering Case," *Houston Chronicle*, 22 November.

Thompson, E. (2006) "The Nexus of Drug Trafficking and Hawala in Afghanistan," in D. Buddenberg and W. Byrd (eds.), *Afghanistan's Drug Industry: Structure, Functioning, Dynamics, and Implications for Counter-Narcotics Policy* (Vienna: UNODC and Washington, DC: World Bank), pp. 155–88.

TIME (1979) "Iran: The Crescent of Crisis," 15 January.

TIME (1980) "An Interview with Brzezinski," 14 January.

Transnational Institute (2001) "Merging Wars: Afghanistan, Drugs and Terrorism" (Amsterdam: TNI).

Transnational Institute (2005) "Plan Afghanistan," Drug Policy Briefing No. 10, January (Amsterdam: TNI).

Truell, P. and Gurwin, L. (1992) *False Profits: The Inside Story of BCCI, the World's Most Corrupt Financial Empire* (Boston: Houghton Mifflin Company).

Turse, N. (2010) "The 700 Military Bases of Afghanistan: Black Sites in the Empire of Bases," TomDispatch.com, 9 February.

UK Foreign and Commonwealth Office (n.d.) "Counternarcotics," http://ukinafghanistan.fco.gov.uk/.

UK Foreign and Commonwealth Office (2010) "The UK's Foreign Policy towards Afghanistan and Pakistan," Written Evidence from the Foreign and Commonwealth Office, www.publications.parliament.uk/pa/cm201011/cmselect/cmfaff/writev/afpak/afpak01.htm.

UNDCP (2001) *Afghanistan Annual Opium Poppy Survey 2001* (Islamabad: UNDCP).

UNODC (2003) *The Opium Economy in Afghanistan: An International Problem* (Vienna: UNODC).

UNODC (2005) *World Drug Report 2005* (New York: United Nations).

UNODC (2008a) *Afghanistan Opium Survey 2008* (Vienna: UNODC).

UNODC (2008b) *Illicit Drug Trends in Central Asia*, (Tashkent: UNODC).

UNODC (2009a) *Afghanistan Cannabis Survey 2009* (Vienna: UNODC).

UNODC (2009b) *Afghanistan Opium Survey 2009* (Summary Findings) (Vienna: UNODC).

UNODC (2009c) *Addiction, Crime and Insurgency: The Transnational Threat of Afghan Opium* (Vienna: UNODC).

UNODC (2009d) *World Drug Report 2009* (New York: United Nations).

UNODC (2009e) *Drug Use in Afghanistan: 2009 Survey* (Executive Summary) (Vienna: UNODC).

UNODC (2010a) *World Drug Report 2010* (New York: United Nations).

UNODC (2010b) *Afghanistan Opium Survey 2010* (Vienna: UNODC).

UNODC (2011a) *The Global Afghan Opium Trade: A Threat Assessment* (Vienna: UNODC).

UNODC (2011b) *Afghanistan Opium Survey 2011* (Vienna: UNODC).

UNODC (2011c) *World Drug Report 2011* (New York: United Nations).

UNODC (2011d) *Afghanistan Opium Survey 2011* (Vienna: UNODC).

UNODC (2011e) *Estimating Illicit Financial Flows Resulting from Drug Trafficking and Other Transnational Organized Crimes* (Vienna: UNODC).

US Department of State (1949) "Transcript of Round Table Discussion on American Policy Toward China," (Washington: Department of State, Division of Central Services).

US Department of State (1996a) "Pakistan-Afghanistan Relations," circa January, in The Taliban File Part III, National Security Archive, 19 March 2004, www.gwu.edu/~nsarchiv/NSAEBB/NSAEBB97/index4.htm.

US Department of State (1996b) "Dealing with the Taliban in Kabul," Cable, 28 September, National Security Archive, www.gwu.edu/~nsarchiv/NSAEBB/NSAEBB97/index.htm.

US Department of State (1996c) "Turkmenistan-Afghanistan-Pakistan Pipelines: Nature of USG Support and Relation to Policy on Afghanistan," September, National Security Archive (made available to the author).

US Department of State (1998a) "Usama bin Laden's Statement About Jihad Against the U.S.," STATE 034310, 26 February, Wikileaks, www.cablegatesearch.net/cable.php?id=98STATE34310&q=afghanistan.

US Department of State (1998b) "Approach to EU on Taleban Support for Usama bin Laden," STATE 055357, 27 March, Wikileaks, www.cablegatesearch.net/cable.php?id=98STATE55357&q=afghanistan.

US Department of State (1998c) "Osama bin Laden: Taliban Spokesman Seeks New Proposal for Resolving bin Laden Problem," Cable, 28 November, National Security Archive, www.gwu.edu/~nsarchiv/NSAEBB/NSAEBB134/index2.htm.

US Department of State (2001a) "U.S. Engagement with the Taliban on Usama bin Laden," circa July, National Security Archive, www.gwu.edu/~nsarchiv/NSAEBB/NSAEBB97/tal40.pdf.

US Department of State (2001b) "Deputy Secretary Armitage-Mamoud Phone Call—September 18, 2001," 18 September, National Security Archive, www.gwu.edu/~nsarchiv/NSAEBB/NSAEBB325/index.htm.

US Department of State (2007) *U.S. Counternarcotics Strategy for Afghanistan* (compiled by Thomas Schweich), August, http://merln.ndu.edu/archivepdf/afghanistan/State/90671.pdf.

US Department of State (2010) *International Narcotics Control Strategy Report 2010*, www.state.gov/j/inl/rls/nrcrpt/2010/vol1/index.htm.

US Department of State (2011) *International Narcotics Control Strategy Report 2011*, www.state.gov/j/inl/rls/nrcrpt/2011/vol1/index.htm.

US Department of State and UK Foreign and Commonwealth Office (2008) "Fighting the Opium Trade in Afghanistan: Myths, Facts, and Sound Policy," 11 March, http://kabul.usembassy.gov/media/afghan_opium_myths_and_facts-final.pdf.

US Embassy (Islamabad) (1996) "Ambassador Meets Taliban: We Are the People," Cable, 12 November, National Security Archive, www.gwu.edu/~nsarchiv/NSAEBB/NSAEBB97/index.htm.

US Embassy (Islamabad) (1997a) "Official Informal for SA Assistant Secretary Robin Raphel and SA/PAB," Cable, 10 March, National Security Archive, www.gwu.edu/~nsarchiv/NSAEBB/NSAEBB295/.

US Embassy (Islamabad) (1997b) "Afghanistan: [Excised] Briefs the Ambassador on his Activities. Pleads for Greater Activism by U.N.," Cable, 27 August, National Security Archive, www.gwu.edu/~nsarchiv/NSAEBB/NSAEBB97/index4.htm.

US Embassy (Islamabad) (1998) "Pakistan: Ambassador Raises bin Laden with Foreign Secretary Shamshad Ahmed," Cable, 6 October, National Security Archive, www.gwu.edu/~nsarchiv/NSAEBB/NSAEBB134/index2.htm.

US Embassy (Islamabad) (2001), "Musharraf [EXCISED]," 13 September, National Security Archive, www.gwu.edu/~nsarchiv/NSAEBB/NSAEBB325/index.htm.

US Embassy (Islamabad) (2001) "Mahmud Plans 2nd Mission to Afghanistan," 24 September, National Security Archive, www.gwu.edu/~nsarchiv/NSAEBB/NSAEBB325/index.htm.

US House of Representatives (1998) "U.S. Interests in the Central Asian Republics," Hearings Before the Subcommittee on Asia and the Pacific of the Committee on International Relations, 12 February, http://commdocs.house.gov/committees/intlrel/hfa48119.000/hfa48119_0.HTM.

US House of Representatives (2004) "Afghanistan: Are the British Counternarcotics Efforts Going Wobbly?" Hearing Before the Subcommittee on Criminal Justice, Drug Policy and Human Resources of the Committee on Government Reform, 1 April (Washington, DC: US Government Printing Office).

US National Security Council (1950) NSC-68, "United States Objectives and Programs for National Security," 14 April 1950, in US Department of State, *Foreign Relations of the United States*, 1950, 1: pp. 235–92 (Washington, DC: Government Printing Office, 1977).

US National Security Council (1954) NSC 5432/1, "United States Objectives and Courses of Action with Respect to Latin America," 3 September.

US National Security Council (1977) PD-18, "U.S. National Strategy," 24 August, www.jimmycarterlibrary.gov/documents/pddirectives/pd18.pdf.

US Senate (1992) *The BCCI Affair: A Report to the Committee on Foreign Relations*, by Senator John Kerry and Senator Hank Brown, December, 102d Congress 2d Session, Senate Print 102–40.

US Senate, Caucus on International Narcotics Control (2010) *U.S. Counternarcotics Strategy in Afghanistan*, July, http://drugcaucus.senate.gov.

US Senate, Committee on Foreign Relations (1989) *Drugs, Law Enforcement and Foreign Policy*, December 1988 (Washington, DC: Government Printing Office).

US Senate, Committee on Foreign Relations (2009) *Afghanistan's Narco War: Breaking the Link between Drug Traffickers and Insurgents*, 10 August, (Washington, DC: US Government Printing Office).

US Senate, Committee on Foreign Relations (2011) *Central Asia and the Transition in Afghanistan*, 19 December (Washington, DC: US Government Printing Office).

Varadarajan, S. (2005) "Pipelines, Power Grids and the New Silk Road in Asia," *The Hindu*, 11 July.

Voice of Russia (2010a) "Russia plans counter-drug deployment in Kyrgyzstan", 24 June, http://english.ruvr.ru/2010/06/24/10631393.html.

Voice of Russia (2010b) "Russia to Set Up Antidrug Military Base in Kyrgyzstan", 25 June, http://english.ruvr.ru/2010/06/25/10660878.html.

Vulliamy, E. (2011) "How a Big US Bank Laundered Billions From Mexico's Murderous Drug Gangs," *Observer* (London), 3 April.

Walsh, S. (1992) "U.S. Warned about BCCI in 1978, Panel Told," *Washington Post*, 20 February.

Ward, C. and Byrd, W. (2004) *Afghanistan's Opium Drug Economy* (Washington, DC: World Bank).

Waxman, S. (1999) "A Cause Unveiled; Hollywood Women Have Made the Plight of Afghan Women Their Own—Sight Unseen," *Washington Post*, 30 March.

Weiner, T. (1990) *Blank Check: The Pentagon's Black Budget* (New York: Warner).

Weir, F. (2010) "Moscow Furious, Says US Not Pushing Drug War in Afghanistan," *Christian Science Monitor*, 19 May.

Weiser, B. (2009) "Afghan Linked to Taliban Sentenced to Death in Drug Trafficking Case," *New York Times*, 1 May.

White House, "Fact Sheet: The U.S.-Afghanistan Strategic Partnership Agreement," 1 May 2012, www.whitehouse.gov/the-press-office/2012/05/01/fact-sheet-us-afghanistan-strategic-partnership-agreement.

WHO (2008a) *Report on the Global Tobacco Epidemic, 2008: The MPOWER Package* (Geneva: World Health Organization).

WHO (2008b) *Tobacco Industry Interference with Tobacco Control* (Geneva: WHO).

WHO (2009) *Report on the Global Tobacco Epidemic, 2009: Implementing Smoke-Free Environments* (Geneva: World Health Organization).

WHO (2011) *Global Status Report on Alcohol and Health* (Geneva: WHO).

Wilder, A. (2005) *A House Divided? Analysing the 2005 Afghan Elections*, December (Kabul: AREU).

Wolf, M. (2011) "We Should End Our Disastrous War on Drugs," *Financial Times*, 3 June.

Wolfe, D. and Malinowska-Sempruch, K. (2004) *Illicit Drug Policies and the Global HIV Epidemic: Effects of UN and National Government Approaches* (New York: Open Society Institute).

Woodward, B. (2003) *Bush at War* (London: Pocket Books/Simon & Schuster).

Yongming, Z. (1999) *Anti-Drug Crusades in Twentieth-Century China: Nationalism, History, and State Building* (Lanham: Rowman & Littlefield).

Zahab, M.A. (2001) "Pakistan: D'un Narco-État à une "Success Story" dans la Guerre Contre la Drogue?" CEMOTI 32:141–58.

Zeigler, D. (2006) "International Trade Agreements Challenge Tobacco and Alcohol Control Policies," *Drug and Alcohol Review* 25(November):567–79.

Index